J.H. Burns

Scholastics Enlightenments and Philosophic Radicals

Essays in honour of J.H. Burns

Edited by Janet Coleman

IMPRINT ACADEMIC, PO BOX NO. 1, THORVERTON EX5 5YX, UK
TEL: +44 (0)1392 841600;   FAX: 841478

ISSN 0143-781X

Articles appearing in this journal
are annotated and indexed in
ARTS & HUMANITIES CITATION INDEX
CURRENT CONTENTS/ARTS & HUMANITIES
HISTORICAL ABSTRACTS & AMERICA: HISTORY AND LIFE
INTERNATIONAL BIBLIOGRAPHY OF BOOK REVIEWS
INTERNATIONAL BIBLIOGRAPHY OF PERIODICAL LITERATURE
INTERNATIONAL MEDIEVAL BIBLIOGRAPHY
INTERNATIONAL POLITICAL SCIENCE ABSTRACTS
PERIODICA ISLAMICA
THE PHILOSOPHER'S INDEX
POLITICAL SCIENCE ABSTRACTS

History of Political Thought, ISSN 0143-781X, USPS Reg. No. 012032
is published quarterly
for $59.00 (Individuals), $126.00 Institution
by Imprint Academic, c/o Royal Mail Int., Yellowstone International,
87 Burlews Court, Hackensack, NJ 07601, USA.
Periodicals Postage Paid at Hackensack.
POSTMASTER: Send address changes to Royal Mail International,
c/o Yellowstone International, 2375 Pratt Boulevard, Elk Grove Village,
IL 60007-5937, USA.

SCHOLASTICS, ENLIGHTENMENTS AND PHILOSOPHIC RADICALS

ISBN 0 907 845 35 5

HISTORY
OF
POLITICAL
THOUGHT

IMPRINT ACADEMIC

Volume XX   Issue 1

Spring 1999

CONTENTS

J.H. BURNS AND THE *HISTORY OF POLITICAL THOUGHT*: A CELEBRATION

To celebrate James Burns, the man and his work, is to provide a long overdue occasion to reflect, with astonishment and delight, on Jimmy's enduring and energetic scholarly devotion to men of ideas and principle in the history of western political thought. It is also an occasion for a concerted roar of thanks: from admirers and friends, former students and colleagues, those who have been inspired by his lectures in Cambridge, at the University of London, at Johns Hopkins and elsewhere in America, from those who have benefited from his freely offered wisdom at the Institute of Historical Research's seminar in the *History of Political Ideas* which he founded, and from those whose own research was perfected by his humane and critical judgments as he actively served, from its very inception, on the Editorial Board of the journal *History of Political Thought*.

A glance at his bibliography takes us across geographical and intellectual borders: from the middle ages of Marsilius of Padua to the Scotland of John Major; from conciliar theory to resistance theory; from Catholic scholasticism and the writings of medieval jurists to the Scottish Reformation; from concepts of monarchy to the ideas of anti-monarchomachs; from Jacques Almain to John Locke; from the discretionary, medieval *potestas absoluta* to the early-modern 'absolute and arbitrary power', thence to despotism degenerating into tyranny and absolut*ism*; from Bentham and J.S. Mill to Scottish committees of the House of Commons in the mid-twentieth century; and then back again, editing several *Cambridge Histories of Political Thought*, from the fourth to the eighteenth centuries. Who, nowadays, has this grasp of the numerous 'dangerous enterprises of innovation', of the extreme positions uttered by learned men in the past from which even they often found it expedient to retreat? As his judicious intellect penetrated into and illumined numerous corners obscured by time or the misapprehensions of other historians, Jimmy always reminded his readers to judge the concepts under consideration concretely, 'to see them in the context of the social system within which they were intended to operate'. Indeed, he observed:

All societies — perhaps even our own — depend for their functioning and survival on the acceptance of shared moral values. Such values may well be effective, more often than not, at the level of what Burke called 'prejudices': the generally unthinking but fundamental assumptions we all make as to how we ought to behave towards one another. And it is (I suspect) a liberal and radical delusion to suppose that people in power (just because they <u>are</u> in power) will be less apt, while ordinary people (just because they <u>are</u> ordinary) will be more apt to abide by those standards. [*Absolutism: The History of an Idea*, The Creighton Trust Lecture, 1986, p. 17.]

2

Jimmy has displayed an extraordinary alertness to the distinctive principles that were embodied in the functional arrangements, the social structures, of societies in the past, such principles corresponding to assumptions and beliefs — about the family, or religion — at a level far deeper than 'political thought'. In this way he has enabled students of medieval to early-modern periods in particular, to *hear* what men have said, indirectly reminding us that anyone engaged in the historical enterprise must seek to take seriously men's theories and practices, perhaps especially when such theories and practices are not now our own.

It is to such a man and scholar, friend, colleague and inspiration, that the following pieces, written by only a very few of those who actively wished to contribute, are dedicated.

In thanks.

Janet Coleman

JAMES BURNS AND JEREMY BENTHAM

F. Rosen

In James Burns' first publication on Bentham, *Jeremy Bentham and University College*, originally delivered as a Lunch Hour lecture in November 1961, the very year of his appointment as General Editor of *The Collected Works of Jeremy Bentham*, he reached the following conclusion:

> This, however, a newcomer may with propriety venture to say. There were many things in Bentham and his doctrine that would not accord well with what many of us think a university should be. There was pretentiousness and superficiality and arrogant dogmatizing; there was the kind of myopic concentration upon the 'usefulness' of an intellectual discipline which often stultifies even the practical application of knowledge. But there were also elements any academic community might value: acute consciousness of the need to criticize concepts and terms; controlled and constructive scepticism as to received notions and established institutions; decisive rejection of the Utopian illusion. To read Bentham is often, no doubt, to be reminded of John Bright's caustic words — 'The trouble with great thinkers is that they so often think wrong'. It is also to be reminded that a remarkable, though eccentric genius did in some sense preside benevolently over the enterprise and faith to which we in the College owe our present existence. And a man who could expect 'honest pride and sympathetic feeling' from the development of critical independence of mind in his students was no unfit patron for a college and a university.[1]

It is a remarkable first assessment of Bentham's political views, philosophy and personality, and I doubt that it has changed much over nearly forty years of writing about many aspects of Bentham's life and work. While fully acknowledging the historical importance of Bentham's philosophy and jurisprudence and his undoubted influence as a reformer, and recognizing his 'remarkable though eccentric genius' and enormous capacity for analytical and critical thought, Burns was never a Benthamite or even a utilitarian. His interest has been mainly historical, and his most important contributions to Bentham studies, apart from the edition of the *Collected Works* itself, have been subtle and sensitive explorations of Bentham's ideas in historical context.

The study of political ideas, as he insisted in his Inaugural Lecture as Professor of the History of Political Thought, 'is genuinely historical or it is

---

[1] James Burns, *Jeremy Bentham and University College* (London, 1962), pp. 14–15.

intended? Should works be published in their entirety or should the most interesting and relevant portions be published as selections?

The answers to these questions depended on one's assessment of the financial and human costs of producing a full edition and ultimately on one's attitude towards Bentham himself. Many members of the Bentham Committee believed that Bentham's ideas were, so to speak, still alive, and that accurate and complete editions of his writings would make important contributions to contemporary work in philosophy, political theory, law and economics.

Although Burns fully appreciated Bentham's importance, his interest lay more in the historical significance of Bentham and his works. Fortunately the two positions dovetailed, and the outcome was a series of texts and volumes of correspondence of great contemporary interest and also edited with the historical dimension fully displayed in the textual work, introduction and annotation for each volume. Bentham has become readable for the first time not only because there are good texts but also because we can now understand the debates in which he participated and the meaning of many of the allusions in the texts.

Burns co-edited with H.L.A. Hart the new edition of *An Introduction to the Principles of Morals and Legislation*, and *A Comment on the Commentaries and A Fragment on Government*.[14] He also co-edited the first volume of *Constitutional Code*.[15] While he was General Editor six volumes (including three of *Correspondence*) were published. The twenty-first volume has now been published with a further ten in various stages of completion. Although most of these were completed or edited by his successors, each one reflects Burns' initial insight into how such an edition should be constituted. One is tempted to conclude that in the Bentham edition, Burns has come closest to playing the role of Legislator, though for a great edition rather than, as in Bentham's case, for 'all nations and all governments professing liberal opinions'.[16]

F. Rosen   UNIVERSITY COLLEGE LONDON

---

[14] J. Bentham, *An Introduction to the Principles of Morals and Legislation*, ed. J.H. Burns and H.L.A. Hart (London, 1970); *A Comment on the Commentaries and A Fragment on Government*, ed. J.H. Burns and H.L.A. Hart (London, 1977).

[15] J. Bentham, *Constitutional Code*, Volume I, ed. F. Rosen and J.H. Burns (Oxford, 1983).

[16] Part of the subtitle of Bentham's *Constitutional Code*. See *ibid.*, p. 1.

BIBLIOGRAPHY OF THE WRITINGS OF
J.H. BURNS 1950–1998

1950

1 'Three Scots Catholic Critics of George Buchanan', *Innes Review*, 1, pp. 92–109.

1951

2 'The Political Ideas of George Buchanan', review-article on *The Powers of the Crown in Scotland* (= Buchanan, *De iure regni apud Scotos*), **ed. C.F. Arrowood**, *Scottish Historical Review*, 30, pp. 60–8.

3 'The Scotland of John Major', *Innes Review*, 2, pp. 65–76.

1952

4 'His Majesty's Instructions', review-article on *The Basilicon Doron of King James VI*, **ed. J. Craigie**, *Scottish Historical Review*, 31, pp. 64–72.

5 'John Major in Scotland', *Scottish Historical Review*, 31, p. 98.

6 (with Saul Rose), 'A Scottish Constituency', in *The British General Election of 1951*, **ed. D.E. Butler** (London: Macmillan), pp. 184–97.

7 Review of **A.P. d'Entrèves**, *Natural Law: An Introduction to Legal Philosophy*, *Philosophical Quarterly*, 2, pp. 90–1.

1953

8 Review of **D. Nobbs**, *England and Scotland 1560–1707*, *Scottish Historical Review*, 32, pp. 172–3.

9 Review of **A. Gewirth**, *Marsilius of Padua, The Defender of Peace*, Vol. 1: *Marsilius of Padua and Medieval Political Philosophy*, *Philosophical Quarterly*, 3, pp. 365–6.

1954

10 'New Light on John Major', *Innes Review*, 5, pp. 83–100.

11 Review of **M.L. Pearl**, *William Cobbett: A Bibliographical Account of his Life and Times*, *Political Studies*, 2, p. 95.

1955

12 'Knox and Bullinger', *Scottish Historical Review*, 34, pp. 90–1.

13 'John Ireland and "The Meroure of Wyssdome" ', *Innes Review*, 4, pp. 77–97.

14 'Market and Fair in Medieval Haddington', *Transactions of the East Lothian Antiquarian and Field Naturalists' Society*, 5, pp. 42–3.

15   (contributor to) 'The Ordination of John Knox: A Symposium', *Innes Review*, 6, pp. 99–106, at pp. 102–3.

16   Review of **L.J. Cohen**, *The Principles of World Citizenship*, *Sociological Review*, n.s. 3, pp. 149–51.

17   Review of *Christian Faith and Communist Faith: A Series of Studies by Members of the Anglican Communion*, **ed. D.M. Mackinnon**, *Aberdeen University Review*, 36, pp. 33–6.

1956

18   'The Political Ideas of the Scottish Reformation', *Aberdeen University Review*, 36, pp. 251–68.

19   'An English View of Federalism in 1829', *Political Studies*, 4, pp. 312–15.

20   Review of **R.H.S. Crossman**, *Socialism and the New Despotism* (Fabian Tract no. 298), *The Mercat Cross*, 11, pp. 148, 176.

1957

21   'Mr Scott on Freedom and Unfreedom', *Political Studies*, 5, pp. 81–3.

22   'J.S. Mill and Democracy, 1829–61. I', *Political Studies*, 5, pp. 158–75.

23   'J.S. Mill and Democracy, 1829–61. II', *Political Studies*, 5, pp. 281–94.

24   Review of *The Liberal Tradition from Fox to Keynes*, **ed. A. Bullock and M. Shock**; **J.C. Rees**, *Mill and his Early Critics; Philosophy, Politics and Society*, **ed. P. Laslett**, *History*, 42, pp. 274–6.

1958

25   'John Knox and Revolution, 1558', *History Today*, 8, pp. 565–73.

26   Review of *The Tyrannous Reign of Mary Stewart: George Buchanan's Account*, **ed. W.A. Gatherer**, *History Today*, 8, pp. 731–2.

1959

27   *Ninian Winzet and the Defence of the Faith in Scotland* (Glasgow: Catholic Truth Society of Scotland).

28   'J.S. Mill and the Term "Social Science" ', *Journal of the History of Ideas*, 20, pp. 431–2.

29   'Utilitarianism and Democracy', *Philosophical Quarterly*, 9, pp. 168–71.

30   'Sovereignty and Constitutional Law in Bodin', *Political Studies*, 7, pp. 174–7.

31   Review of **J.B. Morrall**, *Political Thought in Medieval Times*, *Political Studies*, 7, p. 190.

32 'The Political Background of the [Scottish] Reformation, 1513–1625', *Innes Review*, 10, pp. 199–236.

33 ' "Winzerus": A Forgotten Political Writer', *Journal of the History of Ideas*, 21, pp. 124–30.

1960

34 'The Scottish Committees of the House of Commons, 1948–1959', *Political Studies*, 8, pp. 272–86.

35 Review of **E. Stoke**s, *The English Utilitarians and India*, History, 45, pp. 164–5

1961

36 Review of **G. Lewy**, *Constitutionalism and Statecraft during the Golden Age of Spain: A Study of the Political Philosophy of Juan de Mariana, S.J.*, *History*, 46, p. 141.

37 Review of **R.K. Webb**, *Harriet Martineau: A Radical Victorian*, *History*, 46, pp. 69–70.

38 Review of **W. Stark**, *Montesquieu: Pioneer of the Sociology of Knowledge*, *Political Studies*, 9, p. 307.

1962

39 'Scottish Churchmen and the Council of Basle, Part One', *Innes Review*, 13, pp. 1–53.

40 'Scottish Churchmen and the Council of Basle, Part Two', *Innes Review*, 13, pp. 157–89.

41 (with A. Cobban), 'Rousseau's *Du contrat social*: Some Problems of Translation', *Political Studies*, 10, pp. 203–7.

42 'Bolingbroke and the Concept of Constitutional Government', *Political Studies*, 10, pp. 264–76.

43 'The Political Background of the Reformation, 1513–1625', in *Essays on the Scottish Reformation*, **ed. D. McRoberts** (Glasgow: Burns), pp. 1–38 [reprint of no. 32 above].

44 *Jeremy Bentham and University College* (London: Athlone Press of the University of London).

45 *Scottish Churchmen and the Council of Basle* (Glasgow: Burns) [reprint of nos. 39 and 40 above, with addition of preface and index of names of persons).

46 Review of **G. Dietze**, *The Federalist: A Classic on Federalism and Constitutional Government*, *Political Studies*, 10, p. 102.

1963

47 'The Conciliarist Tradition in Scotland', *Scottish Historical Review*, 42, pp. 89–104.

48 Review of **H.A. Deane**, *The Political and Social Ideas of St Augustine*, *The Month*, n.s. 30, pp. 304–5.

49 Review of **M.L. Clarke**, *George Grote: A Biography*, *History*, 48, pp. 232–3.

50 Review of *The Early Draft of John Stuart Mill's 'Autobiography'*, **ed. J. Stillinger**, *History*, 48, p. 233.

51 Review of **M.P. Mack**, *Jeremy Bentham: An Odyssey of Ideas, 1748–1792*, *Victorian Studies*, 6, pp. 371–2.

52 Review of **Jean Bodin**, *The Six Bookes of a Commonweale*, **ed. K.D. McRae**, *History*, 48, pp. 379–80.

1964

53 'Revolutionary Reflections', review-article on **H. Arendt**, *On Revolution*, *The Month*, n.s. 32, pp. 284–90.

54 '*Du côté de chez Vaughan*: Rousseau Revisited', review-article on *The Political Writings of Jean-Jacques Rousseau*, **ed. C.E. Vaughan**, and **J.H. Broome**, *Rousseau: A Study of his Thought*, *Political Studies*, 12, pp. 229–34.

55 Review of **P.E. Sigmund**, *Nicholas of Cusa and Medieval Political Thought*, *The Month*, n.s. 32, pp. 163–4.

1965

56 Review of **G.R. Cragg**, *Reason and Authority in the Eighteenth Century* and **J. Joll**, *The Anarchists*, *The Month*, n.s. 33, pp. 122–3.

57 Review of **L. Fischer**, *The Life of Lenin* and **J. Ch'en**, *Mao and the Chinese Revolution*, *The Month*, n.s. 33, pp. 268–70.

58 Review of **W.H. Greenleaf**, *Order, Empiricism and Politics: Two Traditions in English Political Thought, 1500–1600* and **F. Raab**, *The English Face of Machiavelli: A Changing Interpretation, 1500–1700*, *History*, 50, pp. 364–5.

1966

59 'Utilitarianism and Reform: Social Theory and Social Change', paper presented at IV Conference of English [= British] and Soviet Historians, Moscow, 1966 [printed in Russian translation].

60 'Catholicism in Defeat: Ninian Winzet 1519–1592', *History Today*, 16, pp. 788–95.

61 Review of **P. Laslett**, *The World We Have Lost*, *The Month*, n.s. 35, pp. 251–2.

62 'Bentham and the French Revolution', *Transactions of the Royal Historical Society*, 5th series 16, pp. 95–114.

63 Review of **J. Hamburger**, *Intellectuals in Politics: John Stuart Mill and the Philosophic Radicals*, *The Mill News Letter*, 1(2), pp. 26–7.

64 Review of **C. Vivanti**, *Lotta politica e pace religiosa in Francia fra cinque e seicento*, *English Historical Review*, 81, p. 391.

1967

65 *The Fabric of Felicity: The Legislator and the Human Condition*, inaugural lecture delivered on 2 March 1967 (London: H.K. Lewis for University College London).

66 Review of *Trends in Medieval Political Thought*, **ed. B. Smalley**, *History*, 52, pp. 66–7.

67 'The Politics of Original Sin', review article on works by **Reinhold Niebuhr**, *The Month*, n.s. 37, pp. 349–54.

68 Review of **H.D. Lasswell**, *The Future of Political Science*, *Journal of Development Studies*, 3, p. 470.

1968

69 'Notes on the History of the Bentham Family', in *The Correspondence of Jeremy Bentham*, Vol. I, 1752–78, **ed. T.L.S. Sprigge** [*The Collected Works of Jeremy Bentham*] (London: The Athlone Press of the University of London), pp. xxxv–xxxix.

70 Review of **K. Minogue**, *Nationalism*, *The Month*, n.s. 39, pp. 251–3.

71 Review of **H.R. Trevor-Roper**, *George Buchanan and the Ancient Scottish Constitution* [= *English Historical Review*, Supplement 3], *History*, 53, pp. 257–8.

72 'J.S. Mill and Democracy, 1829–61', in *Mill: A Collection of Critical Essays*, **ed. J.B. Schneewind** (New York: Anchor Books), pp. 280–328 [reprint of nos. 22 and 23 above].

1969

73 Review of **J. Ridley**, *John Knox*, *History Today*, 19, pp 60–1.

74 Review of *The Art and Science of Government among the Scots: Being George Buchanan's 'De Jure Regni apud Scotos'*, **ed. D.H. MacNeill**, *Scottish Historical Review*, 48, pp. 190–1.

75 Review of **D.J. Manning**, *The Mind of Jeremy Bentham*, *Durham University Journal*, 61, pp. 113–15.

76 Review of **A.P. d'Entrèves**, *The Notion of the State: An Introduction to Political Theory*, *History*, 54, pp. 481–2.

77 Review of **James Fitzjames Stephen**, *Liberty, Equality, Fraternity*, **ed. R.J. White**, *History*, 54, pp. 482–3.

1970

78 (ed. with H.L.A. Hart), *An Introduction to the Principles of Morals and Legislation* [*The Collected Works of Jeremy Bentham*] (London: The Athlone Press of the University of London).

1971

79 'Scotland and England: Culture and Nationality, 1500–1800', in *Britain and the Netherlands*, 4: *Metropolis, Dominion and Province*, **ed. J.S. Bromley and E.H. Kossmann** (The Hague: Martinus Nijhoff), pp. 17–41.

80 'The Rights of Man since the Reformation', in *An Introduction to the Study of Human Rights*, **ed. Sir F. Vallat** (London: Europa Publications), pp. 16–30.

81 'Utilitarianism and Democracy', in *Utilitarianism [by] John Stuart Mill with Critical Essays*, **ed. S. Gorovitz** (Indianapolis and New York: Bobbs–Merrill), pp. 269–72 [reprint of no. 29 above].

1972

82 'The Bentham Project', in *Editing Texts of the Victorian Period*, **ed. J.D. Baird** (Toronto: A.M. Hakkert for The Committee for the Conference on Editorial Problems), pp. 73–87.

1973

83 'Bentham on Sovereignty: An Exploration', *Northern Ireland Legal Quarterly*, 24, pp. 399–416.

1974

84 'Bentham's Critique of Political Fallacies', in *Jeremy Bentham: Ten Critical Essays*, **ed. B. Parekh** (London: Frank Cass), pp. 154–67.

85 'Bentham on Sovereignty: An Exploration', in *Bentham and Legal Theory*, **ed. M.H. James** (Belfast: Northern Ireland Legal Quarterly), pp. 133–50 [reprint of no. 83 above].

1976

86 'The Light of Reason: Philosophical History in the Two Mills', in *James and John Stuart Mill: Papers of the Centenary Conference*, **ed. J.M. Robson and M. Laine** (Toronto and Buffalo: University of Toronto Press), pp. 3–20.

1977

87 (ed. with H.L.A. Hart), *A Comment on the Commentaries and A Fragment on Government* [*The Collected Works of Jeremy Bentham*] (London: The Athlone Press of the University of London).

88 Review of **J.G.A. Pocock**, *The Machiavellian Moment,: Florentine Political Thought and the Atlantic Republican Tradition*, *English Historical Review*, 92, pp. 137–42.

89 'The Fabric of Felicity: The Legislator and the Human Condition', in *The Study of Politics: A Collection of Inaugural Lectures*, **ed. P. King** (London: Frank Cass), pp. 207–24 [reprint of no. 65 above].

1978

90 'Dreams and Destinations: Jeremy Bentham in 1828', *The Bentham Newsletter*, 1, pp. 21–30.

1980

91 '*Ex uno plura*? The British Experience', in *Federalism: History and Current Significance of a Form of Government*, **ed. J.C. Boogman and G.N. van der Plaat** (The Hague: Martinus Nijhoff), pp. 189–215.

92 Review of **A.H. Williamson**, *Scottish National Consciousness in the Age of James VI: The Apocalypse, the Union and the Shaping of Scotland*, *History*, 65, p. 118.

1981

93 '*Politia regalis et optima*: The Political Ideas of John Mair', *History of Political Thought*, 2, pp. 31–61.

94 Review of *Authority and Power: Studies on Medieval Law and Government presented to Walter Ullmann on his Seventieth Birthday*, **ed. B. Tierney and P. Linehan**, *Cambridge Review*, 103, pp. 228–9.

1982

95 Review of **R. Tuck**, *Natural Rights Theories: Their Origin and Development*, *History*, 67, p. 75.

96 Review of **I.D. McFarlane**, *Buchanan*, *History*, 67, pp. 324–5.

97 (ed. with H.L.A. Hart) **Jeremy Betham**, *An Introduction to the Principles of Morals and Legislation* (London and New York: Methuen) [paperback reprint of no. 78 above, with a new introduction by H.L.A. Hart, but without the 1970 editorial introduction].

1983

98 (ed. with F. Rosen) *Constitutional Code*, Vol. 1 (*The Collected Works of Jeremy Bentham*) (Oxford: Clarendon Press).

99 '*Jus gladii* and *jurisdictio*: Jacques Almain and John Locke', *Historical Journal*, 26, pp. 369–74.

100 'St German, Gerson, Aquinas and Ulpian', *History of Political Thought*, 4, pp. 443–9.

101 Review of **B. Tierney**, *Religion, Law and the Growth of Constitutional Thought 1150–1650*, *Journal of Ecclesiastical History*, 34, pp. 271–3.

102 Review of **I.B. Cowan**, *The Scottish Reformation: Church and Society in Sixteenth-Century Scotland*, *History*, 68, pp. 508–9.

1984

103 'Jeremy Bentham: From Radical Enlightenment to Philosophic Radicalism', *The Bentham Newsletter*, 8, pp. 4–14 [a Shearman Lecture, delivered in University College London on 3 November 1983].

104 Review of **K.F. Morrison**, *The Mimetic Tradition of Reform in the West*, *Journal of Ecclesiastical History*, 35, pp. 465–7.

1985

105 'Stands Scotland Where It Did?', review-article on *The New History of Scotland* (8 vols.), general editor **J. Wormald**, *History*, 70, pp. 46–59.

106 'Fortescue and the Political Theory of *dominium*', *Historical Journal*, 28, pp. 777–97.

107 'Scottish Philosophy and the Science of Legislation', in *Scottish Philosophers and the Specialisation of Knowledge* (= Royal Society of Edinburgh Occasional Papers, 2–6), pp. 11–29) [bicentenary symposium 1983].

108 Review of **L. Campos Boralevi**, *Bentham and the Oppressed*, *The Bentham Newsletter*, 9, p. 56.

109 Review of **A. London Fell**, *Origins of Legislative Sovereignty and the Legislative State*, Vols. 1 and 2, *Journal of Modern History*, 57, pp. 324–8.

1986

110 'Misunderstandings', review-article on **R. Stewart**, *Henry Brougham 1778–1868: His Public Career* and **B. Fontana**, *Re-Thinking the Politics of Commercial Society: The 'Edinburgh Review' 1802–1832*, *London Review of Books*, 8(5) (20 March), pp. 17–18.

111 'From "Polite Learning" to "Useful Knowledge" ', *History Today*, 36 (April), pp. 21–9.

112 Review of **A. Black**, *Guilds and Civil Society in European Political Thought from the Twelfth Century to the Present*, *History*, 71, pp. 88–90.

113 'Clio as a Governess: Lessons in History, 1798', *History Today*, 36 (August), pp. 10–15.

1987

114 *Absolutism: The History of an Idea* (The Creighton Trust Lecture 1986, delivered on 10 November 1986) (London: University of London).

1988

115 (ed.) *The Cambridge History of Medieval Political Thought, c.350–c.1450* (Cambridge: Cambridge University Press) [contributed: Introduction, pp. 1–8; Conclusion, pp. 649–52].

116 (ed. with H.L.A. Hart) *Jeremy Bentham: A Fragment on Government* (reprint from no. 87 above of pp. 393–501, 507–15 [sections III and IV], with a new introduction by R. Harrison but without the 1977 editorial introduction).

1989

117 'Bentham and Blackstone: A Lifetime's Dialectic', *Utilitas*, 1, pp. 22–40.

118 'Utilitarianism and Reform: Social Theory and Social Change, 1750–1800', *Utilitas*, 1, pp. 211–25 (a revised version of no. 59 above).

119 'Whiggeries', review of **J.W. Burrow**, *Whigs and Liberals: Continuity and Change in English Political Thought, London Review of Books*, 11(5) (2 March), pp. 18–19.

120 Review of **R.A. Fenn**, *James Mill's Political Thought, Utilitas*, 1, pp. 156–72.

121 Review of *Christian Authority: Essays in Honour of Henry Chadwick*, **ed. G.R. Evans**, *Cambridge Review*, 110, pp. 89–90.

1990

122 'The Idea of Absolutism', in *Absolutism in Seventeenth-Century Europe*, **ed. J. Miller** (London: Macmillan), pp. 21–42.

123 'John Ireland: Theology and Public Affairs in the Late Fifteenth Century', *Innes Review*, 41, pp. 151–79.

124 'Bentham and Blackstone: A Lifetime's Dialectic', in *Empire and Revolutions*, **ed. G.J. Schochet** (Proceedings of the Folger Institute Center for the History of British Political Thought, Vol. 6), pp. 251–78 [the substance of a paper presented at the Folger seminar in 1987: no. 117 above is a revised version].

1991

125 (ed. with M. Goldie), *The Cambridge History of Political Thought 1450–1700* (Cambridge: Cambridge University Press) [contributed: Introduction, pp. 1–6; Ch. 5: 'Scholasticism: survival and revival', pp. 132–55; Conclusion, pp. 653–6].

126 (ed.) *The Cambridge History of Medieval Political Thought, c.350–
     c.1450* (Cambridge: Cambridge University Press) [paperback edition of
     no. 115 above].

127 'Thomas More: A Saint for What Season?', *The Newman* (journal of the
     Newman Association), no. 22, pp. 2–6.

128 'Conciliarism, Papalism, and Power, 1511–1518', in *The Church and
     Sovereignty c.500–1918: Essays in Honour of Michael Wilks*,
     ed. D. Wood (= *Studies in Church History*, Subsidia 9) (Oxford: Basil
     Blackwell for the Ecclesiastical History Society), pp. 409–28.

129 'Viewpoint' [on Michael Oakeshott], *Cambridge Review*, 112, pp. 133–6.

1992

130 *Lordship, Kingship and Empire: The Idea of Monarchy, 1400–1525* (The
     Carlyle Lectures, 1988) (Oxford: Clarendon Press).

131 'The "Monarchia" of Antonio de' Roselli (1390–1466): Text, Context
     and Controversy', *Proceedings of the Eighth International Congress of
     Medieval Canon Law, San Diego 1988* (= *Monumenta Iuris Canonici*,
     Series C: Subsidia 9), pp. 321–51.

132 Review of *Popes, Teachers and Canon Law in the Middle Ages*,
     ed. J.R. Sweeney and S. Chodorow, *Journal of Ecclesiastical History*,
     43, pp. 311–12.

1993

133 'George Buchanan and the Anti-Monarchomachs', in *Political Discourse
     in Early-Modern Britain*, **ed. N. Phillipson and Q. Skinner** (Ideas in
     Context series) (Cambridge: Cambridge University Press), pp. 3–22.

134 'David Ure (1749–1793) "Breadth of mind and accuracy of observa-
     tion" ', *Glasgow Naturalist*, 22, pp. 259–75.

135 'Nature and Natural Authority in Bentham', *Utilitas*, 5, pp. 209–19.

136 'Conciliarism' in *Dictionary of Scottish Church History and Theology*,
     ed. N.M. de S. Cameron et al. (Edinburgh: T. and T. Clark,), pp. 201–2.

137 (ed.) *Histoire de la philosophie politique médiévale* [French translation by
     J. Ménard of no. 115 above] (Paris: Presses Universitaires de France).

1994

138 (ed. with M. Goldie), *The Cambridge History of Political Thought 1450–
     1700* [paperback edition of no. 125 above].

139 'George Buchanan and the anti-Monarchomachs', in *Scots and Britons:
     Scottish Political Thought and the Union of 1603*, **ed. R.A. Mason**

(Cambridge: Cambridge University Press), pp. 138–58 [a fuller version of no. 133 above].

140 'Jacques Almain on *dominium*: A Neglected Text', in *Politics, Ideology and the Law in Early Modern Europe*, ed. **A.E. Bakos** (Rochester, NY and Woodbridge, Suffolk: University of Rochester Press), pp. 149–58.

141 Review of **K. Pennington**, *The Prince and the Law, Journal of Ecclesiastical History*, 45, pp. 499–500.

1996

142 *The True Law of Kingship: Concepts of Monarchy in Early Modern Scotland* (Oxford: Clarendon Press).

143 (ed. with H.L.A. Hart), *Jeremy Bentham: An Introduction to the Principles of Morals and Legislation* [reprint, with a new introduction by F. Rosen and the 1982 essay by Hart but without the 1970 editorial introduction, of no. 97 above].

144 Review of *Stephanus Junius Brutus, the Celt, Vindiciae, contra Tyrannos, Or, Concerning the Legitimate Power of a Prince over the People, and of the People over the Prince, Journal of Ecclesiastical History*, 47, pp. 376–8.

145 *Histoire de la pensée politique moderne 1450–1700* [French translation by J. Ménard and C. Sutto of no. 125 above] (Paris: Presses Universitaires de France).

146 (ed. with T.M. Izbicki), *Conciliarism and Papalism* (Cambridge Texts in the History of Political Thought) (Cambridge: Cambridge University Press) [contributed: Introduction, pp. vii–xxiii; and see 'Editors' note', p. vi].

147 '*Jus gladii* and *jurisdictio*: Jacques Almain and John Locke', in *Locke*, ed. **J. Dunn and I. Harris** (*Great Political Thinkers*, 9) (2 vols., Cheltenham and Lyme, NH: Edward Elgar Publishing), Vol. 2, pp. 1–6 [reprint of no. 99 above].

1998

148 'John Knox: Scholastic and Canonistic Echoes', in *John Knox and the British Reformations*, ed. **R.A. Mason** (Aldershot: Scolar/Ashgate), pp. 117–29.

149 Review of **William Ockham**, *Opera politica*, IV, ed. **H.S. Offler**, *Journal of Ecclesiastical History*, 49, p. 723

THE ROLE OF POWER IN
THE POLITICAL THOUGHT OF MARSILIUS OF PADUA

Joseph Canning*

Abstract: The question of power occupied an even more central role in Marsilius' political thought than previously thought. Behind the appearances of consent in his thought lay, at a deeper level, the idea of power. The core concept of coercive power was located within the field of meaning of *plenitudo potestatis* through which Marsilius' new theory of the nature of power was strained and projected onto the papacy. But the modern debate about whether Marsilius was a legal positivist has been wrongly posed. His stress on the necessity of a clear power structure had a biological basis. Comparison with jurists reveals the strengths and weaknesses of his treatment of power.

The period from the end of the thirteenth century and throughout the fourteenth witnessed a significant shift in political thought towards a greater recognition of the realities of power in church and state.[1] This trend was signalled by a clutch of treatises, produced by Giles of Rome, James of Viterbo and John of Paris between 1302 and 1303, and which were overtly devoted to the theme of power.[2] The fourteenth century witnessed an increasingly sophisticated treatment of the nature, role, structure and importance of power in public affairs. Three bundles of ideas in particular were the focus of discussion. The most well-known of these was plenitude of power (*plenitudo potestatis*) originally developed by the papacy, used systematically by popes from the time of Innocent III and adopted by secular rulers in the course of the thirteenth century. The second was the notion that the ruler's will was held to be reason (*pro ratione voluntas*) and was developed by jurists from the end of the twelfth century.[3] The third was the further elaboration of the distinction between the ruler's absolute and ordinary power (*potestas absoluta* and *potestas ordinaria/*

---

* School of History and Welsh History, University of Wales, Bangor, Gwynedd, Wales LL57 2DG.

[1] See Joseph Canning, *A History of Medieval Political Thought 300–1450* (London and New York, 1996), pp. 135–7.

[2] Giles of Rome, *De ecclesiastica potestate* (1302); James of Viterbo, *De regimine christiano* (1302); John of Paris, *De regia potestate et papali* (1302/3).

[3] See for instance Joseph Canning, 'Italian Juristic Thought and the Realities of Power in the Fourteenth Century', in *Political Thought and the Realities of Power in the Middle Ages/Politisches Denken und die Wirklichkeit der Macht im Mittelalter*, ed. Joseph Canning and Otto-Gerhard Oexle, Veröffentlichungen des Max-Planck-Instituts für Geschichte, 147 (Göttingen, 1998), pp. 227–37.

ordinata), building on the work of Hostiensis in the mid-thirteenth century.[4] This concentration on the theme of power marked a movement away from a more idealized and schematic political thought concerned with the purpose of the ruler's authority and its origins, towards a preoccupation with processes of authority and control in church and state.

It is useful to view Marsilius of Padua's (1275/80–1342/3) political thought specifically within the wider context of this theme of the reality of power. It is a privilege and especially fitting to do so in a volume in honour of James Burns who has had a particular interest in Marsilius, and under whose editorship *The Cambridge History of Medieval Political Thought* reflected the significance of the Paduan's contribution to political thought. Of course it is true that Marsilius' most obvious concern was papal plenitude of power and that the overall purpose of his *Defensor pacis* and *Defensor minor* was to destroy intellectually this whole papal claim. A vast amount of scholarly energy has been expended on this subject. It is, however, my contention, and the purpose of this article to demonstrate, that the question of power occupied an even more central and far-reaching role in Marsilius' thought than has been previously realized. When Marsilius' texts are approached specifically from the standpoint of power, perspectives are changed and his ideas are seen in a different light. Alan Gewirth, for instance, recognized the fruitfulness of reading Marsilius in this way when he said, 'the force of Marsilius' ecclesiastic ideas is to be found equally in his solution of the problems of political power as such: those problems receive at his hands a consistent and striking treatment from a fresh point of view',[5] but did not overtly follow up this perception in a systematic way. My argument is that the question of the nature, exercise and function of power lies at the core of Marsilius' political thought, which is a systematic elaboration of this theme. In other words, however much he may at times be concerned on the surface with other matters, most notably consent,[6] his deep preoccupation was with the problem of power: this provided the fundamental direction of his thought.

'Power' is a term which connotes a notorious diversity of meanings; it is also a concept which poses specific problems in different languages. The complications involved in, for instance, the usages of *Gewalt*, *Macht* and *Herrschaft* in

---

[4] See in particular Eugenio Randi, 'La vergine e il papa. *Potentia dei absoluta* e *plenitudo potestatis* papale nel XIV secolo', *History of Political Thought*, V(3) (1984), pp. 425–45; and Kenneth Pennington, *The Prince and the Law, 1200–1600. Sovereignty and Rights in the Western Legal Tradition* (Berkeley, Los Angeles, Oxford, 1993), pp. 106–18.

[5] Alan Gewirth, *Marsilius of Padua. The Defender of Peace*. I: *Marsilius of Padua and Medieval Political Philosophy* (New York, 1951), p. 9.

[6] For the most comprehensive recent consent interpretation of Marsilius (based on Discourse One of the *Defensor pacis*) see Cary J. Nederman, *Community and Consent. The Secular Political Theory of Marsiglio of Padua's Defensor pacis* (Lanham, MD, 1995).

German (both historically and in modern writings), especially given the prevalence of Max Weber's categorizations, are especially difficult.[7] Any attempt to interpret a political thinker from the standpoint of his or her ideas of power opens up a potentially bewildering range of aspects of their thought. Marsilius was no exception. As was to be expected, he used *potestas* in a wide variety of senses from coercion at one extreme to mere capability at the other. A good example is to be found in his treatment of the powers of priests — they do have powers but not jurisdictional or coercive ones:

> None of these powers or this authority is coercive: they are all doctrinal or economic, speculative or active, just like those which doctors use when giving opinions and dealing with the healthy and the sick . . . And furthermore when the term 'spiritual power' (*potestas spiritualis*) is used, such power should not be understood to mean someone's power or jurisdiction which is coercive through sanctions against property or the person in this world, but such powers of teaching and acting, exhorting and arguing, as we previously noted in the case of a doctor or administrator. However, leaving aside all such powers, we must now only consider that last one, the power to bind and loose men from their sins, and which is commonly called the power of the keys by the saints and the doctors of holy scripture.[8]

My primary concern in this article is to examine further the role played in Marsilius' political thought by one specific aspect of power: coercion. The importance which he attributed to coercive power is of course extremely well known. I hope to show that its role was for him even more central and architectonic than previously thought.

It is possible to argue that consent is the key idea in Marsilius' construction of the model of the political community.[9] At one level this is obviously true. But if one looks at Marsilius' model through the perspective of power then a different picture emerges, just as if one stares at a stereogramme. Precisely

---

[7] See 'Herrschaft' and 'Macht, Gewalt', in *Geschichtliche Grundbegriffe. Historisches Lexikon zur politisch-sozialen Sprache in Deutschland*, ed. Otto Brunner, Werner Conze and Reinhart Koselleck (Stuttgart, 1982), Vol. 3, pp. 1–102 and 817–935.

[8] 'Praefatarum autem potestatum sive auctoritatum nulla coactiva est; sed omnes sunt doctrinales vel oeconomicae, sive speculativae sive operativae, quemadmodum ea quae medici in dicendo et operando circa sanos et aegros . . . Et propterea, cum nominatur potestas spiritualis, non debet intelligi per talem potestatem auctoritas seu iurisdictio cuiusquam, poena reali aut personali in hoc saeculo coactiva, sed qualem docendi et operandi, exhortandi et arguendi, pridem diximus per medici aut oeconomici potestatem; omissis tamen omnibus dictis potestatibus, de ea solum ultima, quae est solvendi et ligandi homines a peccatis, et quae communiter a sanctis et sanctae Scripturae doctoribus potestas clavium nominatur, nunc instat tractare.' *Defensor minor*, 4.3, in *Marsile de Padoue. Oeuvres mineures. Defensor minor. De translatione imperii*, edited with French translation by Colette Jeudy and Jeannine Quillet, Sources d'Histoire Médiévales, 12 (Paris, 1979), p. 192.

[9] See, for instance, Nederman, *Community and Consent*, esp. pp. 46–7 and 77.

because consent is identified with the will of the *universitas civium* as the human legislator, it is in a curious way interchangeable with the power of the people.[10] Marsilius makes this clear when he says of the *pars principans* (or ruling part), that

> It should understand that to it alone belongs the authority to command the subject multitude collectively or distributively, and to constrain anyone, if it is expedient, according to the laws made; and to do nothing apart from the laws, especially in difficult circumstances, without the consent of the subject multitude or legislator; and that the multitude or legislator should not be provoked by injury, because in its expressed will consists the virtue and authority of rulership.[11]

Yet for all the importance of power within Marsilius' discourse, it has to be said that he was relatively restricted in the terminology with which he approached the question: he used only part of the language available to him. He appears not to have explored the implications of the well-known juristic phrase *pro ratione voluntas*, or of the categories of *potestas absoluta* and *potestas ordinaria*. Indeed *potestas absoluta* only makes a tangential appearance as in his discussion of the various possible meanings of *plenitudo potestatis* where he says of the priestly power of binding and loosing, 'it has not been conceded to a priest absolutely or with plenitude, but has been determined by divine law'.[12] Marsilius focused his treatment of power on the concept of *plenitudo potestatis*, doubtless because of his obsession with the papacy. Why his approach was so relatively restricted must remain a mystery, but it does mean that his treatment of power, while it presented a challenge based on first principles, was not as clear as it could have been.

His treatment of *plenitudo potestatis* itself was somewhat bewildering. When he went down a line of argument, it was a characteristic of Marsilius to attempt to be comprehensive, and indeed exhaustive, as only a scholastic writer could be. In *DP*, 2.23.3, he listed eight different senses of *plenitudo potestatis*.[13] The first two, he admitted, could be possessed by God or Christ alone: the power to perform any act and to make anything at will; and acts of will which went far beyond human capacity. He therefore did not discuss them. The fifth sense

---

[10] But see Nederman's rejection of the identification between consent and will in the *Defensor pacis* (*Community and Consent*, p. 51 n. 66).

[11] 'Comprehendet . . . soli sibi convenire auctoritatem precipiendi subiecte multitudini communiter aut divisim; et unumquemque arcere, si expediat, secundum positas leges et nil preter has, arduum presertim, agere absque multitudinis subiecte seu legislatoris consensu; nec iniuria provocandam esse multitudinem seu legislatorem, quoniam in ipsius expressa voluntate consistit virtus et auctoritas principatus.' Marsilius, *Defensor pacis* (hereafter *DP*), 3.3, ed. Richard Scholz, MGH, Fontes Iuris Germanici Antiqui in Usum Scholarum (Hanover, 1932), p. 612.

[12] 'Non est absolute sive cum plenitudine sacerdoti concessa, sed lege divina determinata.' *DP*, 2.23.4, ed. Scholz, p. 444.

[13] *DP*, ed. Scholz, pp. 441–5.

concerned the priestly powers of binding and loosing, excommunication and interdict. The sixth related to the power of making men priests and bestowing or prohibiting the sacraments of the church. As we have just seen, Marsilius rejected any priestly plenitude of power in binding and loosing; he also accorded to the faithful human legislator the power to excommunicate and place under interdict, and denied that bishops had full powers in choosing whom to make priests. The seventh concerned the power to interpret the meanings of Scripture, especially in matters concerning salvation. This was a particularly important question because Giles of Rome, at the very beginning of his tract *De ecclesiastica potestate*, had justified his whole concentration on the notion of papal power, by saying that the pope's plenitude of power, in declaring matters of faith or morals, related to salvation, because anyone ignorant of such decisions would be condemned by God at the Last Judgment.[14] The seventh also concerned the coercive power to regulate all church ritual. The eighth concerned a general pastoral cure of souls amongst all peoples and in all parts of the world. Marsilius rejected these two claims on the grounds that priests were limited by the provisions of human and divine law.

Of the eight possible senses of *plenitudo potestatis* discussed by Marsilius, only the third and the fourth concerned coercive power:

> In a third sense, plenitude of power can be understood as being that of supreme coercive jurisdiction over all the governments, peoples, communities, groups and individuals in the world; or, again, over some of these, but following every impulse of the will. In a fourth sense, it can be understood as that which has just been discussed and in that manner, but only over all clerics, as regards the power to appoint all of them to church offices, to deprive them of office or dismiss them, and to distribute ecclesiastical temporal goods and benefices.[15]

As Georges de Lagarde pointed out, this means that only one of the senses of *plenitudo potestatis* discussed by Marsilius concerns papal power in purely secular matters: all the rest either belong solely to God or relate to spiritual concerns.[16]

Certainly, it was central to Marsilius' argument to reject papal plenitude of power in senses three and four, and there were great set pieces in the *Defensor*

[14] *De ecclesiastica potestate*, 1.1 (ed. Richard Scholz (reprinted Aalen, 1961)), pp. 4–5.

[15] 'Tercio vero modo intelligi potest plenitudo potestatis ea, que supreme iurisdiccionis coactive super omnes mundi principatus, populos, communitates, collegia et singulares personas; aut rursum in aliqua horum, secundum tamen omnem impetum voluntatis. Quarto vero modo intelligi potest ea, que iam dicta est aut secundum dictum modum super omnes clericos tantum, ipsosque omnes ad ecclesiastica officia instituendi, privandi seu deponendi et ecclesiastica temporalia sive beneficia distribuendi.' (*DP*, ed. Scholz, p. 442.

[16] See Georges de Lagarde, *La naissance de l'esprit laïque au déclin du moyen age*. III: *Le defensor pacis* (Paris, 1970), p. 78.

pacis which set out to do this. Papal plenitude of power was for Marsilius the great, singular and new cause of the destruction of political peace of which Aristotle could never have known.[17] It was Marsilius' self-appointed task to unmask this fraud and destroy its credibility: in his own words he saw himself as 'the herald of the truth' to reveal papal lies for what they were.[18]

Marsilius' core notion of coercive power was not therefore identified with *plenitudo potestatis* in all its possible manifestations but was a concept lying within the field of meaning indicated by the term. At a more general and all-inclusive level Marsilius defined *plenitudo potestatis* thus after his listing of its eight possible senses in *DP*, 2.23.3:

> Again, plenitude of power could be understood, in each of the senses given above, as that which is limited by no law, but non-plenary as that which would be limited by laws human and divine, under which heading right reason can also be properly classed.[19]

Marsilius certainly set the papacy up as the archetypal wielder of coercive power. In so doing he created a Leviathan, a monster, which had little correspondence with reality. He attributed to the papacy claims which it and the canonists never made. Marsilius went beyond the usage of *plenitudo potestatis* in papal decretals and the works of the Decretalists. Only perhaps in writers like Giles of Rome and Augustinus Triumphus was papal plenitude of power elaborated to produce the kind of dragon which Marsilius sought to slay.[20] Indeed, no ruler, no government in Christian Europe in the first half of the fourteenth century, had the kind of coercive power which Marsilius maintained that the papacy claimed. Marsilius' obsessive ruminations about the papacy and the threat it posed to the correct order of political society led him to enunciate a notion of coercive power which he projected onto the papacy. In so doing and in constructing a political theory to destroy this papal claim (which was largely of his own making) he produced a new theory of the nature of power and its role in the government of political communities. Marsilius' concept of power was, as it were, strained through the notion of papal *plenitudo potestatis*.

Marsilius' prime contention was that the actions of the papal monarchy revealed that coercive jurisdictional power was in the wrong hands. He did not

---

[17] *DP*, 2.26.19.

[18] 'Quod ne deinceps lateat horum episcoporum fallacia, tamquam veritatis preco clamo valenter' (*DP*, 2.25.18, ed. Scholz, p. 485).

[19] 'Posset autem rursum plenitudo potestatis intelligi secundum unamquamque divisionum dictarum ea, que nulla sit determinata lege; non plena vero, que foret determinata per leges humanam aut divinam, sub qua eciam recta racio potest convenienter comprehendi.' *DP*, ed. Scholz, p. 443.

[20] For an exposition of the views of extreme pro-papal apologists on papal plenitude of power, Michael Wilks, *The Problem of Sovereignty in the Later Middle Ages. The Papal Monarchy with Augustinus Triumphus and the Publicists*, Cambridge Studies in Medieval Life and Thought, 2nd series, 9 (Cambridge, 1963), remains fundamental.

object to the possession and exercise of coercive power as such — far from it. Such power was absolutely necessary for the good and effective government of society. Marsilius' political theory was an attempt to show that coercive power was the backbone of legitimate government, and to reveal where that power lay and the mechanisms whereby it should be exercised. He had to do this in order intellectually to destroy the false claims of the papacy and its court which he had visited:

> I, who was present there and saw for myself, seemed to be seeing that terrible statue which Nebuchadnezzar is said, in Daniel, chapter 2, to have seen in his sleep, its head made of gold, its arms and breast of silver, its belly and thighs of brass, its legs of iron, its feet part of iron and part of clay. For what else does this huge statue represent other than the state of the persons in the curia or of the supreme Roman pontiff, this image which once terrified the wicked, but now fills all conscientious men with dread?[21]

Marsilius' key statement came at the end of the *Defensor pacis*:

> This treatise will be called *Defensor pacis*, because in it there are discussed and explained those main causes whereby civil peace or tranquillity exists and is preserved, and also those through which strife opposed [to peace] arises, is checked and is removed. For through this treatise is made known the authority, the cause, and the concordance of divine and human laws and of all coercive rulership (*principatus*), which are the rules for human acts, in whose proper and unimpeded measure civil peace or tranquillity consists.[22]

Marsilius' contention was that the correct use of coercive power, by the right person or persons, was necessary for the attaining of peace. Such power was, therefore, a positive thing in a political context. In a spiritual one it was utterly out of place and counter-productive. Marsilius' image of the role of the priesthood was that of poverty (and hence powerlessness), and teaching by word and example, not by force.

Marsilius, of course, placed the exercise of coercive power in the hands of the secular human legislator, who could be one, few or many: the emperor, a

---

[21] 'Qui vero vidi et affui, videre videor quam Danielis secundo Nabuchodonosor terribilem statuam in sompnio recitatur vidisse, caput siquidem habentem aureum, brachia vero et pectus argentea, ventrem autem et femora erea, tibias qu dem ferreas pedumque partem unam ferream et reliquam fictilem. Quid enim aliud ingens hec statua est, quam status personarum curie Romani seu summi pontificis, que olim perversis hominum terribilis, nunc vero cunctis studiosis orribilis est aspectu.' *DP*, 2.24.17, ed. Scholz, p. 464.

[22] 'Vocabitur autem tractatus iste Defensor Pacis, quoniam in ipso tractantur et explicantur precipue cause quibus conservatur et extat civilis pax sive tranquillitas et hec eciam propter quas opposita lis oritur, prohibetur et tollitur. Per ipsum enim scitur auctoritas, causa et concordancia divinarum et humanarum legum et coactivi cuiuslibet principatus, que regule sunt actuum humanorum, in quorum convenienti mensura non impedita pax seu tranquillitas civilis consistit.' *DP*, 3.3, ed. Scholz, pp. 611–12.

king, a relatively restricted group or a larger citizen community. But at this point we confront a difficulty. Marsilius certainly made it clear that the human legislator had the ultimate right of command and coercion. But he did little to develop the usage of the words *potestas* and *potentia* in this connection. It would have been logical for him to attribute *plenitudo potestatis* to the human legislator. Did he do this? The answer is 'yes' — but only on a few occasions. Thus when in *DP*, 2.23.4, he was discussing the third and fourth modes of plenitude of power he said,

> But whether such plenitude of power has been granted by human law to any cleric, bishop or priest, or to any layman (in any way in which it is possible for it to be granted and revoked for a reasonable cause by the judgment of the human legislator), must be ascertained from human laws and the rescripts or privileges of the same legislator.[23]

His statement in *DP*, 3.2 (giving his thirteenth conclusion), was clearer:

> That no ruler, and far less any partial group or individual person of whatever status they may be, has plenitude of control or power over the private or civil acts of other people without the determination of the mortal legislator.[24]

The idea of the central and systematic role of power was certainly there in Marsilius' thought and lay behind the theme of coercion which ran through his political theory. But there is no denying that his treatment of power could have been more clearly expressed and developed in a more satisfactory way.

The capacity to coerce is in itself a product of the possession of power. The question is: how clearly is the power relationship perceived when there is coercion? Power may be operative but it may not be overtly named. 'Will', 'consent', 'jurisdiction' and 'command' may be more to the fore. But behind them in reality lies power.

The reason why Marsilius' usage of the terms *potestas* and *potentia* was so focused on the papacy may well have lain in the nature of his adversary. It was the medieval church which pre-eminently developed the language of power in the Middle Ages, with *plenitudo potestatis* being merely the pre-eminent example. It may have been natural, therefore, for Marsilius to concentrate his fire about power on the papacy.

---

[23] 'Vtrum autem humana lege sit clerico cuiquam, episcopo vel sacerdoti aut non-sacerdoti, talis potestatis plenitudo concessa, secundum aliquem modum possibilis quidem concedi, et ex causa racionabili legislatoris humani iudicio revocari, certificandum est ex humanis legibus et rescriptis seu privilegiis legislatoris eiusdem.' *DP*, ed. Scholz, p. 444.

[24] 'Nullum principantem, eoque minus collegium parciale vel singularem personam cuiuscumque condicionis existat, alienorum actuum monasticorum aut civilium absque mortalis legislatoris determinacione imperii plenitudinem seu potestatis habere.' *DP*, ed. Scholz, p. 605.

Certainly, the theme of coercion in Marsilius' thought was even more important than so far suggested. We find this in his treatment of law, the most fundamental aspect of his thought. Marsilius gave detailed treatment to the different senses of the term 'law' (*lex*) and, notoriously, held that law in the proper sense was a coercive precept:

> Law may be considered in two ways. The first is in itself, whereby it only shows what is just or unjust, beneficial or harmful; and in this way, it is called the science or doctrine of right (*iuris*). In another way it can be considered, in so far as, with regard to its observance, there is given a command coercive through punishment or reward to be meted out in the present world, or in so far as it is handed down by way of such a command; and considered in this way it most properly is called, and is, a law. It was in this sense that Aristotle also defined it in the last book of the *Ethics*, chapter 8, when he said: 'Law has coercive power (*coactiva potencia*), for it is discourse derived from some kind of prudence and understanding.' Law, then, is a 'discourse' or statement 'derived from some kind of prudence and understanding' (that is political understanding): it is an ordinance made by political prudence, concerning what is just and beneficial and the opposite, and having 'coercive power' (that is, concerning whose observance there is given a command which one is forced to observe), or it is [an ordinance] made by way of such a command.[25]

This emphasis on law as coercive precept was Marsilius' key idea. By restricting the capacity to make such law to the human legislator, he was able to deny the existence of canon law as law in the proper sense and to deny it any application in this world. This is not to suggest, however, that Marsilius viewed human law as simply an exercise of coercive power in an arbitrary way. His perception was that law, as the expression of coercive power, held political society together and was necessary for achieving the common good and securing the permanence of government:

> We wish to show the necessary purpose of law in its last and most proper sense. Its prime purpose is to achieve civil justice and the common benefit;

---

[25] 'Lex dupliciter considerari potest: uno modo secundum se, ut per ipsam solum ostenditur quid iustum aut iniustum, conferens aut nocivum, et in quantum huiusmodi iuris scientia vel doctrina dicitur. Alio modo considerari potest, secundum quod de ipsius observacione datur preceptum coactivum per penam aut premium in presenti seculo distribuenda, sive secundum quod per modum talis precepti traditur; et hoc modo considerata propriissime lex vocatur et est. Quam eciam sic sumptam diffinit Aristoteles ultimo Ethicorum, 8⁰ capitulo, cum dixit: "Lex autem coactivam habet potenciam sermo ens ab aliqua prudencia et intellectu; sermo" igitur seu oracio "ab aliqua prudencia seu intellectu", politico scilicet, id est ordinacio de iustis et conferentibus et ipsorum oppositis per prudenciam politicam, "habens coactivam potenciam", id est, de cuius observacione datur preceptum, quod quis cogitur observare, seu lata per modum talis precepti, lex est.' *DP*, 1.10.4, ed. Scholz, pp. 49–50.

but its secondary purpose is to provide some security for rulers, especially hereditary ones, and the long duration of rulership.[26]

This means that it is unsustainable to maintain that Marsilius understood human law as simply the expression of a power structure. Rather, law as coercive rule was the necessary means to procure the aim of the common good for which secure and lasting government was required. Marsilius by no means mouthed platitudes about the common good but rather addressed himself to the problem of how it could actually be brought about. Indeed, Marsilius held that a ruler should rule according to the laws and held up Theopompus as a shining example of a ruler who eschewed too much power:

> They say that, when his wife asked him [Theopompus] whether he was not ashamed to hand on to his sons a smaller kingdom than he had received from his father, he replied, 'You should not say that, for the kingdom I pass on will last longer.' O heroic voice, proceeding from Theopompus' unheard-of prudence! How it should be heeded by those who wish to wield plenitude of power over their subjects outside the laws! Many rulers, not listening to this voice, have come to ruin.[27]

Only in this way could peace be achieved.

This brings one to the most difficult question in interpreting Marsilius. Was he or was he not a legal positivist? Did his contention that law in its most proper sense was a coercive precept, lead him to the position that the will alone of the human legislator constituted valid law without any considerations of higher norms (or indeed in violation of them?). This has been a much debated point. If Marsilius did take a legal positivist view then he may well have been alone in the Middle Ages in so doing. To illustrate the poles of scholarly opinion on this point, Gewirth, for example, held as a central thesis of his interpretation that Marsilius was a legal positivist; Cary J. Nederman has recently censured this position.[28]

The solution to this problem is not helped by the lack of clarity in the crucial passage:

[26] 'Eius [i.e. legis] secundum ultimam et propriisimam significationem ostendere volumus necessitatem finalem: principaliorem quidem civile iustum et conferens commune, assecutivam vero quandam principancium, maxime secundum generis successionem, securitatem et principatus diuturnitatem.' *DP*, 1.11.1, ed. Scholz, p. 52; cf. *DP*, 1.11.8.

[27] 'Que quidem, id est hec verba, aiunt et ad uxorem respondisse ipsum, que, scilicet uxor, dixerat: Si nihil, id est si non, verecundaretur, minus regnum tradens filiis, quam a patre accepit? cui verba iam dicta respondit: "Non oportet hoc dicere, trado enim diuturnius." O vox heroica, ex inaudita prudencia Theopompi procedens, et quam notanda hiis qui extra leges uti volunt plenitudine potestatis in subditos; quam inadvertentes multi principancium corruerunt.' *DP*, 1.11.8, ed. Scholz, p. 61.

[28] See Gewirth, *Marsilius of Padua*, I, pp. 132–75; and Nederman, *Community and Consent*, pp. 79–83.

> Sometimes false understandings of what is just and beneficial become laws, when a command is given to observe them or they are made by means of a command, as appears to be the case in the lands of some barbarians, who have it observed as just that a murderer be absolved from guilt and civil penalty, on payment of a fine for such a crime. This, however, is simply unjust, and as a result their laws are not simply perfect. For although they possess due form, that is a command enforcing their observance, they none the less lack due condition, that is the proper and true ordering of justice.[29]

This passage can be interpreted in a positivist sense. But care should be taken with this view given Marsilius' overall position that law was conducive to justice and the common good. A balanced interpretation of his position would suggest that the question of whether or not he was a legal positivist is not correctly posed and is the product of modern jurisprudential concerns. A simple 'yes' or 'no' cannot be given. For most normal circumstances Marsilius was not a legal positivist. He was confident that human law properly made by the right authority would conform to higher norms for the common good of all. He had very great (and perhaps naïve) confidence that the human legislator, more than any individual wise man, would know and will those laws which were in fact best for it, just as an animal would pursue its own health and preservation. Yet my reading of the passage quoted is that Marsilius was prepared (albeit reluctantly) to accept the validity of positive laws which infringed higher norms, represented by justice. He saw that laws as coercive precepts were valid as a fact of life. Only to this extent was he a legal positivist; in the normal course of events the question did not arise. But in essence, for him, the exercise of power in the form of coercion was the core of human law, and the guarantee of the good order of government and society.

Marsilius perceived that if political society were not regulated by the proper exercise of coercive power in the form of law, then it would be prevented from enjoying a peaceful existence. It must therefore be clear where power lay. An abiding problem of late medieval society was the failure to provide an unambiguous answer to this question — or indeed to perceive that it was such an important one. Because Marsilius understood the nature of power, he was unique in the late Middle Ages in insisting that the exercise of coercive power should lie in one clearly defined place within the political community — the human legislator or the prince by its authority. Of course Marsilius primarily

---

[29] 'Quinimo quandoque false cogniciones iustorum et conferencium leges fiunt, cum de ipsis datur observacionis preceptum, seu feruntur per modum precepti: sicut apparet in regionibus barbarorum quorundam, qui tamquam iustum observari faciunt homicidam absolvi a culpa et pena civili reale aliquod precium exhibentem pro tali delicto, cum tamen hoc simpliciter sit iniustum, et per consequens ipsorum leges non perfecte simpliciter. Esto enim quod formam habeant debitam, preceptum scilicet observacionis coactivum, debita tamen carent condicione, videlicet debita et vera ordinacione iustorum.' *DP*, 1.10.5, ed. Scholz, pp. 50–1.

had in mind the problems caused by parallel secular and ecclesiastical jurisdictions, which is the reason why he insisted that excommunication should be a
matter purely for the faithful human legislator, so that its sovereignty could be
preserved.[30]

What comes through overall is Marsilius' view of the necessity and positive
nature of a clear power structure within a political community. He certainly
reached this position as a result of his consideration of the misuse of power on
the papacy's part. There was also another, deeper reason. Marsilius' medical
training left him with a view of the body politic which was primarily this-
worldly and naturalistic. Behind his political thought lay a biological interpretation of human life.[31] He went beyond Aristotle in the way in which he
characterized the political community as an animal:

> Let us assume with Aristotle in Book 1, chapter 2, and Book 5, chapter 3 of
> his *Politics*, that a city is like an animate or animal nature. For just as an
> animal, well-disposed according to its nature, is composed of certain propor-
> tioned parts ordered to one another and acting in mutual communication for
> the good of the whole, so a city is constituted from certain such parts, when
> it is well disposed and instituted according to reason. The relationship there-
> fore between the animal (and its parts) and health, is seen to be similar to that
> between the city or kingdom (and its parts) and tranquillity.[32]

Peace consisted in the good disposition of the parts of the political community;
intranquillity lay in their diseased disposition. This biological approach had
implications for the capacity of such a community to govern itself, and was the
fundamental presupposition underlying Marsilius' confidence that it would
only make laws suitable for itself: that just like an animal it knew what was
best for itself. Above all, the political community naturally sought its own
survival. In this context the natural exercise of power was the proper means by
which it did so.

A return to a fourteenth-century juristic comparison is useful at this point in
order to illustrate just how far Marsilius had gone in his treatment of power and
to put his ideas into some perspective. It is notable that a very similar biological
approach is to be found in the works of Baldus de Ubaldis (1327–1400), who
made pre-eminent contributions to the discussion of power. Baldus, however,

---

[30] *DP*, 2.6.12 and 13.

[31] As Gewirth recognized: see Gewirth, *Marsilius of Padua*, I, pp. 49–52.

[32] 'Debentes itaque describere tranquillitatem et suum oppositum, suscipiamus cum
Aristotele primo et quinto Politice sue capitulis 2^0 et 3^0 civitatem esse velut animatam
seu animalem naturam quandam. Nam sicuti animal bene dispositum secundum naturam
componitur ex quibusdam proporcionatis partibus invicem ordinatis suaque opera sibi
mutuo communicantibus et ad totum, sic civitas ex quibusdam talibus constituitur, cum
bene disposita et instituta fuerit secundum racionem. Qualis est igitur comparacio
animalis et suarum parcium ad sanitatem, talis videbitur civitatis sive regni et suarum
parcium ad tranquillitatem.' *DP*, 1.2.3, ed. Scholz, pp. 11–12. See Aristotle, *Politics*,
1.5.1254a 31 ff; 5.3.1302b 34 ff.

applied the animal metaphor to the political community in a far more overt and developed way:

> A people, therefore, for the very reason that it has existence, consequently has governmental power as part of that existence, just as every animal is ruled by its own spirit and soul . . . Moreover in as much as anything has an essential form it also has a capacity to act. But the people derives its form from itself, and therefore also the exercise of self-preservation as regards its existence and proper form. For it is natural and allowed that anything should strive after the conservation of its existence.[33]

Baldus was using this biological metaphor to justify the legislational autonomy of a city-*populus*.

Further, a comparison between Marsilius and juristic writers does reveal that *plenitudo potestatis* was the key concept for denoting sovereign power, but also produces somewhat mixed results. In the crucial area of the ruler's treatment of his subjects' property rights, there was a difference of juristic opinion. Against the mainstream of juristic thought Baldus held that the emperor, through the exercise of his *potestas absoluta*, could remove his subjects' property without any cause other than his own will. This was a turning-point in the history of political ideas and a crucial step down the road to absolutism. Whereas the established juristic interpretation of *potestas absoluta* was of a power freed from human laws but not higher norms, Baldus, in the case of the dispossession and transfer of property, held that the *princeps*, in the exercise of his absolute power, was not limited by the relevant higher norm of the *ius gentium*. Baldus, in so developing the juristic theme of *pro ratione voluntas* (that the will of the prince is reason enough), went far beyond anything Marsilius had to say about power and, in this respect, had a far more developed notion of the potential exercise of pure power as such.[34]

In another context, the comparison between Marsilius and Baldus is equally revealing. Baldus operated with a notion of a hierarchy of sovereignty within which monarchs (such as the emperor, the pope and kings) were of a higher rank than cities. He was only willing to attribute *plenitudo potestatis* to monarchs: he did not apply it to sovereign city-*populi*.[35] Marsilius in contrast, as

---

[33] 'Eoipso quod populus habet esse habet per consequens regimen in suo esse, sicut omne animal regitur a suo spiritu proprio et anima . . . Preterea quantum unumquodque habet de forma essentiali tantum habet de virtute activa; sed populus habet formam ex se, ergo et exercitium conservandi se in esse suo, et in forma propria; nam hoc est naturale et permissum quod unumquodque studeat conservationi sui esse.' On *Digestum vetus*, 1.1.9, ed. [Lyons], 1498: see Joseph Canning, *The Political Thought of Baldus de Ubaldis* (Cambridge, 1987), pp. 104–7.

[34] See Canning, 'Italian Juristic Thought and Realities of Power', pp. 230–5, where the precedent provided by Jacobus Butrigarius is also discussed (p. 231).

[35] See Canning, *Political Thought of Baldus*, p. 65. Baldus was, nevertheless, willing to accept the claims of some Italian *signori* to plenitude of power (see *ibid.*, pp. 223–4).

we have seen, did on at least a couple of occasions attribute *plenitudo potestatis* to the human legislator.[36] This reveals a difference of mentality. Although Baldus did with great ingenuity and creativity produce an argument for the sovereignty of city-*populi*, he did so within the overall context of the established juristic discourse of the *ius commune*. He did so by developing the implications of the argument that the city-community as a political animal governed itself by its own consent. Thus Baldus' notions of such a city's self-government and then non-recognition of a superior were generated by his understanding of how a city-*populus* reached such a position by its own resources — that is from within. The problem for him was that the model for sovereignty within the *ius commune* remained the emperor or pope (*princeps*). This model had therefore to be applied to such cities from without. This had been done by Bartolus of Sassoferrato through his concept of the *civitas sibi princeps*, which Baldus had followed to the extent of considering such sovereign cities as being in the emperor's place. What Baldus would (or could) not do was to attribute *plenitudo potestatis* to sovereign city-*populi*. It was for this reason that he left them at a level of sovereignty below that of monarchs. Marsilius may therefore in comparison be seen as more emphatically and more directly attributing sovereign power to the city-community as human legislator — an argument from within his overall biological model of such a community.

Marsilius, who was no jurist but had some legal knowledge, had no need to resort to the ingenious and somewhat tortuous mental gymnastics imposed on Bartolus and Baldus by the requirements of juristic discourse: they were after all attempting to develop a theory of popular sovereignty within a legal tradition designed for monarchy. In contrast, because of Marsilius' academic background and the nature of the texts he wrote, it is difficult to place his works within a specific form of discourse, other than to say (somewhat unrevealingly) that he, like the jurists, was also a scholastic author. It was Marsilius' intellectual characteristic that he argued from first principles. He was to this extent freer than a jurist. But it has to be said that he did not make full use of this freedom on the question of power. As we have seen, he could have made more use of the possibilities provided by juristic language. For this reason, important though Marsilius' contribution to the development of the language of power was, the major development of such language in the fourteenth century was made by jurists, notably Baldus, despite the limits which juristic discourse placed upon them. Had Marsilius known more law, he could have formulated his arguments with even greater force.

Joseph Canning   UNIVERSITY OF WALES

---

[36] Above, p. 28.

OCKHAM'S RIGHT REASON AND
THE GENESIS OF THE POLITICAL AS 'ABSOLUTIST'

J. Coleman*

Abstract: My aim is to explain the relation of 'right reason' to Ockham's voluntarism by analysing what Ockham takes individual liberty to mean and how men come to know of it. The Christian law of liberty reveals what individuals come to know by other means — from their own experiences and reason, about certain rights which can never be alienated either to Church or 'state'. It is argued that his distinctive and later political positions can be supported by positions maintained in his earlier logical, psychological and philosophical writings from his Oxford period. He explains the three sources of our knowledge as experience, natural reason and infallible scriptural authority. Based on his explanation of how Scripture is to be interpreted and linking this to his epistemology which starts with intuitive cognition, it is argued that Ockham's understanding of the separate roles of 'state' and Church can be defended. From his earlier positions can also be derived his understanding of corporation theory, his defence of individual members of the community's consent to the constitution of government and the limits on absolute government, no matter what its constitutional form. Because right reason always operates in social contexts with their respective, prevalent knowledge, Ockham has some startling things to say about men's access to the truth.

For historians of political thought, one of Jimmy Burns' most important observations about the concept of absolute power has been his reminder that what was well known in the middle ages as *potestas absoluta*, is not the same thing as our understanding of 'absolutism', the earliest appearance of which in English dates from 1830.[1] I should like to confirm his insight into the medieval rather than modern understanding of 'absolute' legitimate government by examining the writings of the fourteenth-century Franciscan logician and theologian William of Ockham. Although it is beyond the scope of my present examination to trace the ways in which medieval notions of absolute power came to be transformed during the early-modern period and thereafter, I shall allude to a range of Ockhamist positions that bear comparison and contrast with those formulated by the seventeenth-century Hobbes. Ockham's philosophical and political writings would be known and used in the seventeenth century,

* Dept. of Government, London School of Economics and Political Science, Houghton Street, London, WC2A 2AE.

[1]   J.H. Burns, 'Absolutism: The History of an Idea', *The Creighton Trust Lecture*, University of London, (London, 1986), pp. 1–30, p. 2. Also see J.H. Burns, *Lordship, Kingship, and Empire, the Idea of Monarchy, 1400–1525, The Carlyle Lectures 1988* (Oxford, 1992).

especially by Huguenot theorists.[2] But as with the writings of all theorists used by later generations with altered agendas, Ockham's ideas would be filtered, and crucial parts of them ignored, to suit other times, places and perspectives.

The question of legitimate power and authority in civil and ecclesiastical regimes was a favoured topic of fourteenth-century theorists who wrote for a variety of papal, episcopal, royal and city-state patrons, or who engaged these questions in university milieux because lecturers were required to provide commentaries on set texts from Greek and Roman antiquity which raised similar issues. Some authors, whatever their academic training or subsequent patronage, accepted what we might recognize as a political agenda as the purpose for which they wrote. For instance, Ockham's contemporary and fellow exile at the court of Ludwig of Bavaria, Marsilius of Padua, can be considered a political theorist concerned primarily with legitimate power in civil regimes, who thereafter used many Franciscan theological positions to bolster his notions on the nature of the Church. But William of Ockham dealt with questions of human authority because he was more fundamentally interested in theological truth. Does this make his views political only by default?

As a theologian, he engaged in a logical search for Catholic truths in Scripture and was particularly averse to Canon lawyers' interventions in doctrinal issues. He abhorred what he took to be the canonist Pope John XXII's ignorance of theology and his misinterpretation of theological texts of Scripture, especially in John's insistence on interpreting scriptural references to Christ's and the apostles' *use* of things in legal terms. It has often been observed that Ockham's was a limited familiarity with the literature of Canon law, knowing some texts well and not others. But to say that his theological focus on scriptural truths makes him a non-political or anti-political writer is to adopt a twentieth-century view of secular intentions behind political expression.[3] Ockham's political conclusions derived, as did so many of the writings of his contemporaries, from his religious beliefs, which he happened to think could be shown to be reasonable. It was from the perfect law of liberty of the Gospels that Ockham developed his notions of the natural rights of individuals and his subsequent understanding of the origin and limits of all institutions with jurisdiction over men's lives.

---

[2] As Quentin Skinner has shown in his *The Foundations of Modern Political Thought* (Cambridge, 1978), Vol. 2 .

[3] See J. Canning, *A History of Medieval Political Thought 300–1450* (London, 1996), p. 160; Scholz also took the view that Ockham was primarily a theologian but did not go so far as to think him anti-political (*Wilhelm von Ockham als politischer Denker und sein Breviloquium de Principatu Tryannico*, ed. R. Scholz (Leipzig, 1944, repr. Stuttgart, 1952)).

Biographical Details

It is thought that William of Ockham was born *c*.1280 in Surrey and died *c*.1349 in the Black Death which swept across Europe and decimated the European population. He entered the Franciscan Order and then studied in Oxford, teaching in the Franciscan *studia* in London and Northampton. He followed the arts course with his Order and then proceeded to the theology degree in Oxford University. He never became a doctor of theology because his academic career as a logician, philosopher and theologian was cut short *c*.1323 when the Chancellor of the University had excerpts from his philosophical and theological writings sent to the pope, who was then resident in Avignon, for examination and possible censure. Ockham was summoned to defend his philosophical positions, he was censured rather than excommunicated, and in 1328, the year in which Ludwig of Bavaria was established as Emperor in Rome, Ockham escaped from Avignon with the Minister General of the Franciscans, Michael of Cesena, to Ludwig's court in Munich. He took up the Michaelists' position and argued against the papal claim to plenitude of power in matters temporal and spiritual. From the 1330s, then, Ockham set to writing against the pretensions of the papacy and defended the Franciscans concerning the absolute poverty of Christ and the apostles by means of his own scriptural hermeneutics. His wider views on politics, none of which were ever presented systematically, would develop thereafter.

Some have argued that the two phases of Ockham's life, the first as an Oxford academic philosopher and theologian and the second as a political theorist, spent as an exile at the court of Ludwig of Bavaria, produced two radically incommensurable sets of writings which cannot be reconciled. It is believed by some that his politics cannot be deduced from his Oxford logic, philosophy and theology.[4] Undoubtedly, he began as an academic theologian with strong interests in logic, psychology and the philosophy of science, all of which reflected the early fourteenth-century Oxford university milieu as it came to diverge from the University of Paris. There is nothing in these early Oxford writings that show him particularly interested in Franciscan 'political' problems, although his philosophical and theological writings developed from his attempts to refine the perspectives of his distinguished Franciscan predecessor in Oxford, John Duns Scotus. But it is my purpose here briefly to show that his distinctive logical, ethical and theological positions were fundamental to his later, distinctive, political conclusions. The break in his academic career was contingent; he was a Franciscan at Oxford and at Avignon, although it was only in Avignon that he became aware of the nature of the contemporary bias of the papacy against his own Order. My aim is to indicate that his theory of knowledge, and his method of analysing texts of Scripture and history which relies on this

---

[4] Gordon Leff, *William of Ockham, the Metamorphosis of Scholastic Discourse* (Manchester, 1975), Ch. 10.

epistemology, were developed at Oxford and endured throughout his life as he responded to changing issues and circumstances. His commitment to truth before institutional authority simply became increasingly focused. It is unfortunate that some historians of political thought who are interested in what can be called Ockham's political theory have found his epistemology and his logic so difficult as to ignore them.

Ockham's Positions on Church and State

Ockham's political positions on the relations of secular and spiritual jurisdictions are easy enough to draw in main outline. If we look first at the conclusions to be found in his later, political, writings, we can thereafter treat the degree to which they may be derived from positions already maintained in his academic logic, ethics, psychology and theology.

After his experience at Avignon, Ockham began his publicist career by writing about Franciscan poverty and its papal adversaries in his *Opus Nonaginta Dierum* (*The Work of Ninety Days*). He then moved on to discuss the problem of papal heresy (in the first part of his *Dialogus*) and on the rights of the Roman empire. From 1337 on he wrote the major works from which his political views may be extracted: *Contra Benedictum*, the third part of the *Dialogus*, his *Eight Questions on Papal Power* (*Octo quaestiones de potestate papae*), the *Breviloquium* (*A Short discourse on the tyrannical government over things divine and human . . .*), and his *On Imperial and Pontifical Power* (*De Imperatorum et Pontificum Potestate*). I shall be drawing on these and other texts in what follows.

Ockham argued that the function of temporal rulers was to chastise and punish wrongdoers in society and to defend the Church from them. All rulers derive their power from 'their people', who voluntarily consent to constitute public authority. To neglect the rights of the community counts as a vice.[5] The right to use the world was conferred on the whole human race, including

---

[5] Ockham, I *Dialogus*, 6,8; Ockham, *Breviloquium*, 1,4; 2,10; 2,19; 3,7–13. The Latin edition of the *Dialogus* is in *Monarchia Sancti Romani Imperii*, ed. Melchior Goldast, Vol. 2 (Frankfurt, 1614, repr. Graz, 1960). There is no full English translation. Excerpts from III *Dialogus* are in *William of Ockham, A Letter to the Friars Minor and Other Writings*, ed. A.S. McGrade, trans. J. Kilcullen (Cambridge, 1995), pp. 118–298. German translations of excerpts with Latin texts are in *Wilhelm von Ockham, Texte zur politischen Theorie*, ed. J. Miethke (Stuttgart, 1995) and Wilhelm von Ockham, *Dialogus, Auszüge zur politischen Theorie*, ed. J. Miethke, with German translation and commentary (Darmstadt, 1992). The Latin text of the *Breviloquium* has been edited by Scholz (*Wilhelm von Ockham als politischer Denker und sein Breviloquium de principatu tyrannico*) and is now translated into English as *A Short Discourse on Tyrannical Government*, ed. A.S. McGrade, trans. J. Kilcullen (Cambridge, 1992). *Breviloquium*, 4, is particularly concerned with issues on legitimate secular government established by the people's will and consent.

infidels, in God's original grant to Adam. But after the Fall, the power to acquire property and to institute government derived from God's grant to humans of a power to appropriate and divide temporal things as right reason, in fallen conditions, deemed necessary, expedient and useful.[6] As we shall see, right reason operated differently in the conditions prior to Adam's fall and after the Fall. Although the Church has exclusive spiritual power, it is subject to lay rulers with regard to the Church's properties. Like Marsilius, Ockham addressed the current problem of there being two distinct, mainly exclusive, jurisdictional orders, that of temporal and spiritual power. He, like Marsilius, argued that the two must somehow be unified, but Ockham suggested a different locus of this unity: the individual. He thereby, *maintained* two distinct jurisdictions governing men's lives, whereas Marsilius subsumed the ecclesiastical within the temporal, civil order to achieve unity. Ockham argued that men who comprise societies are themselves both spiritual and temporal beings. Hence, divine law governs them spiritually, and human laws govern them temporally as citizens. Each individual is subject both to spiritual and temporal rules at the same time.[7]

But humans have rights to construct autonomous systems of law which vary. From God and from nature humans have the right freely to give themselves a head, because they are born free and not subjected to anyone by human law; for this reason every city and every people can establish law for itself.[8] His focus is on the nature of men as individuals, and he is concerned to show how individual men have certain liberties given them as a consequence of God's creation. I shall discuss below how they come to know of this liberty. No man can ever completely alienate certain naturally possessed liberties, either to the 'state' or to the Church. In both the spiritual and the temporal spheres of human life the individual must be considered first as to his rights, capacities and

---

[6] Ockham, *Breviloquium*, 3,7; Ockham, *Opus Nonaginta Dierum* in *Guillelmi de Ockham, Opera Politica*, Vol. I, ed. H.S. Offler (Manchester, 1940, repr. 1974), Chs. 1–6; and Ockham, *Opera Politica*, Vol. II, ed. R.F. Bennett and H.S. Offler (Manchester, 1963), Chs. 7–124. Excerpts in English translation in *William of Ockham, A Letter to the Friars Minor*, ed. McGrade, pp. 19–115, on lordship in the state of innocence, pp. 34 f. and on the origin of property, pp. 59 f.

[7] See for instance, *Eight Questions on the Power of the Pope*, Q.III, in *William of Ockham, A Letter to the Friars Minor*, ed. McGrade, pp. 300–33; the full Latin text is in Ockham, *Opera Politica*, I, pp. 15–217; *Breviloquium*, 3,7; 4,8.

[8] Ockham, *Breviloquium*, 3,7–8; 3,14–15; 4, 8. Ockham, III *Dialogus*, 2,3 and 5–10. See J. Miethke, 'The Concept of Liberty in William of Ockham', in *Théologie et Droit dans la Science Politique de l'Etat Moderne* (no editor named), Collection de l'Ecole Francaise de Rome, 147 (Rome, 1991) pp. 89–100. After the Fall, man was granted the *potestas rectores eligendi iurisdictionem habentes* but its actual forms, including the functionaries of government, depend on man's decision. Ockham separates the decision in favour of an actual form of government from the question of the absolutely best constitution in III *Dialogus*, 1,2,20, and III *Dialogus*, 1,4,23.

liberties. From an analysis of the individual, Ockham proceeds to speak of collections of individuals as social groups.[9]

This focus on the individual is a consequence of what is often called Ockham's nominalism.[10] Broadly, two philosophical positions endured in medieval university philosophy departments: realism and nominalism. For instance, Aquinas was a moderate realist. But according to Ockham, realism destroyed the possibility of genuine knowledge because it posited nonsingular things outside the mind, such as universal natures, and he believed this went against all of Aristotle's logic and philosophy in particular, and against the science of truth and reason in general. Ockham's philosophy of knowledge insisted that all there is in the world are contingent (not necessary) individuals, and human beings then apply names (*nomina*) to such present and existing individuals which they know through a cognitive experience called 'intuitive cognition'. They construct sentences or propositions, either in thought or in conventional language, by which they refer to the individuality of the world. Our knowledge, then, is of (mental or linguistic) propositions whose terms substitute for our experiences.

Ockham's Epistemology

Ockham became identified in the minds of contemporaries with this claim that the proposition itself was the object of knowledge. He came to this view by asking the question that derives from Aristotle's writings on logic: what do our concepts signify and how do we apply concepts to individuals? He affirmed that concepts are the basic components of our thought, but they are somehow caused by prior existent things. Our knowledge is, therefore, *of* concepts themselves or *of* extramental individuals, and the latter must be prior. He interpreted Aristotle as saying that sensory knowledge is what is known first, and that intellective cognition presupposes sensitive cognition. For Ockham, all knowledge is the result of cognition of individuals which are particular and contingent. Reversing the trend of earlier scholastics, he asked not how the individual derives from an essence or a universal, common nature, but how a world of individuals, which is all that really exists, can ever be known in a non-individual and general manner? He went to great lengths to show that while it is true that the universal character of our knowledge requires universal concepts, universality and commonality are properties only of signs, that is, of

---

[9] J. Coleman, 'Guillaume d'Occam et la notion de sujet', in *Archives de philosophie du droit*, 34 (1989), pp. 25–32.

[10] Less misleadingly, it is a conceptualism: universals (or thoughts) are nothing other than names, that is, naturally significant general concepts (natural signs) which are primary; or secondarily, the conventional signs (terms and propositions in language) corresponding to primary concepts.

linguistic expressions and of acts of thought that may also be expressed in language. Universality and commonality are not properties of things. We shall see that his corporation theory reflects this position. For Ockham the problem of individualism is a logical one, and he was concerned to show how general terms which we use in propositions, be they mental or linguistic, refer to individuals that are signified by them.

Everything that exists in reality is singular and individual. The object of knowledge, then, is the mental, spoken or written proposition and not the substance to which the proposition refers. While it is individual substance which we know, it is only known through terms in propositions.

Ockham believed that humans naturally have an immediate and intuitive knowledge of the existence and presence of individual, contingent objects. Normally we know singulars that exist outside the mind and in the world *through* cognized sense experience of their present existence and thereafter, we know them intellectually as more universal concepts or mental names. The universal concept or thought is a natural sign in the mind, an act of thinking rather than an intelligible species. When a sign or term is a concept, it is an act of knowing which signifies individuals known. A sign or term may also be conventionally established, as is any particular language, and it corresponds to the natural signs or mental concepts which signify the individual things we are aware of having sensually experienced. Ockham insists on the one hand, that what we know of the world had first to be sensually experienced. But on the other, he insists that no external corporeal substance can be naturally apprehended by us in itself. We only know particular and individual substances which exist *through* mental, spoken or written propositions, comprised of signs or terms which substitute (supposit) for extramental things experienced. This is what he meant when he famously said that our knowledge in experience derives from terms which supposit for extramental things.

The starting point of any knowledge of contingent facts is intuitive cognition. Only after intuitive cognition can we have other kinds of knowledge: abstractive, individual, universal, contingent, necessary or self-evident. By this he means that in the natural course of living, upon sensing, we have first an immediate awareness or apprehension of terms which substitute for the really existing and present things we have sensed (and which themselves, as individuals, existing and present, are not signs). This immediate awareness comes before a *judgment* of the existence of the thing and before a judgment as to the truth of the thing. We cannot logically demonstrate this intuitive knowing of things, but we simply experience it as a fact of life. We start with a pure apperception of individuals and the linkage of such through propositions whose terms substitute for them. We have, therefore, an intuition of the singular, prior to our having a definition of it. We first know it simply as existing and present. This immediate apprehension is an act of intellect distinct from and prior to judgment. In the present order of things, our intuitive knowledge is always of what exists here and now (there is no intuitive knowledge of nonexistents) and it is caused by this thing known through its term (*ipsa res nota*).[11]

Imagine yourself to be a student studying the arts course amongst Franciscans in Oxford and hearing Ockham's lectures on Aristotle's logic. He told his students that logic deals with a system of signs that is used to make true or false statements about things signified by these signs. Logic, therefore, is the means by which we unlock our experiences beyond the mere having of them. Spoken and written language is conventionally established to signify what is naturally signified by acts of thought. Thinking is no less a logic than is speaking or writing. Logic is the means by which we can study the properties of linguistic expressions to the extent that they refer to the logically essential functions of the soul's inner discourse. Conventional language has, for Ockham, the capacity to signify natural signs or mental acts, which themselves, as terms, are caused by intuitive cognition of individuals experienced. This view on what conventional language is and does has important effects on what he believes the texts of Scripture can be taken to mean. We shall see that it is the task of the scriptural exegete to determine the true meaning of past historical individuals' experiences intuitively known by them.

Ockham is not, however, claiming that the universal knowledge we have as a result of intuitive cognition necessarily mirrors the inner constitution of nature. Rather, he says that we only have confidence in what we can and have experienced. From here, we can only *assume a hypothetical necessity* that knowledge, which deals in universals, actually reflects the causes of our ideas in the physical world of particulars. In this life (*pro statu isto*) we live in a probable world of contingency beyond our immediate intuitive knowledge of things and concepts. Experience of particulars on the one hand, and syllogistic, logical demonstration on the other, give us the same kind of conclusions based on the primacy of the intuitions of singulars and our subsequent generalizations. Our theories about the world can only be about mental acts as signs that are thought to be common to contingent and corruptible things in the world. We rely on probable premises, and to some extent fallible, evidence to make our way in the world of contingent individuals. Hence, Ockham assumes regularities in nature and the constancy of moral norms. Such regularities are derived from observation and abstraction, founded on the prior intuition of the singulars experienced. This attitude to the certainty of experience and our assumptions about natural and moral regularities will be crucial to what he has to say about

---

[11]   J. Coleman, 'The Relation between Ockham's Intuitive Cognition and his Political Science', in *Théologie et Droit dans la Science Politique de l'Etat Moderne*, pp. 71–88. For a fuller excellent discussion see Marilyn McCord Adams, *William Ockham* (2 vols., Notre Dame, Indiana, 1987).

how men come to constitute secular governments and their understanding of what the Church is.[12]

Therefore, Ockham speaks of our 'knowledge in experience' as deriving from terms (mental or linguistic) which refer to extramental things. Something is evident by experience (*nota per experientiam*) when it is established by induction, that is, generalization from singular, contingent propositions that are evident first by intuitive cognition. Something can then be said to be evident by experience when we suppose hypothetically that there is a common course of nature and we carry out a kind of induction based on this hypothesis. Ockham argues, in the end, that we are as certain of our experiences as we can be of anything. The importance of this certainty for an understanding of what Ockham means by 'right reason' cannot be overstated.

For Ockham, there are three sources of our knowledge: experience, natural reason and infallible scriptural authority. A process emerges whereby cognitive experience precedes everything, to which is applied natural reasoning, and both together enable us to confirm our belief in the truth of scriptural authority by rationally demonstrating its propositions to be reasonable.[13] As an excellent logician who wrote commentaries on many of Aristotle's logical writings, Ockham developed not only an epistemology but a related theory about how humans interpret language in ordinary cases as they live life and communicate with others. He then applied this to how humans can interpret the texts of Scripture. This would have tremendous consequences for the way he interprets the rightful role of the papacy. He takes away from the papacy and the ecclesiastical hierarchy the sole right to interpret the words of God. He argues that anyone who experiences the world and draws conclusions from that experience, so long as he is sane and literate, can also interpret God's words in Scripture. In his political writings, he spends a great deal of time demonstrating how the papacy has misinterpreted Scripture illegitimately and illogically to suit its own case. Any human can know God's intention as well as, if not better than, the papacy, and hence Scripture tells us, if we read it properly as we should read any text, what kinds of jurisdictional power Christ gave to Peter in the spiritual governance of the world.

---

[12] Especially on Ockham's logical theory of signification and on intuitive knowledge see P. Boehner, *Collected Articles on Ockham*, ed. E.M. Buytaert (St Bonaventure, NY, 1958). Many of these views are presented in Ockham's *Quodlibeta septem*, ed. J.C. Wey, *Opera Philosophica et Theologica, Opera Theologica*, IX (St Bonaventure, NY, 1980).

[13] This process of experience, natural reason or logical demonstration, and scriptural authority operate in a similar way in Discourse 2 of Marsilius of Padua's *Defender of Peace*, although Marsilius does not propose that knowledge is only propositional.

Ockham's Dualism Concerning Secular
and Spiritual Government: Continuing the Narrative

In his treatment of the theme of imperial and papal power[14] Ockham argued that individuals have rights of which they may not be deprived. In his *Opus nonaginta dierum*[15] he addressed a papacy which he believed had misinterpreted the breadth and extent of its own powers; and in his *De imperatorem et pontificum potestate* he observed:

> As St Ambrose said, the Christian religion deprives no one of his rights. Wherefore, the pope can deprive no one of his rights for a person has such rights only from God, by nature, or from another man, and by the same reason the pope cannot deprive anyone of his liberty which is given by God and by nature.[16]

Ockham uses the language of liberties and rights, taking both to be concessions by some higher authority, and for him certain authorities, namely God and Nature, cannot be gainsaid by men, be they princes or popes. Furthermore, he says that Scripture tells us, and St Francis the founder of his Order understood this perfectly, that Christ and his apostles only *used* what was necessary to sustain life. Christ and his apostles did not own things, but simply used the world in order to live. Scripture shows us that men have a *natural right of use* of things in the world, rather than ownership or possession of necessities, a right of use given to them by God. This natural right of use came before all subsequent legal or positive rights of possession which men in communities thereafter established. We have a *natural* right of use but no natural right to private property. Lordship or *dominium* was not granted eternally to men according to right reason: they were granted *usus* not *dominium*. Ownership or possession in societies of men is a result of the Fall. Humans thereafter, developed their logical reason to appropriate and divide things in these post-lapsarian conditions. Before the Fall, Adam and Eve had a perfect, non-proprietary power over all things, ruling things with right reason rather than by coercion. Fallen nature however, requires coercion, and *dominium* has therefore, been established for utilitarian purposes and made concrete in positive, civil law. But the ideal of spiritual perfection, before the Fall, is expressed by the natural law in us which lets us know — through our experience and reasoning about what there is to be experienced and known — that we have a God-given right to survive and to use the world for that survival without saying

---

[14] Ockham, *De imperatorum et pontificum potestate*, ed. R. Scholz, *Unbekannte kirchenpolitische Streitschriften aus der Zeit Ludwigs des Bayern* (1327–54), Vol. II (Rome, 1914), pp. 453–80; also Ockham, *De imperatorum et pontificum potestate*, ed. C.K. Brampton (Oxford, 1927).

[15] In Ockham, *Opera Politica*, I and II, and selections in *William of Ockham, A Letter to the Friars Minor*, ed. McGrade, pp. 19–115.

[16] Ockham, *De imperatorum et pontificum potestate*, ed. Brampton, pp. 9–10.

that we own the world or any part of it. Only God has rightful ownership or *dominium* of the world.

Since fallen man, for purposes of utility, established positive civil laws of possession and ownership, it is clear that the body in society that has rightful jurisdiction over properties and property relations must be the temporal ruler. The Church owns nothing and has no rights to ownership. Possession and ownership are secular and logical conclusions to which men agree as fallen creatures, adding to their natural rights of use the specification of ownership. Because priests and popes are men, their relation to property is under the rules of temporal arrangements.[17]

The scope of papal power is circumscribed by what anyone can read in Scripture when one reads the Evangelical Gospel law: there it is said that Christ conferred on Peter not unlimited plenitude of power over things spiritual and temporal, but rather, a limited jurisdiction to administer the sacraments, ordain the priestly hierarchy and instruct the faithful. Christ's act in instituting Peter was not arbitrary. It was an intelligible way of providing for the needs of His Church. It is reasonable to conclude that in order for Peter and his successors to rule the Church for the common spiritual utility it was expedient that there be one Church for all. Ockham accepts papal primacy over the other apostles because Scripture tells us that Christ gave Peter power when he said — *Tu es Petrus* — 'You are Peter and on this rock I build my Church'. The Petrine commission is not mysterious and held on faith; rather, it is based on right reason which in and for this world is an intelligible utility conclusion. But Christ did not give to Peter or his followers jurisdiction over men's material survival in the world. The Church, therefore, is not a juristic entity. God gave men liberty and men know of it through experience, even before the coming of Christ and the establishment of His Church, so that man's liberty is an inalienable, individual right possessed also by those non-Christians before Christ's coming. Men had a natural right freely to arrange their material survival for themselves, prior to the Church's institution, and they do this first by knowing from experience that in order to stay alive they have a right of use in things of the world to achieve this. After expulsion from the Garden of Eden, they then determined logically that it is more useful in these new circumstances to set up positive laws which build on the natural rights to survive by using the world, so that distinct property boundaries were established. The Church is not involved in this. Right reason, that is, men's experiences and their rational capacities to come to more general conclusions about how best to survive on

---

[17] Ockham, *Opus Nonaginta Dierum*, Chs. 26–8 and Chs. 88 and 93. See the detailed, amusing (and hostile) discussion of this in B. Tierney, *The Idea of Natural Rights, Studies on Natural Rights, Natural Law and Church Law 1150–1625*, Emory University Studies in Law and Religion, 5 (Atlanta, 1997), Ch. 6: 'Property, Natural Right and the State of Nature', pp. 131–69; 157–69, and Ch. 7: 'Ockham: Rights and Some Problems of Political Thought', pp. 170–94.

the basis of experience in the contingent conditions of fallen nature, may lead them to establish private property so that the resultant 'state', which has jurisdiction over property disputes amongst individual men, is to be conceived as an autonomous and even pre-Christian sphere of activity. Within the temporal or material sphere of survival and utility for the community that is made up of individuals, legitimacy is assured without reference to the Church. Legitimacy is assured when the consent of the governed is obtained so that the common good may be pursued. The grounds for political legitimacy are not, then, sacred since governments are not immediate divine institutions but rational creations of men.

Comparisons with Marsilius

Like Marsilius, Ockham does not glorify 'states'; he legitimates them. He is not approving the moral character of Roman or infidel administrations. He is simply acknowledging their rights to administer justice. He finds biblical texts that show that non-Christians may be recognized as persons with legitimate standing; and Christianity has no role in perfecting their rights to administer justice. Government comes to be constituted in the world as instrumental conclusions to solve conflictual conditions and serve peace. Nor is Ockham's criterion for legitimate government the moral desert of the ruler; rather, legitimate government is a rational choice, voluntarily exercised by men to establish the civil regulation of life by means of coercive sanction. Like Marsilius, he also thinks that rulers are not radically superior to their subjects in virtue or wisdom, and the form of any government will depend on the quality of the citizens: the better they are, the better the regime. Hence, Ockham, like Marsilius, allows for constitutional variations which accord with the changing circumstances and what is seen by those who constitute the government to be the common utility. He says explicitly that legitimate government is primarily instituted so that it may correct and punish wrongdoers, although it also functions by granting and preserving everyone's rights, enacting necessary and just laws, establishing lower judges and other officials, directing what arts ought to be practised and by whom, and to enjoin acts of virtue.[18] Like Marsilius, he goes beyond Aquinas' teaching that the Church can remove unbelievers at least in their rule over Christians.[19] He does not think that an emperor need be a Christian to be a legitimate emperor, but in the *Dialogus*[20] he crucially adds: 'except insofar as every rational adult ought to be a Christian especially if he has been able to be informed of the faith'. As for Marsilius, the best government is that which is exercised over free men and a community of free men would

---

[18] Ockham, *Octo quaestiones de potestate papae*, III, 8, in *Opera Politica*, I, pp. 112–13.
[19] Aquinas, *Summa Theologiae*, IIaIIae, q.10, a.10 resp.
[20] Ockham, III *Dialogus*, 2,1,14.

not easily allow itself to constitute a government that would reduce it to slavery. Like Marsilius, he also holds that Christian law, through Christ's institution of it as a law of freedom, perfects pagan law and the Old Law, which, by comparison, were laws of servitude. We shall see that like Marsilius, Ockham holds that the Gospel law of liberty is the nearest to perfection that fallen men can rationally grasp by right reason, so that, insofar as men see the need for government in this life, the perfect secular government would be one which was constituted in order to secure a rational, and therefore Christian, understanding of liberty. Christ's advent may not have transformed the basis or nature of legitimate imperial power, but Christians have access to more right reason than non-Christians.

Ockham tries to show that what the Roman Church calls its legislated customs cannot be recognized unless they are reasonable, and they are not reasonable if they are against divine law, or good customs, if they are prejudicial to the common welfare or to any person's liberty. It is insufficient for the Roman Church to try to legitimate its customs through prescription. The papacy cannot simply say that elected kings and emperors are its subjects because this is not according to divine law and divine law may be known by reading Scripture. Nor is the papal claim to superiority over kings and emperors a teaching of the *ius gentium* or the civil law. Nor is it from custom, because custom does not have the force of law unless it is rational. It is not rational if it destroys individual liberty against the will of individuals who have such liberty from God or Nature. In legislating for the faith of Christians, then, the pope cannot deprive them of a liberty so that they possess less liberty than do pagans and infidels. He may only teach God's word, maintain divine worship and ritual, and provide such things as are necessary for Christians in their quest for eternal life. The determination of what is necessary for the Christian quest for salvation must be judged neither by popes nor civil rulers exclusively but through an interpretation of the Gospel text by clergy, lay men and women, whether poor, rich, subjects or rulers. The pope has no power to command, coerce or requisition things that are not *necessary* to this end, otherwise the liberty of the Gospel law would be a law of slavery. Ockham does, however, leave a space for papal coercion in cases of utility or necessity, but he distinguishes these occasional possibilities from a claim to a regular exercise of coercive power.[21] He believes that the power of the papacy should be disputed openly and authentic Scripture made public in order to reveal its reasonable meaning.

The Exceptional Exercise of Coercive Authority

Like others, Ockham found a place for the exercise of exceptional powers in times of necessity beyond the ordinary jurisdictions of both the papacy and

---

[21] Ockham, *De imperatorum et pontificum potestate*, ed. Brampton, pp. 6, 23–7, 34–5; and Ockham, *Octo quaestiones*, I, 8.

empire. He saw that rightly established institutional order might need correction
or even rejection, but he thought such cases would be more extraordinary than
did most of his contemporaries. He did not deny the pope's ultimate (*casualiter*)
jurisdiction in secular affairs but the conditions for such interference would
have to be so grave a crisis, 'where no layman could or would take adequate
action', that only then might the pope act by divine right in temporal matters,
to do whatever *right reason dictated to him was necessary*.[22] This, as we shall
see, is an occurrence which Ockham thinks could virtually never take place
because it would mean the failure of all men's reason. It is implausible to think
that men can operate in this world without assuming the hypothetical necessity
that their thoughts are commonly applicable to the presumed regularities in the
world. Instead, he argued that secular politics not only has its own process of
self-correction, but that it is independent of ecclesiastical power.

Natural Rights

Michel Villey[23] credited Ockham with the first use of a language of subjective,
individual rights. But certain earlier Canonists had also noted a sphere of
individual, personal, moral autonomy, a psychological power or potential capable of exercise as a right, prior to incorporation into any political entity. Even
Marsilius has a subjective meaning for *ius* as a voluntary act, power or habit in
conformity with objective law.[24] Ockham too defined the individual person as
one who has certain powers, spoken of as *ius* or *potestas*, and these were to the
use of the world in order to ensure survival. It is what the seventeenth-century
Hobbes would call the 'right of nature'. According to Ockham, the later
appropriation and division of things which were to be recognized as private
property were the consequence of positive laws drawn up for the utility of fallen
men who desire peace and order. It is the natural right of use of things in the
world which cannot be taken away. Nor can men's natural powers or rights to
make laws and institute rulers be taken away. Each individual knows he has
certain natural powers to make positive laws and constitute government on the
basis of his own reasoned reflections on his experience. The natural right to
survive and to consent, voluntarily, to create a system of laws, a legitimate
positive authority to govern men collectively, is a right men claim for themselves as men who, on the basis of experience, logically judge that their safety
and moral autonomy is best preserved in a system of positive law. Hence, the

---

[22] Ockham, III *Dialogus*, 1,1,16.
[23] M. Villey, *La Formation de la Pensée Juridique Moderne* (Paris, 4th edn., 1975),
pp. 199–272.
[24] Marsilius, *Defender of Peace*, II,12,10; he also spoke of *dominium* as 'the actual
or habitual will to have the lawfully acquired thing' and no one could acquire *dominium*
against his own will, II,12,13–16; See Tierney, *The Idea of Natural Rights*, esp. Ch. 5:
'The Languages of Rights', pp. 104–30.

acts of any *regnum* are the summation of the willed acts of morally responsible individuals regarding the common good and public utility. A state's rules are general propositions which are to be understood by each individual to whom they apply, while each individual who is covered by the rules remains autonomous and responsible for his acts.

Corporation Theory

Ockham understands collective opinion to be the summation of every individual's opinion concerning the common good.[25] Unlike Marsilius, he does not believe that a collection of men into a corporation or general council can take on a separate personality which represents its members. He has a theory of corporations but it is not that of contemporary, representative corporation theory as one finds it in Canon lawyers or in the writings of Marsilius.[26] Collective opinion can only be a summation of individuals consenting to present, contingent circumstances on the basis of their own experiences and thoughts. His corporationism or conciliarism is of the kind where the whole is *nothing more than* the decisions of its individual parts regarding the common good. Therefore, a general council cannot be infallible (*contra* Marsilius). According to Ockham, any whole is the summation of its individual parts, willing what is for the public good. But his individuals are not isolated atoms. They form a community in the sense of a concrete body of individuals whose unity is achieved by their reasoning to the *same* conclusions about the common utility.

He does not have a theory of 'state' where the public authority, the office of the ruler, is a separate and real sphere of rights of its own under law. He treats the ruler as an individual, and he treats the corporation of individuals, not as a legally created *persona* (*non est persona imaginaria et repraesentata*) but as a unified collection of real, individual persons. Only real, autonomous, rational individuals are capable of renouncing or holding legal rights, and since the 'state' is not a real person but rather a fictive, created legal entity, it cannot perform real acts or possess real rights under law.[27] Its acts are the summation of the willed acts of individual members with reference to the collective good, the public utility, and what is expedient is determined by right reason: what is most objectively rational in given circumstances. The communal or political

[25] J. Miethke, *Ockhams Weg zur Sozialphilosophie* (Berlin, 1969); A.S. McGrade, *The Political Thought of William of Ockham. Personal and Institutional Principles* (Cambridge, 1974); A.S. McGrade, 'Ockham and the Birth of Individual Rights', in *Authority and Power, Studies . . . presented to Walter Ullmann*, ed. B. Tierney and P. Linehan (Cambridge, 1980), pp. 149–66; J. Coleman, *Ancient and Medieval Memories, Studies in the Reconstruction of the Past* (Cambridge, 1992), pp. 528 f.

[26] Ockham, *Tractatus contra Benedictum*, in *Opera Politica*, III, ed. H.S. Offler (Manchester, 1956), pp. 189–91.

[27] Effectively, this means the 'state' cannot make a contract with individual citizens; they alone can contract with one another as real persons with wills in order to constitute government. Compare Hobbes.

life is therefore made up of interactions between individual persons of the community, all willing, by right reason, the same common good.

So too, the universal Church is made up of its individual believers, priests, laymen and women, a universal church *in and through time* of individual men who comprise the historical and unbroken witness of the faithful.[28] The universal Church is made up of all its individual believers, whatever their status, and the ecclesiastical hierarchy, as a fictive rather than real person, cannot claim to represent it.[29]

For Ockham, individuals' wills cannot be represented and a collective will is not a real thing. An individual cannot alienate his moral autonomy and responsibility to another. Hence, each individual is responsible for alienating property when he lives in a society that has set up private property as a utilitarian determination of the natural law right of use of the world, known by all. Each individual is responsible in the exercise of his rights, his liberties, and in his resistance to those who act against right reason, be they popes or kings. When one says that the Church must resist papal heresy, Ockham thinks this can only mean that individual members of the Church must resist. The proposition: 'the Church must resist heresy' can only be interpreted as 'this individual Christian must resist, and that individual Christian must resist, and the other individual Christian must resist'.

Ockham's 'Absolutism'

Ockham recognized that the temporal sphere which establishes coercive, positive laws, is imperfect. He thought that men would not have needed the 'state' had Adam and Eve not fallen. Because the temporal sphere is imperfect, he argued that secular sovereignty, once established, could be legitimate even when 'absolutist', in that there need not be regular participation of the people in government, nor need there be institutions to restrain the power of kings. But this did not mean that 'the people' could *confer* absolute power on a ruler, because 'the people', not being a real, but rather a fictive, collective entity under human law, cannot and therefore did not, historically, ever possess such absolute power over individual members who comprised 'the people'. Hence, the people could not alienate a power that they did not actually possess. Furthermore, except in matters judged necessary for the community, no minority in a community can be deprived of their individual rights by a majority.[30] But the

---

[28] Ockham, *Tractatus contra Ioannem*, c. xiv, in *Opera Politica*, III, p. 65.

[29] *Ibid.*; Ockham, *Tractatus contra Benedictum*, c. 3 in *Opera Politica*, III, pp. 191, 233–4; Ockham, I *Dialogus*, 5,25–6.

[30] Ockham, III *Dialogus*, 2,2,27. 'Item, imperator non habet maiorem potestatem in temporalibus, quam habuit populus, cum imperator habeat potestatem suam a populo, ut allegatum est supra, quia populus plus iurisdictionis aut potestatis non potuit transferre in imperatorem, quam habuit . . . Ergo si populus praecipit aliquid alicui de populo, quod non est de necessitate faciendum, non tenetur illud facere, nisi velit, restat igitur, quod

constituting of a government, as in Marsilius, requires and achieves a unanimous consent by all rational individuals. Once established, the circumstances dictate whether or not the governor acts according to the positive laws. While he is not above natural equity he is above human positive laws, especially where he acts for the needs of the common good and the public safety, and in this sense government can be absolutist.[31] Ockham departs from Marsilius in not arguing for a continuous and explicit consent of a human legislator, the people, to the specific powers and laws of government. Their consent is to constituting government which would establish laws in conformity with right reason in the circumstances. Had men not fallen they would not conclude this to be a need and each would rule himself by reason in perfect conditions.[32]

How did Ockham come to hold these Views?

So far I have presented Ockham's various positions on the respective roles of Church and 'state' in the lives of individuals. But he is something of an original, certainly if judged against his contemporaries, in his distinctive way of arriving at and justifying these conclusions. In the *Dialogus*, Ockham notes that men know from experience that they are inclined to conflict and to seek their own interests and not what belongs to the common good. They also know that however much it is beneficial in difficult cases for the truth to be sought by many, it is *useful* that one should have power over all the other advisers seeking the truth.[33] This utility conclusion, he will later call it a supposition, that some unified government be set up over men, is one that has been agreed to unanimously by all. It is a conclusion, given the present and contingent circumstances of this life, that is based on those prior self-evident principles of morality or what follows from them, which are called natural laws.

In III *Dialogus*, 2,1,15, Ockham speaks of three kinds of natural laws: (1) self-evident first principles of morality which are indubitable; (2) inferences from these which are similarly indubitable; (3) further inferences from the inferences. Ockham says that there are natural laws of the second kind which are drawn plainly and without great consideration as certain inferences from the first principles of natural law that are known even by the less learned. Even if we have never before thought of them, such natural laws occur to us immediately when we are obliged to do or omit something in accordance with them, *unless* we will to proceed to act or to omit such act without any deliberation and rule of reason. Presumably, not to deliberate by reason is a mark of insanity. Anyone can immediately and without great study know these second

---

imperator non habet talem potestatis plenitudinem.' Cited with comments in Tierney, 'Ockham: Rights and Some Problems of Political Thought', in *The Idea of Natural Rights*, p. 184, n. 44.

[31] Ockham, III *Dialogus*, 2,1,16.
[32] Compare Hobbes.
[33] Ockham, III *Dialogus*, 2,1,13.

kinds of natural laws. There is no excuse for ignorance of the first and second kinds of natural laws. Then there are other natural laws that are inferred from the inferences from the first principles which a few experts, with great attention and study, arrive at 'through many intermediate propositions', but their expert opinions may conflict. Ignorance of this third kind of natural law is generally excusable. An emperor should apply himself to acquire a knowledge of the third kind of natural law — clearly because here his own prudent judgment will allow him to make decisions on what is, in the circumstances, excusable or not. The other first and second kind of natural laws, the first principles and inferences from them, he need not study because they will easily occur to him when necessary.

Later in the text, Ockham treats the problem of whether the Romans have the right to elect the pope by divine law, extending 'divine law' to mean all natural law. Can all natural law be called divine law? He distinguishes three ways in which natural law is understood in his own times, gathering these under-standings from his interpretations of a variety of Canon law and historical texts. His own discussion is extremely condensed.[34] There are three modes or kinds. First, natural law in conformity with natural reason that never fails, and he gives the examples: 'do not commit adultery' or 'do not lie'. He later makes it clear that it also includes the notion that each man is, by nature, free, but what he means by free is in effect an inalienable, moral, internal freedom as a rational deliberator with a will to do or not to do what is rational. These must be universally true and foundationally self-evident principles (*per se nota*) to men, and such principles are immutable. They are necessary principles and are not based on responses to contingency.

Second, natural law is also taken to mean what is to be observed by those who use natural equity alone and without any custom and human legislation, that is, what for Ockham, would be a necessary conclusion known through experience (*per experientiam*) everywhere before the establishment of govern-ments, but after expulsion from the Garden of Eden. Natural equity seems to be a power of reasoning which serves as a rational readjustment for human weaknesses and men's experiences of them. In the state of nature as originally established, before the Fall, the conclusions from that perfect experience would *not* have required that men draw natural equity conclusions about what is owed to each because, in the original state of nature, all things would have been common, neither commonly or individually *possessed*. Before the Fall there would have been no need to consider what each is owed. Men would have been

---

[34] *Ibid.*, 2,3,6; my reading of this text differs from that provided by McGrade, *The Political Thought of William of Ockham*, pp. 177–85. I have used the corrected Latin text in H.S. Offler, 'The Three Modes of Natural Law in Ockham: A Revision of the Text', *Franciscan Studies*, 37 (1977), pp. 207–18. Also see the interpretation of Tierney in 'Ockham: Rights and Some Problems of Political Thought', in *The Idea of Natural Rights*, pp. 177–82.

living according to natural reason or divine law. Their pre-Fall natural reason would have been consonant with divine law. If, *after* the Fall, all men lived according to reason suited to *these* conditions, then the conclusion they would have drawn was that all things should have been common and nothing *owned* (in common or individually). This would have been a natural equity conclusion to suit contingencies, inferred from immutable first principles, and where no government was required. But since it was not the case that after the Fall all men lived according to natural equity reason, ownership (both as common property and as individual property) was introduced (by men) because of wickedness. Fallen men do not, therefore, have a choice between living without property or setting up property divisions. No one can live simply according to natural equity reasoning after the Fall, and hence appropriation and division in some way or other is a rational human conclusion, their way of fulfilling natural equity here and now. This does not mean it is necessary that appropriation and division had to be entirely private; but it does mean that the world was divided up — as men's *common possession*, from which *private* property could there-after, have been a further conclusion in the circumstances.

While there were Franciscans, like the thirteenth-century Archbishop Pecham, who seemed to think that natural equity alone would suffice to regulate men's affairs if men, with all their limitations, lived as reasonably as they could, Ockham does not seem to hold this view. Ockham may have defended a life without property, but it is its *voluntary* rejection, through, for instance, the Franciscans' vow of poverty, which he defends and not some natural equity state prior to the human law of nations and civil law. Since the Church lives where property has been established (property that is owned in common *or* individually), those who wish to imitate the natural equity state have to reject all forms of ownership voluntarily. Of course, no one can go back to the original, prelapsarian state of nature, not even the Franciscans.

Now, in the fallen world, where governments and civil laws have been established, the second mode of natural law or natural equity includes the *capacity* licitly or rationally to appropriate things and even to be made slaves. Ockham says we find this in the human law of nations (*ius gentium*) as well as in civil law.[35] The way humans now use (the second mode of) natural law when they speak of the law of nations, indicates to Ockham that there are things which men judge permissible to enact as further conclusions in the circumstances. Men's reason in these circumstances demonstrates that the law of nations — by which common possession of all things and the one liberty of all is estab-lished — is changeable since it is judged permissable to enact the contrary, that

[35] Ockham speaks of Pope Gregory the Great as testifying to some free men being placed under the yoke of slavery by the law of nations, who are then *made* free in the nature in which they were born. Gregory believed that all men were born free but through a mysterious dispensation some men were set over others, and only through Christ could such men be made free, while retaining their differential rank in society.

is, to enslave some men and appropriate property from what was commonly possessed. In our present state, reason dictates that all things are common property until they are appropriated with the consent of men, and the yoke of servitude may be imposed on men who are, by nature, free. Ockham is speaking of the facts of the matter: men have been running their own affairs by deductive reasoning from their experiences since they were expelled from the Garden of Eden, possessing the world in one way or another.

A third kind of natural law is inferred by fallen men's evident reasoning from the law of nations or another law, and we can call this 'natural law on supposition'. This third law seems to correspond to Ockham's earlier discussion of the kind of inference from necessary inferences from first principles, an ignorance of which may be judged excusable by a ruler. Natural law in this sense can include returning something deposited, or money lent, and the repelling of violence with force. This third kind of natural law would not have existed in the state of nature as originally established, and it would not have existed among those who, living according to reason, were content with natural equity alone, since there would not have been anything deposited or lent and no one would have inflicted force on another. Natural law on supposition depends on our *supposing* that things and money have been appropriated according to the law of nations or human law. If we suppose this, then by evident reasoning, where these are prevalent understandings in the world, we conclude that a thing deposited and money lent should be returned. There is, then, a conditional natural law which derives from human rational responses to contingent circumstances.

Ockham says something unusual about this third natural law on supposition. He notes that we gather its meaning by evident reasoning from the *ius gentium* or another human law, 'unless the contrary is enacted with the consent of those concerned'. When natural law is held in the third way, it proceeds from a prior supposition about what is natural and fair, and thereafter makes particular judgments according to this supposition, unless the contrary to this supposition is established by some human law. Humans start from propositions as accepted social premises from which they reason to conclusions. The contrary may be enacted by reasonable cause where what one has come to accept by supposing it to be universally true is discovered to be otherwise. The only way in which this could occur, for Ockham, would be if the conditions in which evident reasoning came to its conclusions were altered. As we shall see, one of the ways this could occur would be to establish the truth of living of those humans who had experienced Christ's words and deeds, and to confirm this truth daily in a society that held this way of living to be the truth.

If, however, it is *supposed* that someone is to be set over certain persons as a ruler, rector or prelate, it will then be inferred by evident reason that, unless the contrary is decided on by the person or persons concerned, those whom he is to be set over have the right to elect him, so that no one should be given to them against their will. Since what affects all should be dealt with by all (*quod omnes tangit*), then those whom it concerns make themselves laws and it belongs to them to elect a head. Government is based on a supposition in this world that rulership needs to be constituted. It always belongs to those whom someone is to be set over to elect the one to be set over them, unless the contrary is decided on by the persons concerned. It can even be supposed that in electing rulers they each resign their right and transfer it to another whose decision each is bound to accept. But we shall see that there are certain rights which can never be alienated or transferred and such rights are not conditional, *ex suppositione*. All of this discussion is ultimately in aid of interpreting Scripture and whether Christ, the superior to the Romans, ever deprived the Romans of the right to elect their bishop. Ockham extends it to temporal rulers.[36]

Once individual members of the community have consented voluntarily to create a legitimate positive authority, Ockham argues that public authority may only be retracted in very extreme circumstances, as when a ruler commits egregious sins or crimes.[37] The ruler is an individual with rights of his own. He cannot ignore certain inalienable rights of the individuals who are ruled, although he can override rights conceded by men, for instance to property, but only in cases of necessity. In the *Dialogus* Ockham presents the opinion that the emperor and the king in his kingdom are not tied by the laws, and are not obliged of necessity to judge according to the laws in the way inferior judges are obliged to do. The ruler needs experience and judgment more than he needs a knowledge of civil laws.[38] It seems that his experience and judgment are brought into play in the sphere of what Ockham has called the third kind of natural law or natural law on supposition. Once constituted, the ruler can alter the suppositional premises from which his subjects draw their conclusions from evident reasoning.[39] In the *Breviloquium* he maintained that the Roman emperor's power came to him from God as a remote cause but immediately from the people who elected him. This power was not absolute in the sense that it could not remove the rights and liberties granted to men by God and nature. Common utility required that rulers respect the natural rights of their subjects, but this common utility could prevail over their private rights in cases of necessity.

This being the case, the imperial power was not easily revocable. He appears to have thought that most rulers throughout history had organized society sufficiently in a rational and utilitarian manner so that whatever crimes they may have committed were of lesser consequence to the collective well-being than would have been their removal. He said: 'We ought to delight more in the life of a people than in the punishment of one bad person. If, therefore, the

[36] For an alternative reading see Tierney, *The Idea of Natural Rights*, esp. pp. 175–84.
[37] Ockham, *Breviloquium*, 4, 13.
[38] Ockham, III *Dialogus*, 2,1,15.
[39] Compare Hobbes.

scandal of deposing such a king threatens to overthrow the people . . . such
severity should be abandoned.'[40] Ockham is therefore willing, because he
thinks most men are willing, to grant legitimate power to a sovereign, secular
government even when, thereafter, the government may deprive certain individuals of powers or wrongfully interfere against the civil laws with men's
property, or involve men in wars where they had not been consulted. Once
established by human law, which is itself established by individuals consenting
to specific proposed ordinances to rule their individual and collective behaviour, Ockham says that the 'state' as absolute sovereign must be accepted by
those over whom it exercises its powers. There is no social contract of the kind
between citizens and regulating ruler, and hence government is not a revocable
grant of the people, except in the most extreme circumstances. In effect, he has
no resistance theory to already-constituted government, although that government may not remove the natural rights of men given them by God and nature.
Furthermore, temporal public authority, created by rational, morally responsible individuals, is independent of any ecclesiastical sanction, whatever its
constitution, be it infidel or Christian.

Right Reason

All men, according to Ockham, come to know of their rights, liberties and
powers simply by experiencing the world in which they live and drawing
conclusions as how best to secure their needs in these fallen conditions. In his
Opus Nonaginta Dierum, he says that he is following St Augustine, by distinguishing between right or *ius* as *ius fori* (right according to public law) on the
one hand, and as *ius poli* (right according to heavenly or divine law) on the
other. *Ius fori* is the kind of right that is recognized from contracts or human
ordinances and established customs or divine explanations of these (presumably
such as 'render unto Caesar that which is his'). The superior authority here in
determining violations of the *ius fori* is civil. But *ius poli* is a knowledge of
natural equity and it is consonant with right reason. This knowledge comes
before a knowledge of human and divine positive laws.

Ockham explains that right reason may be construed either as purely by
nature (foundational moral principles which are known indubitably and immu-
tably), or it can be understood as what right reason accepts as following from
nature (the necessary inferences from moral first principles), which to Christians is divinely revealed. Hence, the *ius poli* is natural law (of the first and
second kinds discussed above but supplemented by Scripture and therefore by
natural law on supposition). He says it can also be called divine law because
much of the divine law is consonant with what right reason accepts but, as it is
revealed to men, these reasonable conclusions could not be discovered entirely

---

[40] Ockham, *Octo quaestiones*, 7.7, in *Opera Politica*, I, p. 180.

naturally.[41] Humans now cannot think with the reason that was consonant with Adam's reason prior to the Fall. Ockham notes that this further perfection of right reason's conclusions by the divine law cannot be (logically) demonstrated by purely natural reasoning, just as it cannot be sufficiently proved by human deductive logic that the preaching of Scripture is true, useful and necessary, although it is all of these. This notion of right reason, and its further perfection by divine revelation in Christian Scripture, rationally understood, bears comparison with Marsilius of Padua's use of the term.[42]

We can observe the context in which right reason operates by looking at his *Dialogus*, where Ockham presents a general, theological discussion of heresy. His focus is on papal heresy but his more general undertanding of heresy is the more interesting for political theory. He argues, as did Marsilius, that the fact that the Church determines or defines an assertion does not constitute the truth value of that assertion. Rather, the Church *approves rightly* one of five kinds of truth. The list is revealing.

1. Truth is what is expressed in Scripture or inferred from it by necessary reasoning.

2. Truth is what is handed down to us from the apostles through oral teachings or in the writings of the faithful, but is neither found in Scripture nor deduced from it.

3. Truth is what is discovered in chronicles or histories deemed worthy of trust.

4. Truth is what can be concluded from the truth of the first and second kind alone, or from one or other of the combined truths of the third kind.

5. Apart from the truth that he has already revealed to the apostles, truth is what God has revealed or inspired in others, or will reveal or inspire.[43]

Truth is not established by institutional authority but from Scripture or other sources worthy of trust; and sources that are worthy of trust are determined by individual men's experience and reason. The truth value of sources emerges from the evaluation of human right reason, so that for Ockham truth is defined cognitively before it receives the assent of any institution. Heresy, then, is a problem of human understanding. Ockham, therefore, treats the process of

---

[41] Ockham, *Opus Nonaginta Dierum*, c. 65, pp. 573–6.

[42] For a somewhat different interpretation of the meaning of Ockham's *ius fori* and *ius poli* see Tierney, *The Idea of Natural Rights*, pp. 126–30.

[43] Ockham, I *Dialogus*, 2,16. For a discussion of Ockham on heresy see McGrade, *The Political Thought of William of Ockham*, pp. 51 f., citing especially I *Dialogus*, 4,14–21.

heretical correction in cognitive terms rather than as an exercise of institutional power. Not only does he provide a general prescription for examining authoritative pronouncements of all kinds, but he wishes chiefly to maintain that there can be no *arbitrary* coercion of an individual's will. Right reason is what provides the cognitive certainty and it is available to each and all. Here we note that right reason always operates in social contexts with their respective, prevalent knowledge.

If one is living in a Catholic community, what is prevalently known to every Catholic, no matter how humble or uneducated, determines, for Ockham, the minimal level of knowledge of the Catholic truth that everyone is bound to believe explicitly. If an illiterate layman denies a scriptural truth, then Ockham believes he ought not to be immediately judged heretical before he has been examined and then taught.[44] Although a person's persistence in error in his own mind cannot be known, Ockham lists numerous ways in which someone might reasonably be judged pertinacious on the basis of his words and deeds. We are reminded of Marsilius' distinction between immanent and transitive or transient acts and the requirement that they be witnessed. Ockham asserts that if a man who has reason and understanding and has lived among Christians denies a publicly known Catholic assertion, then he contradicts prevalent knowledge and is judged pertinacious. He must be clearly shown that his assertion is against Catholic truth, and if he persists in his error then he is to be corrected.

How might this be done? Ockham gives an example of showing someone one of the Gospels or some Church historical text in order to demonstrate that his own assertions are contrary to them. One can be corrected noncoercively by friends, but Ockham thinks that someone whose errors are clearly pointed out to him is bound to give them up at once, no matter who has corrected him. Each individual is, for Ockham, morally responsible for grasping the truth.[45] Ockham is relatively tolerant towards the uneducated, but is intolerant of those who hold higher ecclesiastical offices because their amount of theological knowledge should be commensurate with their status. He thinks that experts in Scripture are obliged by their expertise to give clear reasons for the truth to which all individual and less expert Christians also bear witness. But every Christian has cognitive access to that truth, if not to the reasons for it.

Ockham did not believe that Catholic truths explicitly or implicitly asserted in Scripture were the only truths to be believed, however. Intuitive cognition sufficiently guarantees our certain knowledge of contingent truths. Institutional coercive power, then, only adds a kind of authenticity to an assertion when the latter is already true as well as Catholic. For Ockham, truth is superior to and opposed to mere coercive power. What if an individual is actually correct and

---

[44] Ockham, I *Dialogus*, 4,6 and 10; Ockham, *Tractatus contra Ioannem*, c. vi, *Opera Politica*, III, p. 47.

[45] Ockham, I *Dialogus*, 4,6 and 21; Ockham, *Tractatus contra Ioannem*, c. 13–15, *Opera Politica*, III, pp. 60–74.

all the others, experts and ordinary men and women, still hold him to be wrong? Ockham thought this was a (remote) possibility and said that the only thing left was for him to appeal to God and not fear being cut off by an unjust judgment from the society of men.[46] The Student in the *Dialogus* marvels at what appears to be the Master's suggestion that one man, no matter what his office, ought to prefer his own imaginings to all the learned and wise men gathered together. Ockham responds, famously, by saying it is not his own imaginings but his own conscience to which he should listen.[47] Every Christian, no matter what his or her status, has a moral duty to defend the truth and be ready for correction if it is available. But he thinks that the testimony of many men is more likely to be true than the testimony of one.[48]

There seems little doubt that Ockham believed, but could not demonstrate, that Christian communities, having Scripture, had available to them a more complete truth than did other communities with their truths that were not supplemented by Scripture. With the addition of the Christian description of the words and deeds of Christ, a new orientation and a new motive to act in charity would be added to natural principles of morality. He implies that Christians would be more ready to apply the principles of right reason in the circumstances in which they found themselves, although it is not clear that this was because of an additional stimulus to rational action beyond the impulse to reason itself.[49] Indeed, Ockham seems to be holding to the extraordinary (and modern) position that we know the world as we experience it, and if we experience it in a particular community, here Catholic, then that is our truth of experience. There is a cognitive commonality of individuals, and their certitude depends on their experience which, in Christian communities, confirms, from their daily life, the truths of Scripture. For this reason he was able to say in his *Letter to the Friars Minor* that he was better able to understand the customs of men (in general) from the holy rules of Scripture which describe men's customs — and which can be verified daily by experience.[50]

Scriptural Hermeneutics

Ockham seems to have regarded the scriptural text not as describing a particular event that was to be held on faith, but rather as something actually experienced by humans, although in the past. He is unusually clear amongst medieval

[46] Ockham, I *Dialogus*, 4,20.

[47] *Ibid.*, 2,29 .

[48] *Ibid.*, 7,15.

[49] I cannot find any text that supports a notion of grace added to nature for this to occur so that one comes to love God for his own sake, and therefore disagree here with McGrade, *The Political Thought of William of Ockham*, p. 204.

[50] 'Nam sanctarum regulas scripturarum mores hominum describentes, dum quotidie per experientiam verificari conspicio, magis intelligo.' Ockham, *Opera Politica*, III, p. 17.

thinkers that scriptural events happened at another, long-distant time and place. He raised the kind of question about the past as 'over and done with' that we normally associate (wrongly) with Renaissance and (rightly) with modern attitudes to the past as distinct from the present. Ockham tackled the question: how does someone in the present come to grasp the meaning of the intentions or mental acts of past agents? He used his logic to defend the necessary truth of propositions concerning *facts* in the past, such as 'Christ was crucified'. He argued that we know the past through propositions about it, and intellectually we know the past (which is our own) as past. But a present interpreter of Scripture is meant to determine the true meaning behind the different terminology of past authors, as a true meaning of individual past experiences. To determine whether a proposition about the past — but stated now (e.g. Christ *was* crucified) — is true or false, he examined whether a present-tense proposition as stated in the past (Christ *is* crucified) was then true or false.[51]

Anyone sane and literate can do this because the knowledge anyone acquires by logical demonstration provides the same kind of knowledge, in terms of its conclusions, as does experiential knowledge. Because Ockham's epistemology affirms that we are as certain about our present as we are about our past, then someone else who experienced what he did in that past was similarly certain about it. When we consider what they wrote about their experiences we must conclude that something real and true must have happened to individual men in the past. The disciples of the apostles, and of course St Peter, must have possessed a true understanding of Christ's words.[52] A textual expression of those experiences, Scripture, understood by us abstractively, that is independent of time, place and claims to existence of its referents, must be based on 'that someone's' past intuitive cognition of the reality and existence of his experience. Christians, with Scripture, have a fuller access to the past's truths than do others who may only use natural reasoning without the oral and written witnesses to Christ's words and deeds.[53]

[51] See T. Shogimen, 'Ockham's Vision of the Primitive Church', *Studies in Church History*, 33: *The Church Retrospective*, ed. R.N. Swanson (Woodbridge, 1997), pp. 163–75; p. 172.

[52] Ockham, III *Dialogus*, 1,4,13.

[53] For a fuller analysis of Ockham's theory of knowledge and language see Coleman, *Ancient and Medieval Memories*, pp. 500–37; Brian Tierney rejected Ockham's reasonableness in his biblical hermeneutics by saying 'in Ockham's polemical works right reason meant simply his own reason' which recalls Hobbes's own rejection of this kind of argument in *Leviathan*, I, c.5. B. Tierney, *The Origins of Papal Infallibility, 1150–1350* (Leiden, 2nd edn., 1988), p. 230. For a very useful discussion of the primacy of Biblical exegesis for Ockham in all of his polemical works see Shogimen, 'Ockham's Vision of the Primitive Church', pp. 163–75, and his as yet unpublished PhD dissertation (University of Sheffield, 1998), *William of Ockham and Spiritual Authority, A Study of his Polemics.*

Ockham's Ethics

Among the common truths of experience are those that men by nature logically conclude about the need for the establishment of general rules, applicable to all. Specific positive laws are, thereafter, calculations in contingent circumstances, a defined set of specific rules that are judged to be required in *these* circumstances, given prevalent suppositions, so that fallen men may be, when necessary, coerced when they do not act according to their natural knowledge of what is morally right. Since Ockham argued that it is only by intuitive cognition of our own acts that we are aware of ourselves as intelligent beings, it is therefore only through intuitive cognition that we are aware of ourselves as voluntary agents, free to choose between alternatives. We possess as individuals a *libertas*, a freedom, and we know of it only by experience. This individual liberty may be defined as 'that power whereby I can do diverse things indifferently and contingently such that I can cause or not cause the same effect, when all conditions other than this power are the same'.[54]

Just as we cannot prove that we experience individuals intuitively by demonstrative reason — we can only experience this as a fact — so too, we cannot prove the will is free by demonstrative reason 'because every reason proving this assumes something equally unknown as its conclusion, or less known'. A man simply experiences the fact that however much his reason dictates some action, his will can will or not will this act. Hence, human liberty, which we know from our intuitive knowledge of existents, we know evidently as a true term in a proposition, generalized through an extension by induction to all other individuals of the same nature. If we know of our own liberty, we equally come to acknowledge it in others. Together, we then negotiate our collective lives in a variety of different ways, setting up different, legitimate authorities and laws which suit the contingent circumstances.

Ockham thinks of this liberty as the basis of our human dignity and the font of moral goodness and personal responsibility. He holds that this liberty is more central to morality than is the power of reasoning, which only occurs after the simple intuitive apprehension of the term and thereafter what it signifies, even though reasoning is involved in willing or not willing. Our liberty to will, one way or another, is the basis of our human dignity because man is a free agent and therefore, in being responsible for his acts, he can be judged worthy or not.[55] Following Aristotle's distinction between moral and intellectual virtues

---

[54] Ockham, *Quodlibet*, I, q.16, p. 87, in *Quodlibeta septem* in *Guillelmi de Ockham Opera Theologica*, IX, ed. J.C. Wey (St Bonaventure, NY, 1980). Ockham's view is that liberty is not a special quality which man may or may not have; rather, it is identical with man's spontaneous will. See his remarks in his theological work, the 'Ordinatio' on the *Sentences*, Book II, *Sent.* d.10, q.2, in *Guillelmi de Ockham Opera Theologica*, III, ed. G.I. Etzkorn (St Bonaventure, NY, 1977), p. 344.

[55] Ockham, *Quodlibet*, III, q.19, in *Opera Theologica*, IX, pp. 275–6.

in the *Nicomachean Ethics*, Ockham argued that a man is praised for what he wills rather than for what he understands. His cognitive acts are natural, but his power to perform or not, his power to act on what he knows, is what is to be judged. Hence, Ockham's emphasis on rationally guided choice is central to what has come to be called his voluntarism. But like Marsilius (and unlike Hobbes), Ockham is a rational voluntarist. He is not sceptical about human knowing but about our willing what we know. Right reason is an integral requirement of virtue for him, and hence agents must intend to aim at what is most objectively rational. Virtuous acts are those that conform to the principles of right reason, and as we have seen, right reason is concerned with self-evident principles of conduct and the logical inferences that follow from them in contingent circumstances. It is this individual liberty to conform one's will (or not) to right reason which Ockham then invokes when he speaks of the Christian law of liberty by which men know of their rights of use in the world.

In his *Letter to the Friars Minor* he analysed Pope John XXII's official pronouncements against the Franciscans and says he finds heretical, stupid, ridiculous, fantastic and defamatory statements against orthodox faith, against good custom, against natural reason, against experiences that are certain, and against fraternal charity. Judging especially against good custom, natural reasons and the certitude of experiences, he concludes that questions of faith are to be decided not only by a general council or by prelates but also by the Christian faithful laity, and this includes women. All are witnesses to Scriptural truth.

Although we cannot logically demonstrate the truth of such articles of faith, such as 'God is three and one', Ockham thinks that we can define morality in its large sense as 'human acts subject absolutely to the will'. This larger morality is, for him, a demonstrative science because its conclusions are deduced from principles that are either foundationally self-evident to all humans (*per se nota*) or they are evident as a consequence of their experience (*nota per experientiam*). It is here, deductions from experience, that we feel the force of his insistence that individual experiences in communities with Scripture will lead to behaviour that is guided by naturally known as well as Scriptural truths which are prevalent knowledge (suppositions) in the community. Hence, he says that a moral science that is a nonpositive science is that which directs human acts without any superior precepts. The precepts of this nonpositive moral science are known by all men in themselves (*per se nota*, foundationally and without demonstration) or known through experience (*nota per experientiam*). This, he says, is how any man can determine what is honest. Nonpositive morality is known most certainly by any and every human experiencer of the world who lives in a community with its prevalent knowledge.

But then there is a moral science called 'positive', or the science of the lawyers (*scientia iuristarum*). It is not a demonstrative science, because juristic rules are founded on human positive laws which are not propositions that are evidently known, but rather are the products of expediency, calculated in contingent circumstances. Ockham believes in the necessity of positive law in fallen society, but he will not allow the lawyers and their canon or civil laws the foundational, ethical stability of a higher morality which owes them nothing, but to which they owe everything.[56] Ockham had entered the ranks of all those arts and theology lecturers who insisted that ethical and political science required the moral foundations that could only be learned through the philosophy of the arts course and not through the study of positive law.

Conclusion

Ockham did not argue for the kind of subjective, individual rights or capacities which would lead each discrete individual to his own *and different* interpretation of moral rectitude. Central to his claims for psychological capacities on the part of humans as members of the same species is the insistence that thinking, no less than speaking, proceeds according to a logic of thought which, at some abstract level above distinctive and historically specific cultural habits, is rationally the same for all human minds that operate in the social domain with its prevalent knowledge. Above historical cultures is an impartial, logical and critical capacity to evaluate the difference between right and wrong, good and bad habits, a right reasoning that is achieved more completely in Christian societies which have available to them the truths of Scripture added to naturally known and otherwise experienced truths. Like all Christian medieval thinkers, he is insisting on 'right reason' of a spiritually supplemented, but rationally understood, kind, against which customs and laws of any time and place should be judged. In the world as we experience it, and where we rely on a hypothetical necessity that how it normally is *is* how it is, and where we presume, but cannot prove, that this is how God ordained it to be, humans simply do rely on right reason. Their right reason shows them what God must have intended because his intentions in words and deeds were communicated to contemporary witnesses who passed on these intentions in Scripture and other oral and written texts.

Ockham is describing a normative situation in which God's will is not ordinarily considered by men to be inscrutable or arbitrary. He thinks that we can discover from the ways in which we live and come to know what we know in this life, *pro statu isto*, that we have been given the capacities which confirm us in a certain confidence that God had actually intended to ensure that our right reason reflected His plan for humans. This did not ignore God's absolute power to do what He willed, and to intervene extraordinarily in the 'normal' run of affairs, but that absolute will *is* inscrutable to men and they cannot presume to have access to it as a guiding set of rules and principles by which fallen nature is to live. Ockham distanced the divine power in all its might and possibility

---

[56] Ockham, *Quodlibet*, II, q.3, in *Opera Theologica*, IX, pp. 117–18, pp. 120–22; Ockham, *Quodlibet*, II, q.14, pp. 176–8.

from the normal workings of the world, and he thought that men had been granted capacities, right reason, by which they could cope with the instability of contingencies. In this, he left the fallen world to man's making. Some would later speak of Ockham's God as a *deus absconditus*, a God that, after his brief appearance, had left the world to human ways of determining it.[57] But while right reason is our guide, our essential characterization is, for Ockham, our liberty to will to follow right reason. He, like others of his time, was speaking of a range of psychological capacities which, when exercised, led to peculiarly human ways of thinking, behaving and evaluating. His ethics requires rationality in public acts.

Nowhere do we find a discussion of the unique and solitary person with his views and values, reconfigured as sensual preferences, uniquely pitted against the different views and values of his neighbour. No doubt he existed, but it was not this isolated self, this 'man' of sense experience, that could claim human rights and expect others to be obliged to recognize them. It was, rather, on the basis of what humans shared as humans, right reason and will, as social, rational, voluntary moral agents, that individuals could claim they had rights accorded to each member of the species by God and nature, and thereby constitute governments which acknowledged and even extended these rights. Since legitimate political power can only be exercised over free individuals, Ockham affirmed that any authority which attempted to deny what is, in effect, their psychological liberty by requiring behaviour that was contrary to Scripture or reason, was illegitimate. His focus on the supremacy of the individual Christian conscience followed from his interpretation of the New Testament. It was this method and this focus, on the bedrock of Scripture and the individual's reason and will, which would shake the foundations of later medieval theology until and beyond the Protestant Reformation.

Janet Coleman   LONDON SCHOOL OF ECONOMICS
                                         AND POLITICAL SCIENCE

---

[57] On the distinction between God's *potentia ordinata* and God's *potentia absoluta* in Ockham and later nominalist theologians see H. Oberman, *The Harvest of Medieval Theology: Gabriel Biel and Late Medieval Nominalism* (Cambridge, MA, 1963); W.J. Courtney, *Capacity and Volition, A History of the Distinction of Absolute and Ordained Power (Quodlibet 8)* (Bergamo, 1990); Eugenio Randi, *Il sovrano e l'orologiaio, due immagini di Dio nel dibattito sulla 'potentia absoluta' fra XIII e XIV secolo* (Florence, 1986).

BRONZE-AGE CONCILIARISM:
EDMOND RICHER'S ENCOUNTERS WITH CAJETAN AND BELLARMINE

*Francis Oakley**

Abstract: This essay focuses on the persistence of conciliarist constitutionalism down into the seventeenth century, and on the particular way in which the Gallican author, Edmond Richer (1559–1631), framed it in his sweeping and influential critiques of the papalist ecclesiology. In the tradition established by his fifteenth- and sixteenth-century predecessors in the Parisian theology faculty, Richer's formulation of conciliar theory was essentially political in nature. As a result, it lent itself readily to use in the cause of constitutionalist aspiration by such eighteenth-century critics of French monarchical policy as Nicolas Le Gros and Gabriel-Nicolas Maultrot.

The disputed papal election of 1378, the scandalous struggle ensuing between first two and then among three rival claimants to the papal office, and the agonizing persistence for almost forty years of the debilitating religio-political crisis that has gone down in history as the Great Schism of the West — this unprecedented series of events resulted in the generation of a body of writings on matters ecclesiological at once more extensive, more varied, more developed and more systematic than anything emerging from the centuries preceding. Prominent among those writings are those that can be classified as 'conciliarist' in nature, that is to say, those that pivoted on the assumption that a general council of the whole Church, acting in the absence of its papal head, was in some sense superior in authority to that head. When taken together, these conciliarist writings amount to a veritable ocean of controversialist literature that extends across time from the fourteenth to the eighteenth century.

Seen from the perspective of the history of political thought, it is the great contribution of this particular body of literature to have nurtured in what one might well have assumed to be unwelcoming ecclesiastical soil a stubbornly constitutionalist seed. Insisting that 'the true principle of Christian unity' lay not so much in the 'vigorous subordination' of all the members of the Christian community to a single papal head as in 'the corporate association' of those members, this literature envisaged that community as capable, through the mechanism of a general council, of exercising its authority 'even in the absence

* The Oakley Center for the Humanities and Social Sciences, Williams College, Williamstown, MA 01267, USA. Email: Francis.C.Oakley@williams.edu

of an effective head'.[1] It went on to conclude that the pope, therefore, was not an absolute monarch but in some sense a constitutional ruler, that he possessed a merely ministerial authority delegated to him for the good of the whole Church, that the final authority in that Church (at least in certain critical cases) lay not with him but with the whole community of the faithful or with their representatives assembled in a general council, and that such a council could, if needs be, proceed to judge, chastise or even depose a heretical or criminous pope. In response to this belief, the Councils of Pisa (1409) and Constance (1414–18) assembled to put an end to the Schism, the conciliarists at the Council of Basel (1431–49) sought unsuccessfully to defy the authority of a pope the validity of whose title was uncontested, and the cardinals of the opposition convoked in May 1511 the dissident and abortive assembly derided by papalists as the *conciliabulum* of Pisa. In response to this belief, too (or, at least, by relying on its continuing currency for their own, quite varied, purposes), dissidents, universities, groups of disgruntled clerics, and governments manoeuvring for diplomatic advantage — all appealed, in subsequent years, from the judgment of the pope to that of a future general council. Thus, for example, the University of Paris in 1516, Martin Luther in 1518, Henry VIII of England in 1533, the Republic of Venice in 1482 and 1509, and various groupings of French clerics, parlementaires and Jansenists in 1688, 1717 and 1720.[2]

Some years ago, in pursuing the conciliarist tradition down through the years subsequent to the dissolution of the Council of Basel, I distinguished between the 'classical age' of conciliar theory, the period dominated by Pisa, Constance and Basel, and its 'silver age', the years immediately prior to the onset of the Protestant Reformation.[3] Encouraged, let it be confessed, by a tongue-in-cheek suggestion of Thomas Mayer's,[4] I should like now to broaden that classification to encompass a 'bronze age' embracing the literature of conciliarist sympathies that is to be found broadcast across the late-sixteenth, seventeenth and eighteenth centuries.

It is one of the incontestable achievements of postwar conciliar scholarship to have made it abundantly clear that the demise of the conciliar theory which

[1] Brian Tierney, *Foundations of the Conciliar Theory: The Contribution of the Medieval Canonists from Gratian to the Great Schism* (Cambridge, 1955), pp. 240, 10–11.

[2] For these latter-day French appeals to a future general council, see Aimé-Georges Martimort, *Le Gallicanisme de Bossuet* (Paris, 1953); E. Préclin, *Les Jansenistes du XVIIIe siècle et la Constitution civile du Clergé* (Paris, 1929); Dale K. Van Kley, *The Religious Origins of the French Revolution: From Calvin to the Civil Constitution, 1560–1791* (New Haven and London, 1996).

[3] Francis Oakley, 'Almain and Major: Conciliar Theory on the Eve of the Reformation', *American Historical Review*, LXX (1965), pp. 673–90 (at p. 674).

[4] Thomas F. Mayer, 'Marco Mantova, a Bronze Age Conciliarist', *Annuarium Historiae Conciliorum*, XVI (1984), pp. 385–408.

dominated Pisa, Constance and Basel was not as sudden or final as formerly we were led to suppose. The conciliarist literature of the classical and silver ages has since been made the focus among scholars of a very considerable expository and interpretative effort. As a result, the very persistence of conciliarist views from the fourteenth century to the mid-sixteenth is coming increasingly to be taken as a simple matter of fact, and the central issue for scholars is coming, accordingly, to be the more difficult and intricate one of assessing the *nature* of that persisting conciliarist tradition and the degree to which, in its expression by a multitude of thinkers, it manifested variations in meaning, intensity and scope.[5] This is far from being the case, however, with the conciliarism of the bronze age. If one presumes, then, to speak of seventeenth-century conciliarism, one must be prepared to devote some effort to establishing the very fact of its existence, as well as to the more intriguing task of assessing its nature and dimensions.

I

Two great episodes of ideological turbulence, which served as relay stations enhancing and strengthening the conciliarist signal, account, I believe, for the surprising vitality which conciliar theory exhibited during the two centuries subsequent to the dissolution of the Council of Basel in 1449. The first was set in motion in October 1510, when the cardinals of the opposition arrived at an understanding with King Louis XII of France and initiated the process that led them in May 1511, and without papal consent, to take it upon themselves to summon a general council to meet at Pisa. Along with such lesser luminaries as Philippus Decius, Zacharius Ferrerius and Pierre Cordier, the crisis thus engendered eventually drew into the fray on behalf of the conciliarist cause the distinguished Scottish theologian, John Mair (or Major — d.1550) and his brilliant Parisian pupil, Jacques Almain (d.1515). It arrayed them in opposition to none other among papal champions than Thomas de Vio, the Dominican master general and future Cardinal Cajetan (d.1534), a man whom Jedin has described as 'perhaps the greatest theologian of his time'.[6] Across the past thirty years and more, this particular episode and the powerfully coherent controver-

---

[5] See e.g. Francis Oakley, 'Natural Law, the *Corpus Mysticum*, and Consent in Conciliar Thought from John of Paris to Matthias Ugonius', *Speculum*, LVI (1981), pp. 786–810; F. Oakley, '*Verius est licet difficilius*: Tierney's *Foundations of the Conciliar Theory* After 40 Years', in *Nicholas of Cusa on Christ and the Church*, ed. G. Christianson and T.M. Izbicki (Leiden, 1996), pp. 15–34; F. Oakley, 'Constance, Basel and the Two Pisas: The Conciliar Legacy in Sixteenth- and Seventeenth-Century England', *Annuarium Historiae Conciliorum*, XXVI (1994), pp. 1–32; J.H. Burns, *Lordship, Kingship, and Empire: The Idea of Monarchy, 1400–1525* (Oxford, 1992), pp. 124–45.

[6] Hubert Jedin, *A History of the Council of Trent*, trans. Ernest Graf (2 vols., London, 1957–61), Vol. I, p. 114.

sialist literature to which it gave rise have been the focus of a good deal of scholarly attention.[7] J.H. Burns himself has been prominent among those engaged in probing that literature and assessing its significance no less for the history of political thought than for that of ecclesiology;[8] and Quentin Skinner, by placing as much emphasis as he rightly did in his *Foundations of Modern Political Thought* on the constitutionalist theories of resistance which Almain and Mair elaborated in the context of this crisis, has in effect succeeded in 'mainstreaming' among historians of political thought a long overdue appreciation of the significance of this particular episode of ideological activity.[9]

So far, at least, as the history of conciliarist ideas is concerned, nothing similar can be said of the second of the two episodes in question. Although it generated an enormous ideological fallout, the episode, in its multinational totality, has yet to find its historian and, despite what I would argue was a revitalizing effect upon the conciliarist tradition, it fails to get even so much as a mention in Hermann Josef Sieben's recent history of conciliar ideas.[10] The ideological energy involved was released by a dramatic series of events occurring in three countries during a four-year period at the start of the seventeenth century. The events in question, each fully comprehensible only in terms of the issues and developments native to the country involved, can best be understood as a group in the context of the rise to prominence in relation to England, Venice

[7] Josef Klotzner, *Kardinal Dominikus Jacobazzi und sein Konzilswerk: Ein Beitrag zur Geschichte der Konziliaren Idee* (Rome, 1948), esp. pp. 220–86; Olivier de la Brosse, *Le Pape et le Concile: La comparaison de leurs pouvoirs à la veille de la Réforme* (Paris, 1965); Oakley, 'Almain and Major'; F. Oakley, 'Conciliarism at the Fifth Lateran Council?', *Church History*, XLI (1972), pp. 452–63; F. Oakley, 'Conciliarism in the Sixteenth Century: Jacques Almain Again', *Archiv für Reformationsgeschichte*, LXVIII (1977), pp. 111–32; Remigius Bäumer, *Nachwirkungen des Konziliaren Gedankens in der Theologie und Kanonistik des frühen 16. Jahrhunderts* (Münster, 1971).

[8] J.H. Burns, '*Politia regalis et optima*: The Political Ideas of John Mair', *History of Political Thought*, II (1981), pp. 31–61; J.H. Burns, '*Jus gladii* and *jurisdictio*: Jacques Almain and John Locke', *Historical Journal*, XXVI (1982), pp. 369–74; J.H. Burns, 'Scholasticism: Survival and Revival', in *The Cambridge History of Political Thought*, *1450–1700*, ed. J.H. Burns and M. Goldie (Cambridge, 1991), pp. 132–55; Burns, *Lordship, Kingship, and Empire*, pp. 124–45.

[9] Quentin Skinner, *Foundations of Modern Political Thought* (2 vols., Cambridge, 1978), Vol. II, chs. 2, 4 and 9. For a brief epitome of the argument involved, see Quentin Skinner, 'Origins of the Calvinist Theory of Revolution', in *After the Reformation*, ed. B.C. Malament (Manchester, 1980), pp. 309–30. For an attempt to set that argument in a broader context, see Francis Oakley, ' "Anxieties of Influence": Skinner, Figgis, Conciliarism and Early Modern Constitutionalism', *Past and Present*, 151 (May 1996), pp. 60–110.

[10] Hermann Josef Sieben, *Die katholische Konzilsidee von der Reformation bis zur Aufklärung* (Paderborn, 1988). Hans Schneider, *Der Konziliarismus als Problem der neueren Katholischen Theologie: Die Geschichte der Auslegung der Konstanzer Dekrete von Febronius bis zur Gegenwart* (Berlin, 1976), is similarly silent on the episode.

and France of the doctrine of the *indirect power* of the pope in matters temporal — a doctrine refurbished by Francisco de Vitoria (d.1546) and transformed into a commonplace by Robert, Cardinal Bellarmine (d.1621).[11]

The story began in England in November 1605, when the discovery of the Gunpowder Plot stimulated the parliament before its adjournment in May 1606 to impose on Catholic recusants an oath of allegiance requiring them (among other things) to reject as impious and heretical the teaching that princes who had been excommunicated or deprived of their office by the pope might lawfully be deposed by their subjects.[12] In Italy, almost immediately thereafter, Pope Paul V allowed to go into effect the sentences of excommunication of the Venetian doge and senate and of interdict on all Venetian territories that he had already issued on 17 April 1606. That interdict was to remain in effect until April 1607, and for the Republic of Venice the decade and more ensuing was to be characterized by ideological tension and political insecurity.[13] Then, in France, in the wake of the murder in 1610 of Henri IV by a Catholic assassin, the Estates General attempted to impose on churchmen, royal officials and others an oath which its opponents portrayed as modelled on the earlier English Oath of Allegiance.

The Europe-wide ideological strife that followed endured into the early 1620s, generating an enormous body of controversialist literature and drawing into the fray opponents of the distinction of James I, King of England, and Cardinal Bellarmine himself.[14] Ironically enough, it was the latter's obsession with the continuing danger posed by the conciliarist principle of the jurisdictional superiority of council to pope that in the end ensured the prominence attained by conciliarist issues in the controversialist literature generated by the Venetian crisis. That prominence came, in fact, to be such (as I have argued elsewhere)[15] that it had the effect of making people in England for much of the

[11] John Courtney Murray, S.J., 'St. Robert Bellarmine on the Indirect Power', *Theological Studies*, IX (1948), pp. 491–535.

[12] See the succinct discussion by J.H.M. Salmon, 'Catholic Resistance Theory, Ultramontanism, and the Royalist Response', in *The Cambridge History of Political Thought, 1450–1700*, ed. Burns and Goldie, pp. 247–53, and the excellent older discussion by Charles H. McIlwain in the lengthy introductory essay to his *The Political Works of James I* (Cambridge, MA, 1918), pp. xxxv–lxxx.

[13] For the background to the interdict, the course it took, and its aftermath, see William J. Bouwsma, *Venice and the Defense of Republican Liberty: Renaissance Values in the Age of the Counter-Reformation* (Berkeley, Los Angeles, 1968), pp. 339–555. For good shorter recent accounts, see Luigi Salvatorelli, 'Venezia, Paolo V, e fra Paolo Sarpi', in *Storia della Civiltà Veneziana*, ed. Vittore Branca (3 vols., Florence, 1979), Vol. III, pp. 23–6; A.D. Wright, 'Why the Venetian Interdict?', *English Historical Review*, LXXXIX (1974), pp. 536–50.

[14] See McIlwain, *The Political Works of James I*, pp. xxxv–lxxx.

[15] Francis Oakley, 'Complexities of Context: Gerson, Bellarmine, Sarpi, Richer, and the Venetian Interdict of 1606–1607', *Catholic Historical Review*, LXXXII (1996), pp. 369–96.

seventeenth century better acquainted with conciliar history and the writings of the conciliarists than at any previous time, the fifteenth century not excluded. For one of the striking characteristics of this whole great ideological upheaval was the intimacy of the ties binding together the critics of Ultramontane views in London, Venice and Paris and the ease and speed with which tracts and ideas circulated among them.[16] But so far, at least, as the propagation of conciliarist ideas was concerned, the epicentre of energy appears to have been situated in Paris, and the crucial initiating figure to have been Edmond Richer (1559–1631). Rector from 1595 onwards of the Collège de Cardinal Le Moine in the University of Paris, Richer came, from 1608 to 1612, as Syndic of the Sorbonne, to play a leading (if controversial) role in the Parisian Faculty of Theology. It is on France, then, and on Richer's conciliarist commitments that I propose in this essay to dwell.[17]

II

Admittedly, those particular commitments do not appear to have been a compelling focus of attention among the rather small group of scholars who, over the course of the last century or so, have chosen to concern themselves with Richer. As has proved to be the case with so many other thinkers, what one makes of Richer depends very much on the angle from which one approaches him. In particular, it depends on whether one approaches him with the developments of later centuries in mind or with what had gone before. Of the scholars who have viewed him from the former angle of vision, those writing under the long shadow cast over Catholic historiography by the First Vatican Council's definition in 1870 of papal infallibility have tended to view him as a scandalously radical figure, a man intent upon promoting nothing less than a 'democratic' ecclesiology, somebody clearly prone to the heterodox inclinations to which the labels 'multitudinisme', 'presbytérianisme' and 'parochisme' were customarily attached.[18] And for others, historians whose interests have centred

---

[16] Oakley, 'Constance, Basel and the two Pisas', pp. 103–15.

[17] The fullest treatment of Richer is still the old standard work by Edmond Puyol, *Edmond Richer: Étude historique et critique sur la Rénovation du Gallicanisme au commencement du XVIIe siècle* (2 vols., Paris, 1876). See also E. Préclin, 'Edmond Richer (1559–1631): Sa vie, Son oeuvre et le Richérisme', *Revue d'histoire moderne*, V (1930), pp. 241–69, 321–36; Monique Cottret, 'Edmond Richer (1539–1631): Le politique et le sacré', in *L'État Baroque: Regards sur la pensée politique de la France du premier XVIIe siècle*, ed. Henry Méchoulan (Paris, 1985), pp. 159–77.

[18] Thus, quintessentially, Puyol, *Edmond Richer: Étude historique et critique*, a highly critical assessment explicitly determined by what the author took to be the doctrinal implications of the recent infallibility decision. Some traces of the same tendency are evident even in Léopold Willaert, *Après le concile de Trente: La restauration catholique, 1563–1648* (Paris, 1960), Vol. 18 of *Histoire de l'Église*, ed. A. Fliche and V. Martin (26 vols., Paris, 1934–64).

on religio-political developments in the France of the later- seventeenth and eighteenth centuries, Richer's own thinking is prone to being submerged in the broader (and murkier) waters of 'richérisme'.[19]

During the eighteenth century, this last term appears to have come perilously close to being nothing more precise than a broad-gauged term of abuse available for hurling at those suspected of Jansenist sympathies and of the strain of Gallicanism that by then had come frequently to be associated with such sympathies.[20] But the term *richériste* had been in circulation already, and with a more precise connotation, in the second half of the seventeenth century.[21] At that time it had been associated predominantly, if still pejoratively, with the promotion of the view that the *curés* (or lower clergy charged with the cure of souls) were, as successors of the seventy-two disciples of Christ, an integral part of the divinely-established hierarchy of the Church, possessed, therefore, of their own jurisdictional powers and entitled accordingly to a say in the governance of the Church.[22]

Richer certainly suscribed to that view and expressed it forthrightly enough, though without notable insistence, in the work of his that was to be most frequently reprinted and most widely read — the *Libellus de ecclesiastica et politica potestate* (1611).[23] In his own day, however, and sometimes indeed later on, that view was recognized for what it truly was — no bold novelty but the echoing of a theme prominent in the thinking of the revered French theologian, Jean Gerson (d.1429).[24] Although Gerson, because of a dispute in 1409 between a Franciscan, John Gorel, and the secular masters at the University of Paris, had been led as Chancellor of the University to dwell on the matter at some length, there was, again, nothing novel in *his* day about the insistence on

[19] Thus Préclin, *Les Jansénistes du XVIIIe siècle*; Richard M. Golden, *The Godly Rebellion: Parisian Curés and the Religious Fronde, 1652–1662* (Chapel Hill, NC, 1981); Emmanuel Le Roy Ladurie, *The Ancient Régime: A History of France, 1610–1774*, trans. Mark Greengrass (Oxford, 1996); and, though to a lesser degree, Van Kley, *The Religious Origins of the French Revolution*.

[20] Préclin, *Les Jansénistes du XVIIIe siècle*; Van Kley, *The Religious Origins of the French Revolution*.

[21] Martimort, *Le Gallicanisme de Bossuet*, p. 13; Golden, *The Godly Rebellion*, p. 73.

[22] Thus e.g. Le Roy Ladurie, *The Ancient Régime*, p. 124, n. 51: '*Richerism* was a set of doctrines inspired by the ideas of the theologian Edmond Richer . . . It envisaged a stronger position of the parish clergy within the Church'; Golden, *The Godly Rebellion*, pp. 3, 14 ('. . . Richerism, the Gallicanism of the lower clergy'), pp. 72–3, 155–6.

[23] Edmond Richer, *Libellus de ecclesiastica et politica potestate*, caps. 2 and 5. I give my references to the edition most readily available, that in Melchior Goldast, *Monarchia S. Romani Imperii* (3 vols., Frankfurt, 1611–13), Vol. III, pp. 797–806 (at 798:42–9, 800:10–15). While Préclin, 'Edmond Richer', pp. 327, 332–4, stresses Richer's 'parochisme', he acknowledges that that position was still rather 'vague' in the *Libellus* and was fleshed out only in the later writings that remained unpublished during his lifetime.

[24] For the pertinent texts in Gerson, see Louis Pascoe, *Jean Gerson's Principles of Church Reform* (Leiden, 1973), pp. 146–64.

the divinely-established hierarchical status of the parish clergy. The novelty, instead, lay in the willingness of a friar like Gorel to deny it.[25]

If, then, we were to approach Richer not with the tangled eighteenth-century disputes between French *curés* and their bishops in mind, but from a perspective framed by the ecclesiological developments of the two centuries and more preceding, his affirmation of the divine institution of the parish clergy would seem quite unexceptionable. So, too, the more general constitutionalist stance expressed in the set of related and insistently reiterated ecclesiological claims that are, in fact, central to the argument of the *Libellus* in a way that his comments on the status of the parish clergy are not.[26] These are the classic conciliarist claims on which Richer dwells in no less than fourteen of the eighteen chapters of the *Libellus*, and which (*pace* assertions still occasionally made to the contrary) certainly do not involve his viewing the Church as some sort of a 'democracy', still less his denial of a divinely-instituted status to the papal office.[27]

That the position outlined in the *Libellus* proved too bitter a pill for the papal nuncio, leading French churchmen, and even some of his own theological colleagues to swallow[28] is testimony, less to any unprecedentedly radical quality it possessed, than to the degree to which in the late-sixteenth and early-seventeenth centuries Ultramontane inclinations had made themselves at home in the Faculty of Theology at Paris. To that fact, Richer's own changing ecclesiological commitments bear ironic witness. As late as 1592, he himself had been a supporter of the Catholic *Ligue*, a staunch admirer of Bellarmine's writings, and a person of distinctly Ultramontane sympathies.[29] But within a

---

[25] *Ibid.*, pp. 157–64. Pierre d'Ailly (d.1420), Gerson's former teacher, clearly shared similar sympathies, as also did Jean de Paris (d.1306), to whose ecclesiology both men were in varying degree indebted. See Jean de Paris, *Tractatus de regia potestate et papali*, cap. 10, in *Johannes Quidort von Paris: Über königliche und päpstliche Gewalt*, ed. Fritz Bleienstein (Stuttgart, 1969), pp. 114–15; Pierre d'Ailly, *Tractatus de potestate*, in *Joannis Gersonii Opera Omnia*, ed. Louis Ellies Dupin (5 vols., Antwerp, 1706), Vol. II, p. 928. Cf., for the deeper background, Yves M.-J. Congar, 'Aspects ecclésiologiques de la querelle entre mendiants et séculiers dans la seconde moitié du XIIIe siècle et le début du XIVe', *Archives d'histoire doctrinale et littéraire du moyen age*, XXVIII (1961), pp. 35–151.

[26] Richer, *Libellus de ecclesiastica et politica potestate*, esp. caps. 1–10, 14–17; in Goldast, *Monarchia*, Vol. III, pp. 798–802, 804–5.

[27] Thus e.g. Jean Delumeau, *Le Catholicisme entre Luther et Voltaire* (Paris, 1971), p. 173; Préclin, *Les Jansénistes du XVIIIe siècle*, p. 5. Nor is it really accurate to portray him as reducing 'la papauté à n'être plus, dans l'Église, qu'une sorte d'accessoire' (thus *ibid.*, pp. 2–3).

[28] Leading, in fact, to his condemnation by an ecclesiastical commission and forcing him in 1612 to resign from his high office as Syndic of the Sorbonne. See Puyol, *Edmond Richer: Étude historique et critique*, Vol. I, p. 263; Préclin, 'Edmond Richer', pp. 257–62.

[29] Puyol, *Edmond Richer: Étude historique et critique*, Vol. I, p. 97; Préclin, 'Edmond Richer', p. 244.

few years he was to shift his position and become a defender of the rights of Henri IV. Moreover, having combed the Scriptures, the patristic literature, the histories of general councils, and the ecclesiological writings of his distinguished late-medieval predecessors in the Parisian faculty of theology, he was eventually to modulate into a convinced, vigorous and dogged proponent of Gallican and (therefore) conciliarist views. While certainly making common cause with the *politique* Gallicans of the Parlement de Paris, it was his great aim to reinvigorate the *theological* heart of the Gallican tradition by reviving the knowledge of the old doctors of the Sorbonne from Jean de Paris (d. 1306), via Pierre d'Ailly (d.1420) and Jean Gerson, down to Jacques Almain and John Mair, and by reinstating their conciliarist vision as the official ecclesiological doctrine of the Parisian faculty of theology.

To that end, he drew attention to their views repeatedly throughout his career,[30] and worked assiduously to make their ecclesiological writings readily available to a broad public. Thus, in one of the several works of compilation he produced after his own views had been condemned and he had been forced out of his influential role as Syndic of the Sorbonne, he republished, along with a collection of the decrees of the Parisian faculty of theology concerning the pontifical authority, a whole series of Parisian theological writings pertaining to that subject. The full title of the work leaves no doubt about the position it was intended to promote: *Vindiciae doctrinae majorum scholae Parisiensis seu constans et perpetua Scholae Parisiensis doctrina de autoritate et infallibilitate Ecclesiae in rebus fidei ac morum, contra defensores monarchiae universalis et absolutae curiae Romanae.*[31] In that work he reprinted not only the *Tractatus de potestate regia et papali* of Jean de Paris, which contains what is perhaps the earliest (1302) coherent statement of the conciliar theory, but also the principal conciliarist tracts of d'Ailly, Gerson, Almain and Mair.

To avoid renewed controversy, Richer prudently refrained from publishing this work and it saw the public light of day only after his death. But the fruit of his most important editorial endeavour, an edition of the works of Gerson, had been published already in 1606.[32] As the first complete edition of those works,

---

[30] As, for instance, in his *Defensio libelli de ecclesiastica et politica potestate in quinque divisa libros* (2 vols., Cologne, 1701), a vast work which he completed, it seems, in 1622 (see Puyol, *Edmond Richer: Étude historique et critique*, Vol. II, pp. 426–7), but which was published only after his death. Its pages are peppered with references to the acts and decrees of Pisa, Constance and Basel, to the long-established teachings of the School of Paris, and to the conciliarist writings of d'Ailly, Gerson, Almain, Mair and Nicholas of Cusa.

[31] For a description of this work, which was published in Cologne in 1683, see Puyol, *Edmond Richer: Étude historique et critique*, Vol. II, pp. 424–6.

[32] *Joannis . . . Gersonii opera*, ed. Edmond Richer (2 vols., Paris, 1606). The works of d'Ailly, Almain and Mair are reprinted in Vol. II, pp. 675–934.

and one that contained also the central conciliarist writings of d'Ailly, Almain and Mair, it proved to be a very significant and influential publication. Not that the views of these conciliarists had been forgotten, even outside France. It is true that Paolo Sarpi (d.1623) in Venice does not appear to have made their acquaintance until 1606, when Pietro Priuli, the Venetian ambassador to Paris, forwarded to Venice a listing of older theological writings whose republication might conceivably be helpful to the Venetian cause.[33] But in the late-sixteenth century the learned Anglican controversialist, Matthew Sutcliffe (d.1629), showed a marked degree of familiarity with a whole host of conciliarist sympathizers from Nicholas de Clamanges (d.1437) to Nicholas of Cusa (d.1464) and beyond, not excluding the Parisians d'Ailly, Gerson and Almain.[34] What Richer's edition did, however, was to make the conciliarist writings of these Parisians (and those of Mair, too) readily available in convenient form. In Richer's own day, his bitter opponent, the Cardinal du Perron, made rueful acknowledgment of that fact;[35] and, a century later, Louis Ellies du Pin (d.1719), a Gallican of Jansenist sympathies, took Richer's cue and included in his own classic edition of Gerson's complete works, along with other similar writings, the central conciliarist texts of d'Ailly, Gerson, Almain and Mair.[36]

Richer, then, had a good deal more than a nodding acquaintance with the conciliarist tradition that stretched back at Paris into the fourteenth century. If, along with his familiarity with the histories of Pisa, Constance and Basel, he put that knowledge to effective use in his *Libellus de ecclesiastica et politica potestate*, it should be noted that he did so, too, in his responses to the two leading papalist ideologists of the early-modern era: Robert, Cardinal Bellarmine in his own day, and Thomas de Vio, Cardinal Cajetan, who had written a century earlier.

III

It was Bellarmine, in fact, whose assertion of the papalist ecclesiology had stimulated Richer to frame his first and, in some respects, most powerful and coherent affirmation of the conciliarist position. But the Bellarmine in question was not the great 'administrator of doctrine', the systematic controversialist of the *Disputationes de Controversiis Christianae Fidei* (1586–93), but the harried (and sometimes confused) respondent in the war of words the Venetian Repub-

---

[33] It had been drawn up for him, he said, by 'one of the leading and oldest doctors of the Sorbonne' and included works by such conciliarist (or protoconciliarist) authors as Jean de Paris, William of Ockham, d'Ailly, Mair, and the jurist Philippus Decius. See Paolo Sarpi, *Lettere ai Gallicani*, ed. Boris Ulianich (Wiesbaden, 1961), pp. xxvi–xxvii.

[34] Oakley, 'Constance, Basel and the two Pisas', pp. 14–16.

[35] Jacques Davy, Cardinal du Perron, *An Oration made on the Part of the Lordes Spirituall in the Chamber of the Third Estate*, translated into English (St. Omer, 1616), pp. 498–50; cf. pp. 121–2.

[36] *Joannis Gersonii Opera Omnia*, ed. Louis Ellies Dupin (5 vols., Antwerp, 1706).

lic had unleashed by way of self-defence after the proclamation of the papal interdict in April 1606. The first blow struck in that war of words was the anonymous publication, supposedly in Paris though in Italian translation, of two short Latin tracts directed against the abuse of ecclesiastical censure written by Gerson in 1418. Their republication in the vernacular was the work of Paolo Sarpi and it had drawn Bellarmine into the fray, eventuating in a tangled series of polemical exchanges between the two men in which (or so I would judge) Sarpi may be said to have had the edge.[37]

While the tracts in question addressed the characteristically late-medieval *topos* of the abuse of the power of excommunication, in the eighth *consideratio* of the first of them, a mere hundred and fifty words, Gerson had moved on to insist that the Council of Constance had taught that it was heretical to deny the appeal from pope to council.[38] He had done so only in passing, and in the context of speaking (as Sarpi was later to point out) 'in favour of the Apostolic See'. But what little he said was enough to goad Bellarmine, having inflated Gerson's claim into an assertion that Constance had declared it 'to be heresy to deny the superiority of the council to the pope', to condemn that claim as 'manifestly erroneous', and to denounce the translator who had put it forward as pertinent to the present Venetian situation as having revealed himself, by so

---

[37] This revealing exchange is examined in Oakley, 'Complexities of Context', pp. 369–96.

[38] The tracts in question are the *Resolutio circa materiam excommunicationum et irregularitatum* and *De sententia pastoris semper tenenda*, and they are printed in *Jean Gerson: Oeuvres complètes*, ed. Palémon Glorieux (10 vols., Paris, 1960–73), Vol. VI, pp. 291–6. The Italian translations were printed (along with a prefatory statement) at Venice (though supposedly in Paris) as *Trattato e resoluzione sopra la validità delle scommuniche di Giovanni Gersono Teologo e Cancellario Parisino, cognominato il dottore Cristianissimo tradotto dalla lingua latina nella volgare con ogni fedeltà. In opusculi due*. See the editions included in Fra Paolo Sarpi, *Istoria dell' Interdetto e altri scritti editi e inediti*, ed. Giovanni Gambarin (3 vols., Bari, 1940), Vol. II, pp. 171–84. The (inadvertently crucial) eighth consideration reads as follows (*ibid.*, Vol. II, pp. 177–8):

CONSIDERAZIONE VIII. Porta più pericolo lo sprezzo delle chiavi verso la persona del summo pontifice che verso l'inferiore, perché dagli abusi degli'inferiori è aperto il ricorso al papa per il beneficio dell'appellazione. E se alcun dica che parimente si può appellare dal papa al concilio generale, dicevano altre volte, inanzi il concilio generale pisano e costanziense, che questo non era in alcun modo lecito; ed allegavano le sue ragioni a favor loro, molto chiare, per quanto loro pareva. Ma nondimeno al presente costantemente si afferma che il negare la superiorità del concilio sopra il papa sia eresia, condannata per constituzione expressissima e praticata nel detto concilio di Costanza, si come altrove più diffusamente è stato mostrato: per il che si risponde altramente, cioè che non può né debbe celebrar cosi facilmente e per leggier causa un concilio per udir le appellazioni (dove anco fusse lecito appellarsi), si come facilmente si ha ricorso al papa.

doing, to be 'something less than a Catholic' ('Si dimostra poco Catholico').[39]
By so doing, and as the subsequent exchanges with Sarpi made unambiguously
clear, Bellarmine had in fact succeeded in promoting what it had clearly been
his intention to deflect. Nothing less, that is, than the insertion of the old
conciliarist claim into the growing body of publicistic literature now being
generated by the Venetian interdict and by that republic's efforts to defend itself
and to rally support for its cause, not only at home but also in London and Paris.

Although Sarpi had long been interested in the traditional Gallican claims,
and had, since 1604, been in correspondence with leading Gallican authors, in
his careful study of Sarpi's relations with the Gallicans Boris Ulianich finds no
evidence at all to support the old belief that it was Richer who had suggested
to Sarpi the idea of translating and republishing the two Gersonian tracts.[40] But
Ulianich does conclude that the 'principalissimo Theologo' whom the Venetian
ambassador Prinli claimed finally, in January 1607, to have induced to write in
support of Venice was none other than Richer himself, and that the work in
question was the short *Apologia pro ecclesiae et concilii autoritate, adversus
Joannis Gersonii doctoris christianissimi obtrectatores* which, marred by a
series of printing errors and without author or place of publication indicated,
was first published in Italy in 1607.[41]

The *Apologia* was a direct reply to Bellarmine's harsh attack on Gerson, and
it witnesses powerfully to the damage Bellarmine had done to his own papalist
cause by his disproportionate emphasis on the conciliarist element in Gerson's
tracts on excommunication. Gerson's remarks on the matter had been no more
than glancing ones, but Bellarmine had belaboured them for no less than seven
long pages, and Richer, anxious to rebut Bellarmine's portrayal of Gerson's
position as erroneous and evocative of contemporary heretical positions, was
now moved to devote the bulk of his *Apologia* to the Church's constitution in
general and the central role of general councils in particular, turning only in the
last three pages of a forty-eight page discourse to the matter of the abuse of the
power of the keys, which had, in fact, been Gerson's own topic and the reason,

---

[39] Bellarmine, *Risposta de Card. Bellarmino, ad un libretto intitulato Trattato, e
resolutione sopra la validità de le scommuniche di Gio. Gersone* (Rome, 1606), p. 71.

[40] See Sarpi, *Lettere ai Gallicani*, ed. Ulianich, pp. xiii–cxlii (at p. xxii). See also
Bouwsma, *Venice and the Defence of Republican Liberty*, p. 236; Salvatorelli, 'Venezia,
Paolo V, e fra Paolo Sarpi', p. 28.

[41] Sarpi, *Lettere ai Gallicani*, ed. Ulianich, p. xxix. This first edition did not enjoy a
wide circulation. Richer was careful to dissociate his name from it and refrained from
republishing it — see Puyol, *Edmond Richer: Étude historique et critique*, Vol. I,
pp. 92–101, and Vol. II, p. 422. Préclin, 'Edmond Richer', p. 252, n.2, confessed that he
had been unable to run down a copy and I myself have found no copies in North America.
I used the copy in the British Library. The work was posthumously republished as
*Apologia pro Joanno Gersonio, pro suprema Ecclesia et Concilii generalis autoritate et
independentia Regiae potestatis ab alio quam a Deo. Adversus scholae Parisiensis et
ejusdem Doctoris christianissimi obtrectatores* (Lyons, 1676).

presumably, for Sarpi's having chosen to translate the two treatises in the first place.

Bellarmine's attack on Gerson had moved at two levels, the one theoretical, the other historical. Richer's reply is framed in similar fashion, though the theoretical aspect of his work is much more fully and coherently developed. With Bellarmine, the argument 'della raggione' had involved little more than the triumphant insistence that 'the Holy Church is not like the Republic of Venice, or of Genoa, or of any other City' where it can be said that 'the Republic is above the Prince'. 'Nor is it like a kingdom of this world' where the power of the monarch is derived from the people and can be withdrawn by them. Instead, 'the Church of Christ is a most perfect kingdom and an absolute monarchy, which depends not on the people . . . but solely on the divine will'.[42] The historical argument he had developed on three fundamental grounds. First, that although he had read and re-read the proceedings of the Council of Constance he had been unable to identify in them any declaration to the effect that it would be 'heresy to deny the superiority of the council to the pope'. Second, that the superiority decree of Constance's fourth session[43] was not to be read as applicable to any pope whatsoever, and certainly not to any canonically elected pope universally held to be legitimate. It was properly to be viewed, instead, as applicable only to the three dubious claimants of Gerson's own day, over whom the universal Church and the council representing it could unquestionably exercise authority. Third, the decree in question, *Haec sancta synodus*, dating as it did to a time (1415) when there was no pope with an uncontested title, and lacking the subsequent legitimating approbation that Martin V (the new, universally accepted, pope) had given retroactively to other conciliar decrees, had no pertinence to anything but the ending of the Great Schism itself. Accordingly, Pius II, Julius II and subsequent popes had imposed a sentence of excommunication on anyone appealing from pope to future general council. If reason itself indicated the erroneous nature of Gerson's position so too, did the teaching of the Scriptures and of the general councils of the Church — this last as recently as 1516, when the Fifth Lateran Council had explicitly affirmed that the pope is above any council whatsoever.

To these essentially historical arguments Richer, in his response, gave something of a dismissive backhand. Quite correctly, he pointed out that had Bellarmine read the final version of the superiority decree *Haec sancta synodus*, which had been approved at the *fifth* general session of Constance (and not simply the earlier version approved at the fourth), he would have been forced

---

[42] For this and what follows, see Bellarmine, *Risposta de Card. Bellermino ad un libretto . . . di Gio. Gersone*, pp. 72–7.

[43] For the formation of the superiority decree *Haec sancta synodus* and the difference between the texts approved at the fourth and fifth sessions of the Council cf Constance, see Giuseppe Alberigo, *Chiesa conciliare: Identità e significato del conciliarismo* (Brescia, 1981), pp. 165–86. The actual texts are printed side by side on pp. 168–73.

to admit that it applied to *any* general council whatsoever, and not merely to pontiffs of dubious legitimacy but to those whose titles were wholly uncontested.[44] Similarly, Bellarmine himself having earlier claimed that the conciliar status of the Fifth Lateran Council had remained in dispute among Catholics 'down to this day', he was hardly justified now in adducing its decree of 1516 in order to demonstrate the validity of his own counterclaim that the pope was superior in authority to the council.[45] That said, and such simple historical issues handily disposed of, it was clear, Bellarmine's assertion to the contrary notwithstanding, that Gerson's claim that the Council of Constance had dubbed it heretical to deny the superiority of council to pope must stand.[46]

In any case, Richer went on, if Bellarmine were correct in his imputation of heresy to Gerson's teaching on this point, then what on earth was to be made of the similar teachings of those three great cardinals, Pierre d'Ailly, Francesco Zabarella (d.1417) and Nicholas of Cusa — or, for that matter, of the congruent views of such other conciliarists as Panormitanus (d.1450), Decius, Almain and Mair? Or what, indeed, of the posture of the Gallican church itself, for it had 'always received and defended the teaching of Gerson as Catholic and orthodox'.[47] If one were to press him further and to ask why that was the case, one could expect to be told that the answer was set forth in the fifty-three *axiomata* that constitute the heart of his *Apologia*.

Intended to prove that Gerson's conciliarist doctrine was 'altogether in conformity with natural, divine, and canon law',[48] and bolstered with invocations, not only of Gerson's own writings but also of the conciliarist arguments of d'Ailly, Almain, Mair and the Parisian school in general, these axioms elaborate in somewhat fuller and more systematic fashion the core ecclesiological commitments that Richer was to incorporate, a few years later, in his *Libellus de ecclesiastica et politica potestate*.[49] Thus, stipulating at the outset that absolute or despotic government (papal no less than secular) is repugnant to natural and divine law,[50] he goes on to insist (the best political regimen being monarchy tempered by aristocracy) that the universal Church is, accordingly, a monarchical polity instituted by Christ for a supernatural end and, via the instrumentality of the general council, tempered in its government by an aristocratic element.[51] Its 'essential monarch', 'absolute head' and 'essential

---

[44] Richer, *Apologia pro Ecclesiae et Concilio autoritate*, pp. 11, 38–9. See above, n. 43.

[45] Richer, *Apologia*, p. 39.

[46] *Ibid.*, p. 11.

[47] *Ibid.*, p. 3.

[48] *Ibid.*, p. 10.

[49] To which work, therefore, I will give cross-references in what follows.

[50] Richer, *Apologia*, p. 14; *Libellus* cap. 9, in Goldast, *Monarchia*, Vol. III, 802:11–14.

[51] Richer, *Apologia*, pp. 15, 20; cf. *Libellus*, caps. 3, 6 and 15, in Goldast, *Monarchia*, Vol. III, 799:18–22, 800:16–18, 804:58–62.

head' being none other than Christ himself, Peter and his papal successors must properly be viewed as no more than 'mutable', 'secondary', 'ministerial' and 'accidental heads'.[52] Moreover, it is not on the pope but on the universal Church and the general council representing it that Christ, its founder and lord, has directly conferred the infallible teaching power, and the Council of Constance, by decreeing that general councils should be assembled at regular and frequent intervals, has underlined the degree to which the Church's wellbeing depends on them.[53] Capable of performing every act of jurisdiction that the pope can,[54] the general council, by virtue of the fact that it has its power immediately from Christ, is 'superior to the pontiff in infallibility and authority', and is capable also of assembling itself without and even in opposition to the pope.[55] The right, then, of appeal from the judgment of the pope to that of a general council is not to be gainsaid. The council is undoubtedly empowered to correct a scandalous and incorrigible pope and to curb the abuse of the power of the keys — as, indeed, the Council of Constance had done in the case of Pope John XXIII.[56]

Thus, with many an invocation of the deeds and decrees of Constance and Basel and many a reference to 'the doctors of Paris' — not simply Gerson himself but also d'Ailly, Mair and (above all) Almain — Richer laboured mightily to vindicate against Bellarmine the Catholicity of Gerson's conciliarist teaching. But Bellarmine, as he had ruefully acknowledged in the opening paragraphs of the *Apologia*,[57] was by no means the only papalist to have impugned the orthodoxy of that most Christian teaching. A hundred years earlier, after all, during the crisis occasioned by the convocation of the *concili-abulum* of Pisa, Cajetan had done likewise; and when he returned some years later to matters conciliar in his *Defensio libelli de ecclesiastica et politica potestate* (*c*.1622), Richer, while noting that Almain had swiftly risen to the defence of the Parisian ecclesiology against Cajetan's attack, noted also that Cajetan had returned to the fray in his *Apologia de comparata auctoritate et concilii* (1512) and that Almain's premature death in 1515 had prevented his

[52] Richer, *Apologia*, p. 17; cf. *Libellus*, caps. 1, 3, 4 and 15, in Goldast, *Monarchia*, Vol. III, 758:24–6, 799:27–30, 799:33–8, 804:49–51.

[53] Richer, *Apologia*, pp. 10–11, 32–3, cf. *Libellus*, caps. 5 and 8, in Goldast, *Monarchia*, Vol. III, 800:5–7, 801:41–4.

[54] Richer, *Apologia*, p. 33. Richer is using words precisely here, and is acknowledging that the council cannot administer the sacraments or preach — acts which require individual human agency. What is simply assumed here is the traditional canonistic and theological practice of distinguishing between the *potestas ordinis*, the sacramental power conferred on priests by ordination, and the *potestas jurisdictionis* in the external forum, the power of governance which does not presuppose for its exercise priestly ordination.

[55] Richer, *Apologia*, pp. 28, 31, 35–6.

[56] Richer, *Apologia*, pp. 26–7, 34–6; cf. *Libellus*, caps. 7 and 16, in Goldast, *Monarchia*, Vol. III, 801:30–4, 805:1–11.

[57] Richer, *Apologia*, p. 3.

replying to *that* work. That task, accordingly, Richer now in 1622 undertook himself, boldly claiming, moreover, that he would respond further to *all* of Cajetan's arguments,[58] including those set forth in his *De comparatione auctoritatis papae et concilii* (1511), the work to which Almain had originally replied in his *Tractatus de auctoritate ecclesiae*.[59] It would doubtless be possible to argue about the quality of these responses — sometimes dogmatic, not infrequently condescending, occasionally bordering on outright abuse. But as Richer works his way remorselessly, first through the successive chapters of the *Apologia*, then of the *De comparatione*, carefully summarizing Cajetan's arguments and then stating his own responses to them, a wearying measure of credibility comes to attach to his claim.

He divides his rebuttal into some seven *questiones*, on only the first of which will we need to dwell at any length. The other six questions constitute a sort of dialectical mopping-up operation designed to dispose of Cajetan's residual arguments, many of them drawn not from the *Apologia* but from his earlier *De comparatione*. The argumentation they contain is highly repetitive, circling back again and again to a handful of claims central to Richer's earliest formulations of his conciliarist commitments in 1607 and 1611. Namely, that it is Christ himself who is the only 'internal and essential head' of the Church; that Peter was no more than an 'external, ministerial and mutable head' charged with the external work of hierarchical administration; that the same is true, accordingly, of his papal successors; that upon them, as upon other prelates taken individually, Christ conferred the keys (the power of jurisdiction) only 'partially', insofar as it pertains to 'use, exercise' and 'the execution of natural, divine, and canon law'. It was, rather, upon the sacerdotal Church as a whole that he conferred that jurisdictional power 'in its totality' and in 'the architectonic fashion that pertains to lordship and proprietary right'. That being so, it is of course 'the power of the pope [that] is subordinated to the power of the Church and the council, just as a part [is subordinated] to the whole, and not

---

[58] Edmond Richer, *Defensio libelli de ecclesiastica et politica potestate* (Cologne, 1701), Lib. III, cap. 3, p. 311: '. . . Quo circa ergo non tantum his postremis lucubrationibus [i.e. the arguments Cajetan had made in 1512 in his *Apologia*], verumtamen omnibus argumentis Cajetani respondebo'. He devotes the whole of Chapter III (pp. 311–40) to this task.

[59] Modern edited texts of both of Cajetan's works are to be found in Tommaso de Vio, Cardinal Cajetan, *De comparatione auctoritatis papae et concilii cum Apologia ejusdem Tractatus*, ed. V.M.J. Pollet (Rome, 1936). Almain's *Tractatus de auctoritate ecclesiae* is most readily available in Gerson, *Opera omnia*, ed. Dupin, Vol. II, pp. 976–1012. All three works are now conveniently available in English translation along with a brief introduction in *Conciliarism and Papalism*, ed. J.H. Burns and Thomas M. Izbicki (Cambridge, 1997).

vice versa.[60] This line of argument Richer bolsters with frequent appeals not only to the case he himself had made in 1607 in his *Apologia pro ecclesiae et concilii auctoritate*, or to such 'private doctors' as John of Paris, Gerson, Nicholas of Cusa, Almain and Mair, but also to the historic decrees of Constance and Basel affirming the jurisdictional superiority of council to pope — decrees which as he reminds us yet once more, 'the whole School of Paris' had long held and 'doggedly defended' as a tenet of the Catholic faith itself.[61]

But, then, it was precisely that traditional Parisian ecclesiology that Cajetan had set out to attack. He had done so, especially, in the first and most important chapter of his *Apologia*, where he had gone to the very heart of the matter by challenging its claim to be grounded in the law of nature itself. Long ago, in advancing his classic argument that conciliarist thinking had played an important role in the history of late-medieval and early-modern political and constitutional thinking, John Neville Figgis argued that the crucial move made by the conciliarist thinkers was that of having treated 'the Church definitively as one of a class, political societies'.[62] That some (though by no means all)[63] of them were led, as a result, to ground their case in the mandates of the natural law itself was only to be expected. That move was certainly characteristic of such great Parisian theologians as d'Ailly and Gerson at the time of the Council of Constance. A century later, as Burns and Skinner have emphasized, it was characteristic also of their sixteenth-century Parisian successors, Almain and Mair.[64] Had that not been the case, indeed, the willingness of Calvinist monarchomachs in the sixteenth century and English parliamentarians in the seventeenth to deploy conciliarist ideas in an attempt to bolster their own constitutionalist claims to a right of resistance against tyrannous monarchs would have been totally inconceivable.[65]

[60] Richer, *Defensio*, Lib. III, qu. 3, 6 and 7, pp. 321, 334–5, 337, 339; cf. qu. 1 and 2, pp. 313, 314, 317, 319. The words quoted occur (in order) at pp. 335, 321, 339 and 317.

[61] Richer, *Defensio*, Lib. III, qu. 7, pp. 337–9; cf. qu. 5 and 6, pp. 332 and 335.

[62] J.N. Figgis, *Political Thought from Gerson to Grotius, 1414–1625: Seven Studies* (New York, 1960), p. 56. These studies were first published in 1907.

[63] See Oakley, 'Natural Law, the *Corpus Mysticum*, and Consent in Conciliar Thought', where it is argued that the willingness to treat the Church as an essentially *political* society and to give the appeal to natural law a central role in the making of the conciliarist case was by no means characteristic of all conciliar thinkers.

[64] Burns, '*Politia regalis et optima*: The Political Ideas of John Mair'; Burns, '*Jus gladii* and *jurisdictio*: Jacques Almain and John Locke'; Burns, 'Scholasticism: Survival and Revival'; Burns, *Lordship, Kingship, and Empire*, pp. 124–45. Quentin Skinner, *Foundations of Modern Political Thought*, Vol. II, chs. 2, 4 and 9; Skinner, 'Origins of the Calvinist Theory of Revolution'.

[65] As I have argued elsewhere. See Francis Oakley, 'Figgis, Constance, and the Divines of Paris', *American Historical Review*, LXXV (1969), pp. 368–86, as well as 'Natural Law, the *Corpus Mysticum*, and Consent', and especially, ' "Anxieties of Influence": Skinner, Figgis, Conciliarism and Early Modern Constitutionalism'.

In this respect, Almain had been particularly forceful, and despite an opening bow in his *Tractatus de auctoritate papae et concilii* in the direction of acknowledging the features that serve to distinguish the universal Church from secular political societies, he had come close (like Mair, his former teacher) to treating the ecclesiastical and secular polities univocally. In his *De comparatione auctoritatis papae et concilii*, Cajetan had employed language that could be taken to suggest a degree of compatibility with that approach, and by the time he came in 1512 to respond to Almain's treatise he may conceivably have felt a bit rueful about the degree of ideological overlap that others might thereby assume.[66] Whatever the case, he certainly chose, in his *Apologia*, to try to blunt the force of Almain's argument from natural law.

A century later, when forced to confront the similar challenge posed by Paolo Sarpi's invocation of secular political analogies, Bellarmine (as we have seen) was to content himself with a firm insistence on the *supernatural* grounding of ecclesiastical power: 'The Holy Church', he was to insist, is 'a most perfect kingdom and absolute monarchy, which [unlike worldly monarchies] depends not on the people but on the divine will alone.'[67] Cajetan's response, on the contrary, while more complex and scholastically sophisticated, was somewhat less robust. Unlike Bellarmine, he chose not to contrast supernature with nature, but to try to operate within the orbit of the argument from natural law which his conciliarist opponent had pursued. He did so by insisting that 'the nature of government' had to be considered at a level deeper than the one to which Almain had penetrated. Government, he said, 'takes different forms according to the *source* of its nature' (italics mine). It being (as is the case with other things) 'the natural propagation of a government' that reveals 'the nature of the thing produced', it should be recognized that 'the Church derives the first principle of [its] origin, perfection and power, not from individuals or the community but from the head who shares its nature, Jesus Christ'. 'So far', then, 'as the right of ruling' is concerned, the Church is not 'a free community' like more ordinary political communities. Hence, and 'as a consequence of natural law', it is for Christ, the natural head and 'prince' of the ecclesiastical community, and not for the community itself 'to provide for a vicar'. So that that vicar, who is none other than the pope, draws his authority *naturally* 'not

---

[66] As Katherine Elliot van Liere has suggested in her stimulating analysis, 'Vitoria, Cajetan, and the Conciliarists', *Journal of the History of Ideas*, LVIII (1997), pp. 597–616 (at p. 605): 'Jacques Almain's reply to Cajetan', she says, forced the latter 'to confront the paradox that his own arguments shared some fundamental presuppositions with the radical conciliarists. Cajetan had unwittingly played into the conciliarist's hands by using language that was comprehensible only if one imagined the Church as being in some sense analogous to a secular monarchy.'

[67] Bellarmine, *Risposta de Card. Bellarmino ad un libretto . . . di Gio. Gersone*, p. 76.

from that community but from Jesus Christ', and 'the [alleged] foundation from natural law for the Church's power over the pope' is altogether 'rooted up'.[68]

To this rather indirect line of argument, Richer's response, in turn, is nothing if not blunt in its confident reaffirmation of the direct pertinence to ecclesiological discourse of secular political analogies. Cajetan, he concedes, was correct in his insistence on the importance of focusing on the very nature of any governmental regime and, accordingly, 'on the essential causes of its institution'. But 'with respect both to its nature and its exercise', the papal primacy 'is clearly a moral and political entity, not something metaphysical'. Disputation concerning its institution, then, should be pursued in moral and political terms not in terms of scholastic metaphysics, and certainly not in terms of the vain cavillings and sophistic subtleties favoured by Cajetan.[69] That said, it is easy enough to recognize that the papal primacy is something altogether different from any absolute monarchy. If it is, indeed, of divine institution, so too is the Church's aristocratic form of government. Neither can be abrogated by the other, but it has to be recognized that the aristocratic government of the Church can in practice *limit* the exercise and execution of the primacy. For just as the kingdom of Poland confers authority on someone by electing him as King, so too does the Church when it chooses someone as pope, for it is the Church as a totality which possesses ecclesiastical authority architectonically and, as it were, by proprietary right. Far from being irrelevant to ecclesiological discourse, then, such arguments drawn from the analogy of political bodies are to be regarded as entirely apposite to the matter at hand.[70]

IV

In the clarity of his affirmation that the Church was, indeed, to be understood very much 'as one of a class, political societies', Richer remained faithful to the guiding intuition of his Parisian predecessors all the way back to the fourteenth century. That fact is not to be taken for granted. It is easy enough to recognize that Richer's understanding of the ecclesiastical polity is diametrically opposed to that of Cajetan and Bellarmine. But it is almost as easy to miss the fact, references to the elective kingship of Poland notwithstanding, that his view of the secular polity is equally at odds with their view — always assuming, that is, that the secular polity one has in mind is the Kingdom of France itself. If that is indeed the case, then his position overall is almost the mirror image of Cajetan's. For the latter, the Church, in which the supreme power of the papal monarch is conferred upon him directly by Christ, was to be contrasted with

---

[68] Cajetan, *Apologia de comparata auctoritate papae et concilii*, cap. 1, ed. Pollet, pp. 204–7. My quotations in most cases follow the English translation of the work in *Conciliarism and Papalism*, ed. Burns and Izbicki, pp. 201–84 (at pp. 202–5).

[69] Richer, *Defensio*, Lib. III, qu. 1, p. 312.

[70] *Ibid.*, pp. 313–14.

the secular polity in which (as he was perfectly willing to concede) the governmental power 'is devolved to one or more by the [whole] community'.[71] For Richer, on the other hand, the reverse is true. For him it is rather the ecclesiastical power which resides in the community. The King of France, on the other hand, he portrays as no merely ministerial figure but as a sacral monarch, the representative of God to his people, by virtue of his legitimating inheritance divinely endowed with special graces.[72] Unlike some of the conciliarists of the Basel era, and his own intense royalism notwithstanding, he made no effort to frame his conciliarist commitments in such a way as to render them *less* relevant or even *irrelevant* to matters political.[73] Quite the contrary, indeed, and we should recognize that a considerable historical significance attaches to that fact. It meant, in effect, that Richer did nothing to conceal, blunt or deflect the obviously constitutionalist implications for secular political life of the conciliarist teachings handed down by d'Ailly, Gerson, Almain and Mair. He himself had done more than anyone else to make the writings of those great Parisian predecessors readily available to his contemporaries, thereby projecting their teaching forward into the great ideological conflicts of seventeenth- and eighteenth-century France. His name, certainly, came to be closely associated with theirs, and for many his polemical writings served as the central conduit through which the old Parisian conciliarist teachings came to be known.

Unfair, then, to the precise lineaments of Richer's own thinking though he may have been, it is not altogether surprising that, when defending the royalist

[71] Cajetan, *Apologia*, cap. 1, ed. Pollet, p. 205; *Conciliarism and Papalism*, ed. Burns and Izbicki, p. 203.

[72] For Richer's vision of the French kingship, see Cottret, 'Edmond Richer (1539–1631): Le Politique et le sacré', pp. 161–77, where she portrays him as 'défenseur de la monarchie absolue et gallicane' (p. 170) and as being, in his political thinking, in direct contradiction with the views of the eighteenth-century *richéristes* who, 'sur le plan politique . . . bâtiront un système fondé sur la democratie à l'image du gouvernement de l'Église primitive' (p. 167).

[73] I have in mind the efforts of such thinkers as Panormitanus, Andrew of Escobar, Thomas Strempinski and, above all, John of Segovia to cope with the vigorous ideological and diplomatic counter-offensive which the supporters of Eugenius IV launched in the 1430s and 1440s. That counter-offensive involved the damaging portrayal of the Baselian conciliarist ecclesiology as 'constituting a subversive, even revolutionary challenge to the very principle of monarchical authority . . . in the temporal as well as the spiritual realm' — thus Burns, *Lordship, Kingship and Empire*, p. 9; cf. A.J. Black, *Monarchy and Community: Political Ideas in the Later Conciliar Controversy, 1430–1450* (Cambridge, 1970), esp. pp. 85–129; and A.J. Black, *Council and Commune: The Conciliar Movement and Fifteenth-Century Heritage* (London, 1979). For the attempt of these Baselian conciliarists to *de-politicize* conciliar theory and the degree to which this distinguishes their posture from that of Richer's Parisian predecessors, see the line of argument developed in Oakley, 'Natural Law, the *Corpus Mysticum*, and Consent', to which reference may be made for the pertinent printed texts and for some extracts from the unprinted manuscripts.

cause in 1754, Abbé Bertrand Capmartin de Chaupy should try to finger Richer as the villain originally responsible for introducing into France the deplorable and alien notion that whatever 'power governed Society belonged to that society which retained its property while relinquishing only the exercise'.[74] The historical inaccuracy of that accusation notwithstanding, it was by no means without precedent. It reflected much the same fearful apprehension of the broader constitutionalist implications of the conciliarist position as that which the papal propagandists of the 1430s and 1440s had tried to exploit in order to frighten the monarchs of Europe into aligning themselves with the cause of Eugenius IV.[75] Or again, as Pope Innocent XI himself tried to exploit during his great dispute with Louis XIV in the 1680s, when he needled the French ambassador by pointing out to him that 'if councils were superior to the pope whose power comes from God, then the Estates General would have leave to press the same claim against Kings'.[76]

It was not only the opponents of the conciliarist ecclesiology who came to be aware of such constitutionalist implications for the world of secular politics. Figgis and others have long since made the case for the significance of the role conciliarist ideas came to play in the constitutionalist resistance theories alike of sixteenth-century Protestant monarchomachs and of seventeeth-century parliamentarian opponents in England and Scotland of Stuart absolutist pretensions.[77] More recently, Dale Van Kley has likewise drawn attention to the persistent proclivity of eighteenth-century French critics of monarchical policy to invoke the conciliarist constitutionalism of Richer, Gerson and the other 'old theologians of Paris' and to exploit its implications no less for the governance of the kingdom than for that of the universal Church. Thus Vivien de la Borde and Nicolas Le Gros writing (1714–16) in the context of the great pamphlet war occasioned by the sweeping condemnations of 'Jansenist' beliefs and practices contained in the papal constitution *Unigenitus*. Thus Claude May and Gabriel-Nicolas Maultrot writing in the 1750s and again in the 1770s. Thus Emmanuel d'Antraigue and other pamphleteers writing in the late 1780s.[78]

---

[74] Abbé Bertrand Capmartin de Chaupy, *Observations sur le refus que fait le Châtelet de reconnaître la Chambre royale* (France, 1754), pp. 196–8; cited from Van Kley, *The Religious Origins of the French Revolution*, pp. 226–7.

[75] See note 73, above.

[76] See Van Kley, *The Religious Origins of the French Revolution*, p. 37. Cf. Martimort, *Le Gallicanisme de Bossuet*, p. 544.

[77] The pertinent literature is surveyed in Oakley, ' "Anxieties of Influence": Skinner, Figgis, Conciliarism and Early Modern Constitutionalism', pp. 69–94.

[78] Van Kley, *The Religious Origins of the French Revolution*, esp. pp. 37–8, 77–81, 91, 151, 192–9, 214–18, 226–8, 257–9, 313–15; Dale K. Van Kley, 'The Estates General as Ecumenical Council: The Constitutionalism of Corporate Consensus and the *Parlement's* Ruling of September 25, 1788', *Journal of Modern History*, LXII (1989), pp. 1–52.

To suggest, of course, that there was anything like a direct route from Constance to 1789 would be an even greater exaggeration than that indulged by H.J. Laski in 1936 when, thinking of the use that English parliamentarians had made of conciliarist ideas in the seventeenth century, he boldly proclaimed that 'the road from Constance to [the Glorious Revolution of] 1688 is a direct one'.[79] Nevertheless, the scholarship of the past half-century has clearly put beyond question the fact that such a path did indeed exist from Constance to at least 1644.[80] If Van Kley is correct, it would also appear that there was something of a parallel track in France, one that wound its tortuous way through the thickets of eighteenth-century Gallican and Jansenist religio-political debate all the way down to the years immediately prior to the Revolution itself. If that is so, Edmond Richer's influential reiteration of the conciliarist position in the early-seventeenth century, and the essentially political way in which he persisted in framing it, undoubtedly constituted an important transit point *en route*.

Francis Oakley   WILLIAMS COLLEGE

---

[79] H.J. Laski, 'Political Theory in the Later Middle Ages', *Cambridge Medieval History* (8 vols., Cambridge, 1911–36), Vol. VIII, p. 638.

[80] For which, see Oakley, 'Figgis, Constance, and the Divines of Paris', and ' "Anxieties of Influence" : Skinner, Figgis, Conciliarism and Early Modern Constitutionalism'.

LIBERTY BY DEGREES: RAYNAL AND DIDEROT ON THE BRITISH CONSTITUTION

*J.H.M. Salmon**

Abstract: Raynal and his collaborator, Diderot, offer views on the history and nature of the British Constitution in various parts of their encyclopedic account of Western expansion, *The History of the Two Indies* (1770, revised versions 1780 and 1784). These opinions are analysed in comparison with the judgments of Montesquieu, Voltaire, Hume, Bolingbroke, De Lolme and others. The evolution of Raynal's ideas on the subject is discussed in the light of his earlier anglophobic *History of the Parliament of England* (1748) and the mutually contrasting French historians he used for that work, the Jesuit Pierre-Joseph d'Orléans and the Huguenot Paul de Rapin-Thoyras. Raynal's conversion to a liberal admiration for British institutions is seen both in the context of the American Revolution and his relationship with Diderot. His insistence on a historical approach clashes with Diderot's more radical and philosophical rhetoric, and the stress between their attitudes becomes apparent in the compromises they attain. Notable among their conclusions are the rejection of English appeals to antiquity, and the fortuitous development of liberty through a series of well defined stages.

In the first half of the eighteenth century French liberal attitudes to the British constitution are best known through key passages in Voltaire's *Philosophical Letters* (1734) and Montesquieu's *Spirit of the Laws* (1748). In his eighth letter ('On the Parliament') Voltaire wrote:

> The English nation is the only one on earth which has succeeded in regulating the power of kings by resisting them, and which, after many endeavours, has finally established that wise government where the prince, all powerful to do good, has his hands tied to do wrong, where the lords have great esteem with neither insolence nor vassals, and where the people share in government without confusion.[1]

Apart from Montesquieu's account of the separation of powers in his chapter 'On the English Constitution',[2] this section contains his celebrated invocation of the Gothic ancestry of the British system: 'If you read Tacitus's admirable work *On the Customs of the Germans*, you will see that it is from them that the

---

* 1853 County Line Rd, Villanova, PA 19085, USA.

[1] Voltaire, *Lettres philosophiques*, ed. Raymond Naves (Paris, 1956), p. 34. Unless otherwise indicated, all translations are by the author.

[2] Montesquieu, *De L'Esprit des lois*, ed. Gonzague Truc (2 vols., Paris, 1945), Vol. 1, pp. 163–74 (l. xi, cap. vi).

English have drawn the idea of their political government. This fine system was discovered in the woods.'[3] A few pages later Montesquieu was more explicit:

> The German nations who conquered the Roman Empire, were, as one knows, very free . . . When they were in Germany the whole nation could assemble. When they were dispersed in conquest, they could no longer do so. Since the nation had to deliberate upon its affairs, as it had done before the conquest, it did so by representatives. This is the origin of the Gothic government among us. At first it was a mixture of aristocracy and monarchy, but it had the inconvenience that the common people were slaves. It was a good government, with the capacity to become better. It became customary to grant letters of enfranchisement; and soon the civil liberty of the people, the prerogatives of nobility and clergy, and the power of kings found themselves in such acccord that I do not believe there has been on earth so well tempered a government as that to be found in each part of Europe in the time it existed. It is admirable that the corruption of the government of a conquering people should have formed the best kind of government that men can possibly imagine.[4]

Montesquieu's conservative Gothicism had little appeal to the next generation of *philosophes*, and an increasingly absolutist Voltaire modified his adulation of English mixed parliamentary government to adopt more ambiguous attitudes on the British system. New viewpoints on Britain are exemplified in the writings of Guillaume-Thomas Raynal and his principal collaborator, Denis Diderot.

The abbé Raynal is remembered for his weighty account of the discovery and colonization of the New World, the expansion of Western influence in Asia, and the effects of colonial trade and conquest upon the material and moral economies of the nations of Europe. The multiple editions of his *Philosophical and Political History of the Settlements and Commerce of the Europeans in the Two Indies* made him in his time as well known a figure as Montesquieu, Voltaire or Rousseau.[5] In 1765, when the free-thinking abbé conceived his

---

[3] *Ibid.*, p. 174

[4] *Ibid.*, pp. 175–6 (l. xi, cap. viii).

[5] The edition used here is *Histoire philosophique et politique des établissemens et du commerce des Européens dans les Deux Indes* (10 vols., Geneva, 1781) (hereafter *HDI*). A critical bibliographical study of the French versions of all Raynal's works is by Anatole Feugère, *Bibliographie critique de l'abbé Raynal* (Angoulême, 1922). Feugère also published a two-part study of sources and plagiarisms in *The Two Indies*, and the role of Raynal's collaborators in that work: A. Feugère, 'Raynal, Diderot et quelques autres historiens des "Deux Indes" ', *Revue d'histoire littéraire de la France* (hereafter *RHLF*), 20 and 22 (1913 and 1915), pp. 343–78 and pp. 408–52. On this aspect see also Herbert Dieckmann, *Inventaire du Fonds Vandeul et inédits de Diderot* (Geneva, 1951), and 'Les contributions de Diderot à la "Correspondance littéraire" et à "l'Histoire des Deux Indes" ', *RHLF*, 51 (1951), pp. 417–40. More detailed analyses of Diderot's contributions are by Michèle Duchet: 'Diderot collaborateur de Raynal: à propos des "Fragments imprimés" du Fonds Vandeul', *RHLF*, 60 (1960), pp. 531–56, and *Diderot*

encyclopedic work and asked Diderot and others to collaborate, his central theme was the way in which commerce had been the primary agent of progress from barbarism to civilization. This, it may be noted, had been suggested by Montesquieu in the twentieth book of *The Spirit of the Laws*.[6] As *The Two Indies* chronicled the savagery and rapine of the colonizing powers, and as its scope expanded through the three principal editions of 1770, 1774 and 1780 to include comment on the American Revolution, the influence of Diderot radicalized the work until it became an outspoken assault on despotism, imperialism, slavery and superstition. This, in turn, affected the views expressed in it on the British constitution and its history. The prudent and statistically-minded Raynal accepted this metamorphosis, and insisted upon his authorial responsibility. Abandoning the ties with French governmental circles that had facilitated his earlier works, the abbé suffered censorship and exile, before returning to France and adopting a more conservative stance against the excesses of the French Revolution.

Raynal's first foray into British politics and history had been his *History of the Parliament of England*,[7] published in the same year as *The Spirit of the Laws*, at a time when the abbé was beginning to secure government patronage and make his name known in the salons of Paris. In contrast to the praise of English institutions offered by Voltaire and Montesquieu, it scorned claims for the antiquity of parliament, and treated that institution as the source of instability, civil war and regicide. Raynal did mention Anglo-Saxon assemblies as importations from Germany, but insisted that the *witena gemot* was composed entirely of nobles and existed only in the petty states of the Heptarchy, not in the later unified kingdom. Claims that the modern parliament had originated in remote ages were dismissed as 'frivolous conjectures', designed by modern writers unwilling to admit that later forms of parliament were created by kings who could abolish them at will. In contrast with 'pure monarchy', the idea of mixed government was 'bizarre' and inherently unstable. Had the Anglo-Saxon chiefs been more enlightened, Raynal wrote, they would have seen that someone must command, and other institutions should temper, not share, royal authority.[8] The idea of monarchy tempered by intermediary bodies sounds a little like Montesquieu, but there was no mention of the separation of powers,

---

et l'Histoire des Deux Indes, ou l'écriture fragmentaire (Paris, 1978). See also Hans Wolpe, *Raynal et sa machine de guerre: l'Histoire des Deux Indes et ses perfectionnements* (Stanford, 1957). The proceedings of two recent conferences on *The Two Indies* have been published: *Lectures de Raynal: l'Histoire des Deux Indes en Europe et en Amérique au XVIIIe siècle*, ed. Hans-Jürgen Lüsebrink and Manfred Tietz (Oxford, 1991), and *L'Histoire des Deux Indes: réécriture et polygraphie*, ed. Hans-Jürgen Lüsebrink and Anthony Strugnell (Oxford, 1995).

[6] Montesquieu, *De l'Esprit des lois*, Vol. 2, p. 8.

[7] Raynal, *Histoire du parlement d'Angleterre* (2 vols., London, 1748).

[8] *Ibid.*, Vol. 1, pp. 23–6.

and the abbé's more absolutist stance was apparent in his account of the Norman conquest.

Raynal noted that a common interpretation of the conquest credited William's sincerity when, after his victory, he accepted the offer of the crown from the lords and bishops and 'took an oath to bear the sceptre under the same conditions as the Saxon kings and to maintain the established laws.' The abbé saw this merely as play-acting by the conqueror, who was 'too clever to let his new subjects understand that he intended to establish a despotic government'.[9] William allayed Saxon fears by making laws that seemed to create 'the solid and legitimate bases of a perfect and equitable form of government', but before long he ceased to respect them, and ruled in an imperious fashion.[10] Among his successors the tyrant King John provoked the barons to usurp authority and demand a return to Anglo-Saxon practices. The result was Magna Carta, a document that proved to be 'the pretext for all the civil wars that subsequently tore England'.[11] Raynal then provided a French text of the charter, 'as it is found in the most authoritative historian of England'.[12]

When Raynal faced the appearance of the Commons in the second half of the thirteenth century, he dealt summarily with the myth of an immemorial parliament. It was a matter of semantics:

> If by parliament is meant the right usurped by the barons to grant the king extraordinary taxes, it goes back to the immediate successors of William the Conqueror; if the first use of the word parliament is intended, then it began at Oxford in 1258; but if an assembly composed of the three bodies of the kingdom is understood, the origin must be fixed in 1264, the first time that the Commons are mentioned in the archives of the nation.[13]

Raynal's contempt for the parliaments associated with the rebellion of Simon de Montfort against Henry III was evident in his description of Montfort as 'the English Catiline', and 'the usurper of royal authority'. He criticized such parliaments as 'convoked solely to degrade the throne and justify that rebellion'.[14]

In the following reign Edward I, to whom Raynal accorded the customary appellation of 'the English Justinian', had established the system whereby the deputies of the Commons were elected. Here the abbé added an unexpectedly liberal passage in contradiction to his theme: 'This period, I believe, should be regarded as very important in this history. The nation has since been free, and only because it has maintained the right to choose freely the members of

[9] *Ibid.*, pp. 41–2.

[10] *Ibid.*, p. 43.

[11] *Ibid.*, p. 90.

[12] *Ibid.*, p. 91. This was Paul de Rapin-Thoyras's *History of England* (1726). See note 27, below.

[13] Raynal, *Histoire du parlement d'Angleterre*, Vol. 1, p. 186.

[14] *Ibid.*, pp. 188–9.

parliament who represent it.'[15] Even so, parliament could be undermined by the influence of the crown or the resentment of the common people against the servitude to which 'feeble or self-interested deputies reduced them'.[16] Sovereignty, defined by the power to legislate, remained in the king, even if he chose to make it appear that parliament shared in the process. The crown also retained sole control of the executive, which Raynal called 'an inseparable prerogative of royalty'.[17] Whatever the apparent merits of the English constitution, the weakness of particular kings in the fourteenth and fifteenth centuries allowed baronial factions to rebel and use parliament as the instrument for deposing their ruler. All this changed with the advent of the Tudors.

After the battle of Bosworth the defector, Sir William Stanley, according to Raynal, offered advice to Henry VII as to the grounds on which he should claim the throne:

> England, once the most monarchical state in Europe, has degenerated into a republic through the audacity of an assembly. The people have taken advantage of circumstances to ruin the sovereign authority. Why, then, should sovereigns not have the right to put them in their place and reimpose it?[18]

This invented speech in fact summarized the author's central argument. The first Tudor king managed to represent his claim so ambiguously that parliamentary endorsement could not be construed as a precedent. With craft and prudence he controlled the assemblies he convoked, and used parliament to enfeeble the nobility with a statute that allowed them to sell their lands to men of lesser rank. In consequence the Commons gradually acquired greater status, and eventually 'ruined both royal and aristocratic power'.[19]

Henry VIII, less talented but more vicious than his father, acquired near absolute authority by using parliament to break with Rome. Under Edward VI the two Protectors controlled the assembly to such a degree that it completed the drift to Protestantism against the will and sentiments of the people. In due course Elizabeth avoided the reefs of internal disharmony and foreign threats by judicious use of her authority. 'History', wrote Raynal, 'should take good note of the sublime principles of so perfect a government.'[20] Unscrupulous in the pursuit of her policy to advance the welfare of her people, 'she united the little vanities of a woman with the great sentiments of heroes'.[21] James I, on the other hand, was depicted as an irresolute pedant who, depite his monologues to the contrary, allowed parliament to control the state. Under the influence of his favourites Charles I tried to put into practice his father's view that parliamentary privileges existed only through royal concession, and could be withdrawn. The Lords were corrupted and the Commons fanatically Puritan.

---

[15] *Ibid.*, p. 200.
[16] *Ibid.*, p. 201.
[17] *Ibid.*, pp. 302–3.
[18] *Ibid.*, Vol. 2, p. 15.

[19] *Ibid.*, p. 23.
[20] *Ibid.*, p. 51.
[21] *Ibid.*, p. 53.

Anglican clergy could preach divine right and passive obedience, but the dominant faction in parliament espoused doctrines of lawful resistance, and the royal martyr lost his throne and his head.

For Raynal the outcome of the revolution was the sovereignty of the House of Commons, a result forecast by Henry VII's promotion of the second chamber to counteract the nobility. The Commons were in turn replaced by Oliver Cromwell, the hypocrite usurper, who instituted a new tyranny. At the restoration Charles II had the opportunity to reinstate pure monarchy, but he preferred his personal comforts to the fame he might have achieved. His nemesis was the first Earl of Shaftesbury, 'a new but less crafty Cromwell',[22] whose design it was to destroy the monarchy. Shaftesbury died in exile, but his party survived to depose James II, whom Raynal praised for his policy of religious toleration but blamed for being too proud to disguise his intentions and to seek compromise. The republican element in the Convention Parliament introduced 'the odious and dangerous question as to whether there was an original contract between king and people, and whether James had broken it by his despotic administration, and if so whether his subjects were released from their oath of allegiance'. The upper chamber eventually agreed. 'The more one thinks about it', wrote Raynal, 'the less one can find any reason or equity in so violent a resolution.'[23] In his concluding pages the abbé reviewed the constitutional settlement under William and Mary, and the subsequent corruption of parliament by Walpole's administration under the Hanoverians. All these developments were the necessary outcome of trying to share power between king, Lords and Commons, each of whom had interests contrary to the others.

As can be imagined, *The History of the Parliament of England* was likely to offend Englishmen of every political persuasion. It played to current French anglophobia at the end of the War of the Austrian Succession. Its heroes were rulers whose ruthlessness was matched by their Machiavellian qualities, such as William I, Edward I, Henry VII and Elizabeth; most of the other kings combined ineptitude and tyranny; and the parliament was the leitmotiv of rebellion and instability. There were, however, some liberal bench marks in Raynal's general adherence to absolutist principles. He wrote approvingly of tempered government, and used the word 'despot' pejoratively. He spoke of liberty as maintained by the free election of the House of Commons from the time of Edward I. He praised Elizabeth for thinking first of the welfare of her people, and he condemned religious intolerance. These paradoxes arose from the contrasting ideological alignment of the two French sources from which Raynal derived most of his information: *The History of the Revolutions of England* by the Jesuit father, Pierre-Joseph d'Orléans, and *The History of England* by the Huguenot exile, Paul de Rapin-Thoyras.

[22] *Ibid.*, p. 168.
[23] *Ibid.*, pp. 195–6.

D'Orléans was an unequivocal apologist for the principles underlying the regime of Louis XIV. His *History of the Revolutions*, first published in 1689 and reprinted many times in the eighteenth century, contained two dedications to the Sun King. For D'Orléans the English monarchy was an object lesson in the way institutional flaws and the arbitrary abuse of power resulted in continued political upheavals. William the Conqueror abolished all Anglo-Saxon laws, but his successors restored some of them. King John was compared with the tyrant Tiberius, and Magna Carta depicted as 'a celebrated reef for royal authority, and the source of all the popular movements that so often convulsed England'.[24] That the rebel Simon de Montfort could be seen by the English as a martyr to parliamentary liberty merely confirmed for D'Orléans their penchant for anarchy, and the idea that parliament should moderate the authority of the crown was ' a truly pernicious thing and a continual source of wars'.[25] Parliament was used to depose Edward II, Richard II, Henry VI, Richard III, Charles I and James II. The craft with which Henry VII controlled parliament without diminishing royal dignity, and the ability of Elizabeth to exercise an almost unrestrained authority, received fulsome praise, whereas the intemperance of Henry VIII and the complacence towards parliament displayed by James I were criticized. D'Orléans held the religious changes introduced by the Tudors to be in large part responsible for the political convulsions of the seventeenth century. He treated the later Stuarts with particular reverence, and called the reasons given for the deposition of James II 'odious questions'.[26] Raynal's *Parliament* followed D'Orléans closely on these issues, and at times used similar language.

Unlike D'Orléans' *Revolutions*, *The History of England* by Rapin-Thoyras was much respected in England, where it was known in the English translation of Nicholas Tindal, the vicar of Great Waltham in Essex.[27] Rapin professed an early fascination with the origins of the English constitution in Anglo-Saxon times, and he read and cited the works of English antiquaries in the late seventeenth century, when scholarship, rather than political expediency, began to dominate research on the evolution of parliament. Among the documents Rapin reproduced in his text was the French version of Magna Carta replicated by Raynal. Rapin's background placed him in the opposite camp to that of D'Orléans. He fled to England at the time of the revocation of the Edict of Nantes, and then to Holland, whence he returned in the army of William III, and subsequently fought at the battle of the Boyne. Although David Hume used

[24] Pierre-Joseph d'Orléans, *Histoire des révolutions d'Angleterre depuis le commencement de la monarchie* (4 vols., Amsterdam, 1772), Vol. 1, p. 321.

[25] *Ibid.*, p. 130.

[26] *Ibid.*, Vol. 4, p. 309.

[27] *The History of England, written in French by Mr. Rapin de Thoyras, translated into English with additional notes by N. Tindal* (2 vols., London, 1732–3). The first French version was published in 1726.

Rapin in his own *History of England*, the latter acquired the reputation of being a Whig historian. This was true enough of Rapin's first published work, *A Dissertation on the Whigs and the Tories* (1717), which began:

> The government of England is of a particular kind, of which there is not the like at present in all the world. It is, however, the same which was formerly established in all the kingdoms of Europe, formed out of the ruins of the Roman Empire. The present difference between England and other states in this respect is owing to this, that the English have preserved their form of government since their settling in Great Britain, whereas in other nations it has been lost by degrees, or extremely altered.[28]

However, Rapin was much more objective in his *History*, and appreciated how the past was distorted when it was bent to serve the political needs of the present. 'For my part', he wrote when discussing royal succession in pre-conquest England, 'I can hardly be persuaded there is any occasion to recur to the customs of the Anglo-Saxons to establish those that are to be followed at this day.'[29] He did not pretend that the Conqueror preserved any Anglo-Saxon institutions, but stressed the importance of Magna Carta as a return to earlier forms. He was sceptical of the authority of the Commons in Simon de Montfort's time, and argued that they were formally instituted at about the time that, according to Etienne Pasquier, the third estate joined the clergy and nobility in the French estates general (that is, under Edward I in England).[30] Rapin was no admirer of Henry VII, and credited the first Tudor with complete control of parliament. Referring to the imposition of Henry's hated minister upon the Commons, he wrote: 'Nothing shows more the most absolute power of the king than the choice of Dudley for speaker of the House of Commons.'[31] Here Rapin was echoing Francis Bacon's biography of Henry VII. He used Bacon again when describing the king's policy towards the aristocracy: 'Instead of increasing the credit of the nobility, he took all care to lessen it. His council was almost wholly composed of churchmen and lawyers, who, being devoted to him and aiming only to please him, never opposed his will.'[32] Rapin followed Bacon, and Raynal expanded the point in both *The Parliament* and *The Two Indies*.

Raynal preferred D'Orléans' account of the conflicts between James I and his parliaments to Rapin's, for the Huguenot was far more critical of the king than was the Jesuit. Similarly, he accepted D'Orléans' denunciation of Crom-

---

[28] Rapin, *A Dissertation on the Rise, Progress, Views, Strength, Interests and Characters of the Two Parties of the Whigs and the Tories* (1717), reproduced in *The History of England*, trans. Tindal, Vol. 2, p. 796.

[29] Rapin, *The History of England*, trans. Tindal, Vol. 1, p. 159.

[30] *Ibid.*, p. 333.

[31] *Ibid.*, p. 687.

[32] Francis Bacon, *The History of the Reign of King Henry VII*, ed. F.J. Levy (New York, 1972), p. 226.

well rather than Rapin's more positive portrait. Again, he chose the Jesuit's view of the Restoration, and ignored Rapin's criticism of D'Orléans for failing to substantiate his charges against Shaftesbury. Of course, Raynal's interpretation of the Glorious Revolution had little in common with Rapin's sympathetic treatment. Nevertheless, something of Rapin's fair-minded discussion of English constitutional conflicts left its mark on the abbé. His criticism of eighteenth-century parliamentary placemen and of the inequities of borough representation in the Commons came directly from Rapin.[33]

In the years between Raynal's *History of the Parliament* and his *Two Indies* Voltaire and Hume offered further insights on the development of the British constitution, some of them based upon Rapin-Thoyras. In his *Essay on Customs* Voltaire endorsed the view that Edward I had originated the modern form of parliament by building up the Commons to balance the power of the Lords. He was not, however, as confident about the perfection of English government as he had been in his *Philosophical Letters*:

> This prince, who was firm and clever enough to handle the barons and to have no fear of them, formed the kind of government which collects together all the advantages of monarchy, aristocracy and democracy but has also the disadvantages of all three, and which can survive only under a wise king. His son was not wise, and England was torn apart.[34]

Raynal, it will be recalled, had uncharacteristically used the elevation of the Commons by Edward I to praise liberty as preserved by freedom of election. On the other hand, Voltaire offered comments on the foolishness of James I in boasting about his prerogative, and thereby provoking the Commons to define limits to royal authority, that were similar to Raynal's and, in turn, to those of Rapin-Thoyras.[35]

Hume published the medieval volume of his *History of England* in 1761, and it, like the earlier volumes on the Tudors and the Stuarts, was soon translated into French. Raynal read and, indeed, plagiarized the work in *The Two Indies*, but the section that he reproduced was an attack upon superstition as revealed in the customs of the ancient Britons, not on the English constitution.[36] While Hume repeated the standard theme of the aristocratic freedom of Anglo-Saxon government, he held knowledge of Saxon forms to be inexact, and he denounced

---

[33] Rapin, *The History of England*, trans. Tindal, Vol. 2, p. 806. This passage is actually from Rapin's *Dissertation*.

[34] Voltaire, *Essai sur les mœurs*, ed. R. Pomeau (2 vols., Paris, 1963 [1756]), Vol. 1, p. 710.

[35] *Ibid.*, Vol. 2, p. 612.

[36] C.P. Courtney, 'David Hume et l'abbé Raynal, une source de *L'Histoire philosophique des Deux Indes'*, *Revue de littérature comparée*, 36 (1962), pp. 565–71.

those who, from a pretended respect for antiquity, appeal at every turn to an original plan of the constitution, only cover their turbulent spirit and their private ambition under the appearance of venerable forms . . . A civilised nation like the English, who have happily established the most perfect and most accurate system of liberty that was ever found compatible with government, ought to be cautious in appealing to the practice of their ancestors, or regarding the maxims of uncultivated ages as certain rules for their present conduct.[37]

Hume was responding to writers such as Algernon Sidney and his disciple, Robert Molesworth, whose *Principles of a Real Whig* stated:

My notion of a Whig, I mean of a real Whig (for the nominal are worse than any sort of man) is that he is one who is exactly for keeping up to the strictness of the true old Gothick constitution, under the three estates of king (or queen), Lords and Commons: the legislature being seated in all three together, the executive entrusted with the first, but accountable to the whole body of the people in case of maladministration.[38]

Hume went much further than Rapin's *History* in doubting the relevance of Gothicism and, while he idealized the liberty achieved in the English constitution, he may also have been correcting Montesquieu. His was a doctrine of liberty not derived from adherence to past forms but acquired by degrees. This attitude was to be adopted in Raynal's *Two Indies* in a far more positive fashion than it had been in his *Parliament.*

Chains of influence in the history of ideas are not always easy to establish, especially when a particular judgment becomes the basis of a wider generalization. As noted earlier, Raynal in his *Parliament* had given weight to the weakening of the nobility by Henry VII. He seems to have taken this from Rapin, who had developed it from a passage in Bacon's biography. Hume regarded the undermining of the aristocracy by the first Tudor as a veritable turning point:

But the most important law in its consequences, which was enacted during the reign of Henry, was that by which the nobility and gentry acquired a power of breaking the ancient entails, and of alienating their estates. By means of this law, joined to the beginning luxury and refinements of the age, the great fortunes of the barons were gradually dissipated, and the property of the commons increased in England. It is probable that Henry foresaw and intended this consequence, because the constant scheme of his policy consisted

---

[37] Hume, *The History of England* (3 vols., London, 1894), Vol. 1, p. 704.
[38] *Francogallia by François Hotman,* ed. Ralph E. Giesey and J.H.M. Salmon (Cambridge, 1972), p. 125 (spelling and punctuation modernized). Molesworth's *Principles* was originally the preface to his translation of Hotman's attempt to present the ancient constitution of the Franks as a guide to sixteenth-century French government. *The Principles* was published separately in 1721 and in subsequent editions.

in depressing the great, and exalting churchmen, lawyers, and men of new families, who were more dependent on him.[39]

Hume was extrapolating directly from Bacon. Whether or not Raynal had taken note of Hume's elaboration, he gave the point even more prominence in *The Two Indies* than it had possessed in *The Parliament*.

Other writers on the British constitution and its history may serve as counterpoint to Raynal's views, and in some instances may have influenced him. One such was Lord Bolingbroke, whose *Remarks on the History of England* and *Letters on the Study and Use of History*, although written in the 1730s, appeared in collected form in French and English in 1752. As if to exemplify his view that the only useful history was modern history, Bolingbroke insisted that to understand the present constitution one need only go back to Henry VII. He, too, emphasized the importance of Henry's diminution of aristocratic power and the consequent rise of the Commons, but, unlike Hume, he doubted whether the king foresaw the consequences of his actions.[40] It was purely by chance, Bolingbroke argued, 'that we were brought back, in times very different and in circumstances very different, to the principles of government which had prevailed amongst our Saxon ancestors, before they left Germany'.[41]

Nor is there any clear evidence to show that Raynal read Jean-Louis de Lolme's *Constitution of England*, which was published at the same time as the first edition of *The Two Indies*. De Lolme has generally been mentioned as a disciple of Montesquieu,[42] and it is true that he followed *The Spirit of the Laws* in terms of the English system as being a mixed form of government with checks and balances. But, contrary to received opinion, De Lolme said little about the separation of powers, and a great deal about the historical vicissitudes of the constitution. Quoting Sir William Temple's *Introduction to English History* (1695), De Lolme characterized knowledge of Anglo-Saxon forms as

> so many antique, broken or defaced pictures, which may still represent something of the customs and fashions of those ages, though little of the true lines, proportions or resemblances . . . It is at the era of the conquest that we are to look for the real foundation of the English constitution.[43]

A note added to De Lolme's text suggested that those who held that William had continued Saxon practices, and had acceded to, rather than conquered, the kingdom, were writing in times of opposition.

> Indeed, there was a far greater probability of success in raising among the people the notions familiar to them of legal claims and long established

[39] Hume, *History of England*, Vol. 2, p. 54.
[40] Bolingbroke, *Historical Writings*, ed. Isaac Kramnick (Chicago. 1972), pp. 89, 90, 211–13.
[41] *Ibid.*, p. 233.
[42] C.P. Courtney, *Montesquieu and Burke* (Oxford, 1963), p. 21.
[43] J.L. de Lolme, *The Constitution of England* (London, 1784 [1771]), p. 7.

customs than in arguing with them from the no less rational, but less deter-
minate and somewhat dangerous doctrines concerning the original rights of
mankind, and the lawfulness of at all times opposing force to an oppressive
government.[44]

This sounds rather like Hume's denunciation of 'the turbulent spirits' who
used the idea of an immemorial constitution to foment disorder. De Lolme went
on to describe William as 'an absolute monarch . . . (who) imposed the yoke of
despotism both on the victors and the vanquished'.[45] In subsequent generations
the tyranny of William's successors united the barons with the people. Magna
Carta, coupled with Edward I's legislation declaring taxation illegal without the
consent of Lords and Commons, was the basis of the constitution.[46] However,
this form of government underwent constant change, especially with the decay
of the nobility and the despotism of the Tudors. James I had imprudently drawn
back the veil that disguised their usurpations, setting in train the later conflicts
of the seventeenth century. With the Glorious Revolution a new constitutional
era began, when 'the true principles of civil society were established'.[47]
Whether or not Raynal drew upon De Lolme for the theme that united resistance
to Norman despotism was the paradoxical source of English liberty and the
driving force of constitutional progress, he introduced it in the opening chapter
of *The Two Indies*, and reiterated it thereafter. However, De Lolme's distrust of
natural rights doctrines was not shared by Diderot, who made them an important
theme in his polemical discourse.

Despite his anglophobic *History of the Parliament of England*. Raynal was
made a member of the Royal Society in 1754, an honour that Diderot refused.
He learnt more about England from personal experience during the early
preparation of *The Two Indies* and period of its revision. Several Englishmen,
including Hume, attended the salons of the *philosophes* after the end of the
Seven Years War, and made his acquaintance. Late in 1773 Raynal's friend, the
abbé Morellet, put him in touch with the liberal circle of Lord Shelburne in
England.[48] Four years later he visited London, where he met Edmund Burke
who had just published his *Letter to the Sheriffs of Bristol*. Burke had stressed
the importance of free expression and the political weight of public opinion,
and this may have inspired a late insertion to this effect in *The Two Indies*.[49] It
is difficult to know how much Raynal benefited from such contacts, for Burke's

---

[44] *Ibid.*, p. 8.

[45] *Ibid.*, p. 14.

[46] *Ibid.*, pp. 21–35.

[47] *Ibid.*, p. 59.

[48] Anthony Strugnell, 'Dialogue et désaccord idéologiques entre Raynal et Diderot:
le cas des Anglais en Inde', in *L'Histoire des Deux Indes*, ed. Lüsebrink and Strugnell,
p. 420.

[49] Edoardo Tortarolo, 'La Révolution américaine dans l'Histoire des Deux Indes', in
L'Histoire des Deux Indes, ed. Lüsebrink and Strugnell, p. 211. *HDI*, Vol. 10, pp. 50–1.

correspondence with a friend he asked to show the abbé round Bristol suggests that his guest's command of English was poor. Raynal stayed with Shelburne in 1777 and again in 1780. There he was probably in contact with the two radical dissenting ministers who formed part of Shelburne's entourage: Joseph Priestley, Shelburne's librarian, whose *Essay on the First Principles of Government* (1768) saw civil liberty as that part of the citizen's life that was free from state interference, and political liberty as the right to take part in government; and Richard Price, whose *Observations on the Nature of Civil Liberty* (1776) supported natural rights and wanted government to serve the will of the people. Price supported the American Revolution, although he hoped that the colonies would, as self-governing entities, form part of a British federation.[50] This was also the position of Raynal and Diderot.

The various editions of *The Two Indies* received mixed reviews in Britain, but radical Whig journals praised it.[51] While in England Raynal arranged for French and English versions of the chapters on North America to be published as *The Revolution of America* (1781). Despite his being a citizen of a country allied with the American rebels, the abbé was generally well received, and his admiration for English institutions increased markedly. His stance in *The History of the Parliamant* was completely revised, and he became a devotee of British constitutional liberty. His new anglophilia, together with his acceptance of ideas of natural right, made it easier for him to accept the radical changes introduced into *The Two Indies* by Diderot.

Diderot's early political attitudes were set out in the article 'Political Authority', published in the *Encyclopedia* in 1751. There he maintained that all legitimate power is held by consent and is necessarily limited both by moral natural law and specific constitutional arrangements.[52] His admiration for Montesquieu declined in later years as he perceived the inherent conservatism of *The Spirit of the Laws*. For Diderot liberty was not simply a matter of doing what the laws permitted but of the right to consent to the laws, or even participate in their making. Some of the articles he commissioned as editor of the *Encyclopedia*, such as 'Political Liberty' by the Chevalier de Jaucourt, endorsed the separation of powers, but Diderot came to believe that in a democracy, which he seemed to consider the best form of government, it was not necessary to separate the executive from the legislative.[53]

---

[50] Richard Price, *Political Writings*, ed. D.O. Thomas (Cambridge, 1991), pp. xvi–xx.

[51] Anthony Strugnell, 'La réception de l'Histoire des Deux Indes en Angleterre au dix-huitième siècle', in *Lectures de Raynal*, ed. Lüsebrink and Tietz, pp. 253–64.

[52] *The Encyclopédie of Diderot and d'Alembert*, ed. John Lough (Cambridge, 1954), pp. 6–15.

[53] Arthur M. Wilson, 'The Development and Scope of Diderot's Political Thought', *Studies in Voltaire and the Eighteenth Century*, 27 (1963), p. 1891.

Although a confidant of Catherine the Great of Russia, Diderot was an opponent of enlightened despotism. Among the memoirs he composed for the Tsarina was one in which he stated that two or three consecutive despots as benevolent as Elizabeth of England would lull the people into forgetfulness of their rights, and reduce them to servitude. Like many of his other occasional pieces, he inserted this in *The Two Indies*.[54] Indeed, he published a number of his additions to Raynal's volumes elsewhere. Others he thought too dangerous to appear in print except under the abbé's name. They were a means of venting his frustrations against the censorship, and it is not surprising that Raynal became a martyr to the cause they represented. Diderot's collaboration obliged him to confront political issues he had not previously resolved, and provided a sometimes revolutionary and democratic edge. At the same time, the pages that Diderot wrote upon Britain had to conform to the historical format preferred by Raynal. Thus, while his rhetoric radicalized *The Two Indies*, his impulse to generalize in terms of moral outrage was tempered by a measure of historical empiricism.

The Two Indies traced the expansion of the colonizing powers separately in each sector of the globe. Since the background to each European nation was provided to introduce the chapter appropriate to its activity in each particular area, remarks on the history of England and its political system are to be found in several places, notably before the chapters on British trade and colonization in Asia (Book III), in the Caribbean (Book XIV), and in North America (Books XVII and XVIII). Relevant passages are also located in other parts of the work, especially in the introductory section on the states of Europe on the eve of the Portuguese and Spanish voyages of discovery, and the concluding volume, which is concerned with the effects of overseas acquisitions upon Europe. This organization provoked contemporary criticism, and there is indeed a certain amount of repetition, at least as far as the segments on Britain are concerned. Both the first and last discussions of British political history stress a particular theme resulting fortuitously in the modern constitution. In the former it is the paradox of William the Conqueror's tyranny setting in train the struggle of the English people for liberty that had finally led them 'to establish the government under which they now have the happiness to live'.[55] In the latter it is the consequences of Tudor despotism in the conflicts of the succeeding century, and the final establishment of a constitution 'which ought to convince all persons of good sense that there has never been so well ordered a system on earth'.[56] The attainment of liberty by degrees had become the central thread in discussion of the British constitution, but this was scarcely consistent with its

[54] Arthur M. Wilson, *Diderot* (New York, 1972), p. 635; Duchet, 'Diderot collaborateur de Raynal', pp. 553–4. See p. 103, below.
[55] *HDI*, Vol. 1, p. 21.
[56] *Ibid.*, Vol. 10, p. 51.

denial to the American colonists. Hence there are passages in the text where praise is qualified by doubt, where the sceptical spirit of the earlier Raynal reappears, and the enthusiasm of his more illustrious collaborator for British institutions is dampened by the perceived reality of British oppression.

In a new piece, composed for the third edition of *The Two Indies* to introduce the section on British establishments in the West Indies, Diderot provided an overview of the development of the constitution:

> In modern history England is the country of extraordinary political phenomena. There liberty has been more violently at grips with despotism than anywhere else, sometimes being trodden under foot, and at other times crushing its opponent. There liberty has ended in triumph, and everything, even religious fanaticism, has concurred to produce this outcome. There one king has been dragged for judgment to the scaffold and another deposed by a decree of the nation with all his line to provide a lesson for the world. There, in the midst of civil convulsions separated by momentary intervals of calm, the most exact and profound sciences have been advanced, and minds accustomed to reasoning and reflecting have been able, before anything else, to devote their attention to government. Finally, it is there that after long and violent crises a constitution has been formed which, though not without some disadvantages, is the happiest possible outcome, given the country's situation.[57]

The vicissitudes to which Diderot alluded were essentially the epochs of Raynal's *History of the Parliament*, although now presented in the context of the struggle between liberty and despotism. First came the tyrannical system set up at the Norman conquest, followed by two centuries of attempts to modify that regime. Then came the achievement of the modern form of parliament under Edward I, succeeded by another two hundred years of strife. In the next phase, although Henry VII set in train the supremacy of the Commons over the Lords, Tudor despotism repressed liberty, even under the cleverly disguised absolutism of Elizabeth. Finally, the foolish posturing of James I launched the conflicts of the seventeenth century, resulting in the triumph of liberty at the Glorious Revolution.

This schema consistently refused to recognize the relevance of six centuries of Anglo-Saxon history. The word 'Gothic' appeared only once in *The Two Indies*, in a passage that seemed to acknowledge the concept of the ancient constitution propounded by early seventeenth-century opponents of the Stuarts. Discussing the ferment of political ideas at that time, it referred to the stirring of 'the monstrous colossus of Gothic government, asleep for centuries in the lethargy of ignorance'.[58] There were brief mentions of Saxon depredations and the anarchy of the petty kingdoms of the Heptarchy, where 'the law of the

---

[57] *Ibid.*, Vol. 7, pp. 211–12.
[58] *Ibid.*, p. 216.

strongest' applied. If there had been a Germanic constitution, it 'degenerated into tyranny and slavery'.[59]

William I established order out of chaos. So harsh was this regime that liberty could have made no progress against his successors had it not been for 'a league in which all citizens, without distinction of nobleman and commoner, inhabitants of both town and coutryside, became united in their resentment and their common interest'.[60] This was also the theme suggested by De Lolme. In Raynal's *History of the Parliament* it had been the barons alone who extracted Magna Carta from King John. *The Two Indies* ascribed it to this 'universal confederation'. The provisions of the charter also took on a more popular tone:

> It abolished the most onerous feudal laws, and assured to vassals vis-à-vis their seigneurs the same rights the seigneurs had vis-à-vis the kings. It placed all persons and property under the protection of juries and judgment by peers. It even helped the serfs by reducing the oppression of servitude.[61]

By virtue of their new status the people profited from the ensuing wars, and secured parliamentary representation, followed by full legislative participation, the right of taxation, and even authority to challenge royal ministers.

These gains were partly lost in the Wars of the Roses, and eclipsed under the Tudors:

> Tyranny made itself felt with so many atrocities that the citizenry of the various orders abandoned all idea of general liberty to concentrate solely on their personal safety. This cruel despotism lasted more than a century. Elizabeth herself, whose administration could in many ways serve as a model, always ruled by entirely arbitrary principles.[62]

This passage from the concluding book of *The Two Indies* far exceeded earlier strictures on Tudor despotism. In contrast, a section in Book III praised Henry VII as 'one of the greatest kings who sat on the throne of England',[63] while another in Book XIV returned to the theme outlined by Rapin and so extravagantly delineated by Hume of the first Tudor's plan to advance the unprivileged at the expense of the nobility:

> For the first time he authorised the nobles to alienate their land. This dangerous favour, combined with the desire for luxury then permeating Europe, produced a great revolution in fortunes. The immense fiefs of the barons were gradually dispersed, and the wealth of the commons increased.[64]

Additional commentaries on the role of Elizabeth also offered slightly differing perspectives, though tending to the same conclusion. In Book III she was seen once again as a benevolent despot, 'absolute and popular, enlightened and obeyed', who inherited contradictions she could not solve but knew how

[59] *Ibid.*, Vol. 2, p. 8, and Vol. 10, p. 42.   [62] *Ibid.*, p. 44.
[60] *Ibid.*, p. 43.   [63] *Ibid.*, Vol. 2, p. 7.
[61] *Ibid.*   [64] *Ibid.*, Vol. 7, p. 214.

to divert. The religious dissent, which had produced civil wars in Europe, was allegedly channelled into an English thirst for trade and seafaring. However, the monopolies she granted excited criticism in the Commons, and the queen made her memorable 'golden speech' in which she confessed to have erred through ignorance of the facts, and professed her loving care for her subjects. The text presented was far from accurate, although it conveyed the sentiment well enough.[65] But the reader was not to be deceived, as the deputies had been, by these fair words. A despot was a despot, and it was at this point that Diderot's words written for Catherine the Great about the fatal effect of a succession of such rulers were inserted. The contradictions inherited by Elizabeth were explained in Book XIV, where liberty was linked to religious innovation and the revival of democratic or republican ideas from classical antiquity. Both trends excited hatred of unlimited authority:

> But the controlling power that Elizabeth assumed and preserved, coupled with forty years of material prosperity, kept this unrest in check or diverted it into enterprises useful to the state.[66]

If Elizabeth had cleverly reduced the heat of English discontents, James I's blunders brought them rapidly to the boil. This interpretation, already outlined in Raynal's *History of the Parliament*, as also by Hume, De Lolme and others, received additional stress in *The Two Indies*:

> James I appeared and recalled to the people the rights they seemed to have forgotten. Less wise than his predecessors, who had been content to enjoy an unlimited power secretly and, so to speak, under a veil of mystery, this prince, who was deceived by the word monarchy and, confirmed in his illusion by his courtiers and clergy, made known his pretensions with a blind and unparalleled simplicity.[67]

The point was reiterated in another passage:

> From his very infancy the monarch had as much distaste for limited authority as the people had horror for despotism and absolute monarchy . . . This theologian-prince, thinking he held all from God and nothing from men, saw in himself alone the spirit of reason, wisdom and good counsel. These false principles, which made government a religious mystery . . . were so strongly rooted in his mind, along with all the other prejudices of a bad education, that it never even occurred to him to support them with any of the human resources of prudence or force.[68]

---

[65] *Ibid.*, Vol. 2, pp. 9–10. Cf. G.R. Elton, *The Tudor Constitution: Documents and Commentary* (Cambridge, 1960), pp. 316–17.

[66] *HDI*, Vol. 7, p. 217.

[67] *Ibid.*, Vol. 10, pp. 44–5.

[68] *Ibid.*, Vol. 7, p. 215 .

Such harsh judgments allowed Raynal and Diderot to set forth the contrary ideas that the king had supposedly provoked:

> The citizens heatedly declaimed against these principles, feeble as they seem as soon as they are discussed, and maintained that the people make up the essence of government, as much, and indeed more, than the monarch. One is the matter, the other the form. The supreme law is the welfare of the people, not of the prince. The king may die, the monarchy may perish, but society continues without monarch or throne. Thus reasoned the English at the dawn of liberty.[69]

From this point Raynal and Diderot did not pursue the political implications of the Civil War, Interregnum and Restoration as Raynal had in his *History of the Parliament*. They went straight to the overthrow of James II and explained its constitutional outcome:

> From a foreign line the opposition chose a prince who at last had to accept that social contract that all hereditary kings pretend not to know. William III received the sceptre under conditions, and contented himself with an authority established on the same basis as the rights of the nation. Since a parliamentary title is the only basis for the crown, these conventions have not been violated.[70]

There followed a summation of the British system of mixed government as a unique model for the world. Here the authors did not hesitate to describe the monarchical element as by nature tyrannical, and the democratic as inherently anarchic and, interestingly enough, characterized the aristocratic part as 'floating between the two and striking the reefs extended by both'. The result was a balance that had acquired stability because it was the fruit of both reason and experience:

> This is the mixed government of the English, containing the advantages of these three powers, which observe, temper, aid and restrain each other, and work for the national good. By their action and reaction, these different constituencies form an equilibrium whence liberty is born.[71]

There was nothing very new or radical about this conclusion. It seems tame and stilted when set beside the analysis of Thomas Paine in his defence of the American Revolution in *Common Sense*. Paine, it may be noted, issued a pamphlet denouncing Raynal after reading that part of *The Two Indies* published separately as *The Revolution of America*. He criticised the abbé for plagiarising his remark about government, in contrast with society, being a necessary evil, corrected his errors on America, and hinted that Raynal was a British sympa-

---

[69] *Ibid.*, p. 217.
[70] *Ibid.*, Vol. 10, p. 45.
[71] *Ibid.*, p. 46.

thizer.[72] Paine saw the king and the Lords as the outdated remnants of tyranny, and the Commons as a republican element whose defence of liberty depended on the virtue of the deputies. 'To say', he wrote, 'that the constitution of England is a union of three powers, reciprocally checking each other, is farcical, either the words have no meaning, or they are flat contradictions.'[73]

The pieces written on the British constitution by Raynal and Diderot in *The Two Indies* comprised, of course, only a small part of a work in which the radical thrust lay elsewhere. Their particular interest lies in their schematic approach to history, which drew upon, and at times subtly differed from, the generalizations of their English contemporaries and their French predecessors. Liberty and despotism represented the two poles, and the advance towards the model constitution they described was measured step by step over the centuries. True, the result at times was not very different from Hume's, and the idea of an equilibrium of checks and balances was quite close to Montesquieu's, shorn of its Gothic roots. Montesquieu himself was mentioned several times in *The Two Indies*, but only to criticize his views on slavery and his misunderstanding of the causes of the decadence of the Roman Empire.[74] Nevertheless, the ideas of tempered monarchy, of intermediary bodies, and of a mixed system of checks and balances expressed in *The Spirit of the Laws* frequently recurred in *The Two Indies*, as they did, for that matter, in other contemporary works on the British constitution. There were, of course, many precedents for the mixed form in English political thought long before Montesquieu. Raynal and Diderot located the mixed form in the legislature, and insisted on the undivided control of the executive by the crown, but they said nothing of an independent judicial power, which for Montesquieu reposed in juries, not in independent judges, and had little role to play in the separation of powers. In this last respect the English common law offered better precedents, but it received no mention in *The Two Indies*. Moreover, Diderot insisted, and Raynal evidently agreed, that the executive was responsible to parliament.

Whatever Thomas Paine might say to the contrary, the final volumes of *The Two Indies* supported the cause of the American colonists. Perhaps it was because they were aware that the principles of constitutional liberty they had praised so much did not seem to apply in the relationship between Britain and the colonies that the authors felt it necessary to offer criticisms in their conclusion. 'Is this government perfect?' they asked. 'No, because there is nothing, and there can be nothing, perfect in this world.' The king was dependent on the will of the people, and had to care for their safety, liberty and happiness, but how could this be if his German ties involved the nation in continental wars?

[72] Feugère, 'Raynal, Diderot et quelques autres historiens' (1915), pp. 416–19.

[73] Thomas Paine, *Common Sense* (New York, 1942 [1776]), pp. 5–6.

[74] *HDI*, Vol. 1, pp. 8, 17. These were references to Montesquieu's *Considérations sur les causes de la grandeur des Romains et de leur décadence* (1732).

Even though the legislature held the supreme power, the nominal separation of the executive offered the possibility of political strife. In terms similar to Bolingbroke's, the corruption of the Commons by venal ministers was excoriated. The very balance of the three elements in the legislature might break down into anarchy. A false sense of its own grandeur moved the nation to undertake enterprises beyond its capacity, and it seemed likely to lose its colonial empire. Sooner or later it would fall back into 'the abyss whence it had emerged through torrents of blood and the calamities of two centuries of fanaticism and war'.[75]

This was a strange way to end a section devoted to the triumph of liberty in the British constitution. Much of this passage was written by Diderot,[76] but its pessimism about English affairs was, like the later Voltaire's, reminiscent of the Raynal who had composed *The History of the Parliament of England.* Among other things, the treatment of British constitutional history reveals the continuing tension between the editor of *The Encyclopedia* and the author/ editor of *The Two Indies.* They were, however, agreed that liberty was not derived from some ancient constitution developed over time. It had ebbed and flowed in the course of the centuries, and its triumph was a fortuitous thing. The degree of liberty could be assessed from one epoch to the next, but in the outcome its present state had been a matter of accident. So, too, could be its loss.

J.H.M. Salmon   BRYN MAWR COLLEGE

---

[75] *HDI*, Vol. 10, pp. 52–4.
[76] Duchet, *Diderot et l'Histoire des Deux Indes*, p. 99.

THE MANUSCRIPT AUTHORITY OF POLITICAL THOUGHTS

*Robert Wokler**

Abstract: Contextualist interpretations of political thought need to be imaginatively constructed no less than the philosophically abstract readings they are often designed to supplant. Examples of recent scholarship on Hobbes, Locke and Rousseau, in particular, illustrate problems in establishing contextual meaning with precision. Manuscripts often embrace their authors' notions in an unrefined state, in their gestation and the immediacy of their first formulations. The study of manuscripts sometimes invites a free association of ideas across what, in a post-Enlightenment world, may be perceived as circumscribed disciplinary boundaries.

By way of commenting on the study of manuscripts I mean in these remarks to put a plea for toleration, or methodological eclecticism, as distinct from both the philosophical and especially the contextualist approaches to the interpretation of political argument now prevalent among Anglo-American theorists. Uncovering manuscripts might be thought to lead merely towards arcane knowledge gained from subtextual probes with scalpels and lenses, and in conducting archival research I have indeed sometimes felt myself transported by otherworldly attractions, sniffing the glue of the secret diaries of long-departed friends. The case I wish to advance here, however, has less to do with remoteness than pertinence. I shall be concerned most particularly with the insights that manuscripts may shed upon writings destined to become more sharply focused through later refinement but which, in their initial and sometimes explosive utterance, offer glimpses of the interpenetration of themes that cross their authors' minds perhaps more clearly than do published works.

I first met Jimmy Burns in the mid-1960s when I was a postgraduate student at the London School of Economics working on Rousseau and some of his modern interpreters, just after Jimmy himself had addressed the same themes in a notable article in *Political Studies* that had caught my attention.[1] Why he was so patient in dealing with a stranger who could not refrain from disputing his own account of Rousseau's meaning did not then prompt the curiosity on my part it merited, and later I found it required no explanation at all, since

* Dept. of Politics, University of Exeter, Amory Building, Rennes Drive, Exeter, Devon, EX4 4RJ, UK.

[1] James Burns, 'Du côté de chez Vaughan: Rousseau Revisited', *Political Studies*, 12 (1964), pp. 229–34. The first chapter of my doctoral dissertation, later recast as 'Natural law and the Meaning of Rousseau's Political Thought', in *Enlightenment Essays in Memory of Robert Shackleton* (Oxford, 1988), pp. 319–35, embraces a reply to Burns.

Jimmy was indiscriminately gracious to all tiresome and importunate students. Over the years I have often thought that his proposed translation of the real title of the work for which *Du Contrat social*[2] was only intended as a half-title — that is, *Principes du droit politique* — made perfect sense as *Principles of Constitutional Law*, if only because that title is virtually irresistible to anyone who devotes so much of his own professional life to the study of Bentham. It was, moreover, by way of his treatment of Bentham, rather than Rousseau, and most particularly his painstaking devotion to deciphering Bentham's manuscripts, that I came to find in Jimmy a kindred soul whose sensitivity to the surprises that lurk in archives spared him the methodological straitjackets of either dogmatic truth or demonstrable accuracy such as too often confine one-eyed studies of political thought. Of all the memorably congenial political theorists or intellectual historians of his generation, Jimmy has always struck me as the most benign and most tolerant. In keeping his distance throughout his professional life from a political thinker he served as an indefatigable amanuensis, he gave me reason to hope that my transcription of Rousseau's manuscripts need not of itself contaminate me fatally. He has shown us all that it is possible to probe conceptual undergrowths without losing sight of the bridges or buttresses overhead. Even the writing of methodological essays is largely alien to him. In resisting that temptation, he has proved wiser than I can be here.

In commenting on manuscripts mainly in order to correct contextual treatments of political thought, I have it in mind less to stress the putative differences between historical and philosophical readings of texts than to cast doubt on the validity of such distinctions. Historians of ideas often decry the attempts of philosophers to address the sense of past thinkers' arguments in plucking them from the circumstances of their composition, but through these remarks I mean to show that contextual meanings also have to be ascribed and legislated by their interpreters. They are not, merely on the evidence of their being couched in historical terms, thereby rendered more accurate or more reliable. In his entry on 'History' in the *Companion to Contemporary Political Philosophy* edited by Robert Goodin and Phillip Pettit, Richard Tuck has described the historical revolution, to which he has contributed much himself, as 'the new history', a term appropriated by Dario Castiglione in a notable essay on the subject published a few years ago in the *Political Theory Newsletter*.[3] There may indeed be as many denominations of 'the new history' as there are persons who practise it, proceeding, for instance, from Stefan Collini in his focus on the determinants

---

[2] Or, rather, *Du Contract social*, suppressed from the title-page on Rousseau's instruction because it had become too crowded with words, although a number of copies of the first edition escaped that alteration.

[3] See Richard Tuck, 'The Contribution of History', in *A Companion to Contemporary Political Philosophy* (Oxford, 1993), pp. 72–89, and Dario Castiglione, 'Historical Arguments in Political Theory', *Political Theory Newsletter*, 5 (1993), pp. 89–109.

of a political culture, to John Pocock on political language and discourse, to Quentin Skinner on the intentional meaning of particular authors. If the approaches they adopt are in each case distinctive, however, our new historians of political thought are nevertheless agreed that political writings must always be situated within the particular intellectual landscapes that define them, excluding philosophical perspectives as anachronistically decontextualized from the worlds and the works they purport to explain.

To my mind, however, in insisting upon the contextual analysis of political doctrines, we risk just relocating ambiguities of interpretation from one domain to another. What counts as a proper context is not an independent variable but inescapably our own construction, as open to challenge as are the abstractions it is meant to supplant. This is hardly an original thesis. It has many precursors and in terms I admire was articulated at length in 1933 by Michael Oakeshott in *Experience and its Modes*. My aim here is to pursue its implications with reference to the study of manuscripts, which I believe need not be based on presuppositions as to what their authors must mean in the light of the intentions we impute to them or the interpretations of their thought which we ascribe to their immediate contemporaries. Manuscripts are of course no more pregnant with meaning than are published works; their recoverable sense also reflects the skills of their interpreters. But as well as constituting drafts of other texts, they can point towards meanings their authors might later refine, sharpen, blunt, suppress, abandon or deem insignificant. They may articulate a free association of ideas and give expression to dreams that wend across disciplines. As distinct from the works to which they give rise, they are genuine *pièces fugitives*, not to be confined to quarters, bursting from their contexts.

As I understand them contextual readings of political arguments do not, as a matter of fact, always displace philosophical ones, and even the most historically learned interpretations may seem at bottom to have eluded the truth. Consider for a moment a number of recent studies of Locke. Thanks initially to Peter Laslett and his pupils, and now to several generations of scholars inspired by his contextualist account of the *Second Treatise*, we have come a very long way from Brough Macpherson's model of the capitalist presuppositions of Locke's theory of possessive individualism. After John Dunn in particular it has become impossible for Locke scholarship to make a retrograde step with impunity. But where exactly do we find ourselves in having assimilated the most up-to-date contextualist interpretations of Locke's political thought? James Tully, among the most learned of all our new historians of the subject, does not, as I read him, make use of his undeniable scholarship to decisive advantage in his confrontation with Jeremy Waldron about the true meaning of the texts they explore. Perhaps no one has ever studied the sources of Locke's political philosophy in general, or his theory of property in particular, with greater care, and I am unacquainted with any finer treatment than Tully's of Locke's debts to, and departures from, Suárez, Grotius and Pufendorf, in their uses of the terms *dominium* and *proprietas*, and of the formulations of his objections to Filmer.

Much of Tully's substantially juristic account of Locke on property is designed to refute the anachronisms of Macpherson's essentially economic interpretation of the same subject, and in highlighting their differences he lays great stress upon the fact that, on his reading of the text, 'property in political society is a creation of that society',[4] not so much a natural right preserved as an entitlement determined by positive law, its distribution accordingly secured by convention. Several passages of the *Second Treatise* are presented as evidence which informs this interpretation, which to my mind is neither required by Tully's account of Locke's sources, nor warranted by the text itself, including the passages presented by Tully in defence of his claims, even allowing for the opacity of Locke's own views.

In a long commentary on Tully's thesis, Jeremy Waldron provides what seems to me far more convincing testimony, equally drawn from the *Second Treatise*, that property rights are indeed *natural* entitlements which ought to survive men's transition to civil society from their original state, as not only Macpherson but other careful readers of that text had correctly understood to be its meaning. When Locke speaks of property rights as 'determined' by positive law, he is not claiming that they are *created* by civil society but only that they are *regulated* there, Waldron contends,[5] recalling a somewhat similar debate which some years ago exercised other political theorists about the meaning of *bestimmen* or *determine* in Marx's theory of history. My point here is not to show that a subtly contextualist reading of a political doctrine may be successfully challenged by a purely analytical account, or that the doctrine is better interpreted with respect to its internal coherence than in the light of claims prevalent in works its author embraced or combated. I mean only that Tully's case, designed to disabuse Locke's readers of a widespread misconception, remains unproven in the face of Waldron's challenge, and I am surprised to find that in his most recent study of *Locke in Contexts*, where Tully replies to his critics, he leaves this objection unanswered.[6]

Consider, too, the work of the late Richard Ashcraft who, after devoting more than twenty years of his life to the most brilliantly meticulous study of Locke's

---

[4] James Tully, *A Discourse of Property: John Locke and his Adversaries* (Cambridge, 1980), p. 98.

[5] See Jeremy Waldron, *The Right to Private Property* (Oxford, 1988), pp. 232–41.

[6] See J. Tully, *An Approach to Political Philosophy: Locke in Contexts* (Cambridge, 1993). In *The Locke Newsletter*, 13 (1982), however, he replied to other criticisms of his interpretation of Locke's meaning, by Thomas Baldwin and Waldron in particular (see pp. 9–46), which had mainly returned to the question posed by Macpherson as to whether capitalist relations could already have been enshrined in the state of nature. Matthew Kramer's *John Locke and the Origins of Private Property* (Cambridge, 1997) offers a philosophical critique both of Locke's account of the connection between private property and civil laws and, even more, of Tully's alleged misreadings of that argument.

democratic radicalism that could ever have been hoped for this side of pedantry, had to contend with Ellen Meiksins Wood's carefully assembled riposte that Locke was no democrat, as well as with Mark Goldie's even more closely argued challenge to the effect that he was not much of a radical either.[7] Because it turns around manuscripts I shall comment exclusively on this second case. As readers of *History of Political Thought* and *The Historical Journal* will know, the question of whether Locke had been a covert conspirator against James II has come to hinge on the meaning of the word *tree* in letters he addressed around 1685 to one of the members of his circle, Samuel Clarke, identified by Ashcraft as a fellow-conspirator. Writing to Clarke about 'seeds' and 'trees', Ashcraft claims that these terms were a code for 'money' and 'troops', to which Goldie replies that Locke had an abiding interest in vines and trees, in this context expressing a preference for limes over horse-chestnuts, so that when he talks of 'trees' Locke just plainly means 'trees' — a point unconvincing to Ashcraft, who retorts that the letters are in ciphers, marked by the repetition of secret injunctions Clarke would have understood.[8]

Not least as a student of Rousseau, I am myself quite partial to trees, and since those which Rousseau recollects in the Seventh Walk of his *Rêveries* may, I suspect, have been originally inspired by a lust for Sophie d'Houdetot which he hoped might be more lyrically persuasive in botanical form, I can understand, with Aschcraft, how reference to trees might pass from one discourse to another. In Locke's own lifetime, after all, Andrew Marvell had also employed a kind of sexual code in his rich imagery of vegetable love. But how are readers to legislate between Ashcraft and Goldie in this matter? Goldie's common-or-garden reading of Locke on trees seems quite compelling, but even if Locke had only meant to state his preference for limes over chestnuts, may we not see that preference itself as at least a faint sign of his radicalism, bearing in mind that the lime is a Whig tree, in contrast with the oak, which is Tory? May we not turn to chapter 5, paragraph 28 of the *Second Treatise*, where Locke speaks of being nourished by acorns picked under an oak, and, noting that there is no reference to limes anywhere in the text, thus deduce that he held the state of nature itself to be Tory? At any rate, when a weary Ashcraft calls for interpretive charity',[9] I feel inclined to regret our collective failure to grant him that peace of mind in good time.

[7] See Mark Goldie, 'John Locke's Circle and James II', *The Historical Journal*, 35 (1992), pp. 557–86; Ellen Meiksins Wood, 'Locke against Democracy: Consent, Representation and Suffrage in the *Two Treatises*', *History of Political Thought*, 13 (1992), pp. 657–89; and Richard Ashcraft, 'The Radical Dimensions of Locke's Political Thought: A Dialogic Essay on some Problems of Interpretation', *History of Political Thought*, 13 (1992), pp. 703–72.

[8] See Richard Ashcraft, *Revolutionary Politics and Locke's Two Treatises of Government* (Princeton, 1986), pp. 452–3; Goldie, 'Locke's Circle', p. 564; and Ashcraft, 'The Radical Dimensions of Locke's Political Thought', p. 771.

[9] Ashcraft, 'The Radical Dimensions of Locke's Political Thought', p. 772.

Or consider Richard Tuck on Hobbes. In a number of recent essays, and in his 1989 'Past Master' on *Hobbes*, Tuck has suggested that the anonymous manuscript entitled *A Short Tract on First Principles*, uncovered by Ferdinand Tönnies among the Harleian papers in the British Museum and published a century ago, is not in fact by Hobbes.[10] Supposing that it is indeed Hobbes's work, other scholars had dated it from around the end of 1630 or the beginning of 1631, and there at least appears to be no dispute that if it were actually by Hobbes it would have had to be drafted before 1636, when we know from his correspondence that he had come to reject the particulate or corpuscular theory of light which the work embraces.

Since Tuck, however, had already established to his own satisfaction that Hobbes had no consistent natural philosophy before the publication of Descartes' *Discours de la méthode* in 1637, he claims that there is nothing particularly Hobbesian about the *Short Tract* and no good reason for ascribing it to Hobbes, preferring instead to attribute it to Robert Payne, a member of the circle of Sir Charles Cavendish and the Earl of Newcastle at Welbeck Abbey. Johann Sommerville, a former pupil of Tuck, finds his tutor's arguments plausible, without, however, hazarding the manuscript's attribution to Payne.[11] In his remarkable edition of Hobbes's *Correspondence*, Noel Malcolm agrees with Tuck that the *Short Tract*, apparently drafted in Payne's own hand, can for that reason be 'plausibly attributed to him', although he disputes Tuck's identification of Payne's handwriting in the light of letters which he contends are not actually in Payne's hand but are, rather, transcripts from Payne made by Thomas Birch.[12] According to Tuck, at the time the *Short Tract* is alleged to have been drafted Hobbes had been preoccupied with epistemological matters and not natural philosophy — in particular, with the fashionable revival of Pyrrhonianism under the influence of Montaigne and Charron, whose sceptical challenge was met in this period by Mersenne and Gassendi, together with their mutual friend, Hobbes, before the argument would later be given a new twist in the direction of natural philosophy by Descartes.[13]

[10] See Hobbes, *The Elements of Law: Natural and Politic*, ed. Ferdinand Tönnies (London, 1889), p. xii and appendix I, pp. 193–210; Richard Tuck, 'Hobbes and Descartes', in *Perspectives on Thomas Hobbes*, ed. G.A.J. Rogers and Alan Ryan (Oxford, 1988), pp. 17–18; and R. Tuck, *Hobbes* (Oxford, 1989), p. 18. Tuck has elsewhere been more circumspect in doubting Hobbes's composition of the *Short Tract*. In his 'Optics and Sceptics: The Philosophical Foundations of Hobbes's Political Thought', in *Conscience and Casuistry in Early Modern Europe*, ed. Edmund Leites (Cambridge, 1988), p. 249, he remarks only that 'until the work's authorship and date are properly established, it is wise to ignore it in discussions of Hobbes's intellectual development'.

[11] See Johann Sommerville, *Thomas Hobbes: Political Ideas in Historical Context* (Basingstoke, 1992), pp. 170–1, n. 23.

[12] See *The Correspondence of Thomas Hobbes*, ed. Noel Malcolm (Oxford, 1994), II, p. 874.

[13] See Tuck, 'Hobbes and Descartes', pp. 16–18.

But Tuck's reading of the *Short Tract* has not borne well the close scrutiny of other historians, it having already been established by Jean Jacquot in 1952 that the handwriting of the text in question bears striking similarity to that of a letter addressed by Hobbes to Cavendish among the same papers.[14] To more recent commentators on the subject, there seems scant reason for denying Hobbes's authorship, notwithstanding Tuck's suppositions of the correct timing of Hobbes's pertinent intellectual interests such as would contextually preclude his having had the range of scientific interests the work articulates. As Richard Popkin and Tom Sorell have shown over the past couple of decades, moreover, the sceptical crises which troubled Mersenne and Gassendi are hardly mentioned by Hobbes, who, by contrast, following Descartes's imputation of plagiarism in a letter to Mersenne, replied that certain ideas on light which he admittedly shared with Descartes had not been culled from his work but had been independently conceived in research he had undertaken around 1630, as he had already conveyed to the Earl of Newcastle and to Cavendish at the time, which forms one of the main reasons for the scholarly ascription of the *Short Tract* to that period in the first place.[15]

In a notable commentary on the subject published in 1993, Perez Zagorin agreed with Sorell that the appropriate context for an assessment of the *Short Tract* is that of Euclidean geometry and Galilean mechanics, providing sources for the formulation of Hobbes's natural philosophy independent of Descartes, and an anti-sceptical focus around a theory of perception, owing little to the epistemological doctrines of Mersenne and Gassendi, whose expression, in much the same terms, can be traced from the *Short Tract* to the *Elements of Law*, which had supplied Tönnies' original reason for publishing the works together.[16] Two years later, in the most authoritative treatment of the *Short Tract* thus far produced, Karl Schuhmann demonstrated, not least by meticulously collating this text with passages from other writings by Hobbes, that it must

[14] See Jacquot, 'Sir Charles Cavendish and his Learned Friends', pt. I, *Annals of Science*, 8 (1952), p. 21n. In identifying as the work of Payne manuscripts previously thought to have been drafted by Hobbes, Malcolm does not address this claim by Jacquot, whose expertise in such matters was also considerable. He notes, however, that Payne's handwriting closely resembles that of Hobbes. Payne, who was one of Hobbes's best friends, appears to have transcribed other manuscripts, perhaps occasionally for Hobbes's benefit. But in ascribing the *Short Tract* to Hobbes rather than Payne, the central matters at issue for most commentators have been the substance of the text rather than its handwriting, its compatibility of style and meaning with other works by Hobbes, and the absence of writings known to be by Payne which might point to similar interests or talent.

[15] See *The Correspondence of Hobbes*, I, Letters 33 and 34, pp. 94–114; Richard Popkin, 'Hobbes and Scepticism', *History of Philosophy in the Making. A Symposium in Honor of James D. Collins* (Washington, DC, 1982), pp. 134–5; and Tom Sorell, 'Descartes, Hobbes, and the Body of Natural Science', *The Monist*, 71 (1988), pp. 521–3.

[16] See Perez Zagorin, 'Hobbes's Early Philosophical Development', *Journal of the History of Ideas*, 54 (1993), pp. 505–18.

indeed have been manufactured by him, albeit probably in 1632 or 1633 rather than 1630.[17] Allowing that Tuck may one day reply to what now seems a formidable set of objections to his exclusion of the manuscript from the corpus of Hobbes's writings, it seems to me that, at least for the time being, the historical case against his contextualist reading of Hobbes is as persuasive as Waldron's philosophical case against Tully's reading of Locke. How is it that the new history, which like logical positivism in the 1930s was meant to overcome our confusion of categories in the interpretation of arguments, has sometimes managed to conduct us from one wilderness to another? Where are the clearings in the history of political thought from which we can safely map out a new frontier? Who benefits from this surfeit of fresh readings, of which, to my taste, too many come into the world with the express wish that the others should leave it? Plainly our publishers benefit, for insofar as our new historians have failed to dispose of decontextualized analyses, on the one hand, while at the same time generating multiple candidates for historical investigation, on the other, we are now confronted with several accredited perspectives on every major thinker where before it was thought that a single framework might suffice — at least two Hobbes industries, three independent approaches to Locke and four distinct ways of situating Mill in the history of liberal thought, allowing, of course, that Mill's contribution to liberalism was problematic even before the historians parted company from the philosophers. What are we to do in the face of such confusion? Never mind who wrote the *Short Tract on First Principles*. If we must all unravel the intricacies of the connections between Hobbes and the *de facto* Tories, Hobbes and the Engagement Controversy, or Hobbes and the Royal Society (in this case a lack of connection), who can blame those among us who give up in frustration in the face of so much historical detail and just resign themselves to their original brisk grapple with the unsituated mysteries of eighteen central chapters from the *Leviathan*? In the short space that remains, let me suggest how the study of manuscripts may point in another direction.

Of course manuscripts sometimes matter scarcely at all. No one would have been more dismayed than Marx to find the history of Western communism in the twentieth century so much shaped by the scholarly interpretation of papers that, around the time of their composition, he jettisoned to the scrap heap of history. Such papers, moreover, take widely different forms, from documents in public records offices to jottings and drafts of letters which their authors abandoned. Each of these forms invites an appropriate scholarly use, as is plain, for instance, from Ralph Leigh's magisterial edition of the *Correspondance complète de Rousseau*, which assembles the biographical details of perhaps five thousand minor figures who populated Rousseau's world from manuscripts of one kind, but also documents the immediacy of Rousseau's vision and the stages

---

[17] See K. Schuhmann, 'Le *Short Tract*, première œuvre philosophique de Hobbes', *Hobbes Studies*, 8 (1995), pp. 3–36.

of creativity of his writing from manuscripts of another. Let me call this second kind dreams trapped in archives, although the same manuscripts may sometimes be better described as nightmares which decline to take leave of their host.

There are of course many important aspects of the subject which must be overlooked here — not least what counts as a manuscript in this age of new technologies when, in the composition of our texts upon screens, we destroy the rough drafts that express the spontaneity of our imagination in the very act of refining statements we hope will be fit for public consumption. There are also notable technical problems about the retrieval of manuscripts, for instance in Henry Hardy's reconstruction of dictated recordings of lectures given by Isaiah Berlin for which, in certain instances, there was no surviving manuscript. Thanks to the ingenuity of staff at the National Sound Archive who located a relic in the National Science Museum and thereby managed to reassemble a long defunct dictabelt transcription machine, the transfer of obsolete tapes to modern cassettes was achieved and Berlin's *ipsissima verba* have survived,[18] which, if the matter had been left to him alone, may not really have been his first preference.

The point I wish to stress is that if we start from an author's manuscripts rather than the imputed context of his or her published work, we might at least avoid the trap into which Tuck has apparently fallen of supposing that a manuscript cannot be by its author, because it does not seem tailored to fit that context. To put this point in more general terms, one of my main objections to the contextualist strictures of our so-called 'new history' of political thought is that it seems, to my mind, too narrowly political in focus. Having divorced the truly historical treatment of texts from the world of political theory to which my former tutors supposed they could freely contribute by way of commenting on past authors, our new historians have also sometimes disengaged those features of an intellectual context which they regard as appropriate to political argument from all the rest, isolating the various languages of politics they address from other discourses — from anthropology, psychology and the philosophy of music and language, for instance, just to name certain themes of particular interest to me. The compelling attraction of such circumscribed frameworks for historians is that they can provide an apparently more solid foundation — embracing institutions and sometimes even events — within or around which to locate ideas in context that more abstract interpreters have ignored. In transporting political thought from the peaks of Parnassus to the lowlands of the Fens, some of them have brought down-to-earth, even subterranean, respectability to a subject which, in History Faculties or Departments, is otherwise held to be irredeemably philosophical. But political institutions

[18] See Henry Hardy's editorial preface to Isaiah Berlin, *The Magus of the North: J.G. Hamann and the Origins of Modern Irrationalism* (London, 1993), p. x.

and the popular languages of public morality are by no means the only framework within which political theories were formed.

When in the late 1960s I came across and then later transcribed the manuscript of Rousseau's *Du principe de la mélodie* in the archives of the Bibliothèque de la Ville de Neuchâtel, I was particularly drawn to those passages of the text which I took, and still take, to be of remarkably political character. It is in this manuscript that we find the first surviving draft of what were to become chapters eighteen and nineteen of the *Essai sur l'origine des langues* in which Rousseau describes the chords of the scale of Western music as a crude and vulgar innovation unknown to the Greeks and then traces the moral decadence of modern music to the barbarian invasions of the Roman Empire, bringing about, among other things, the destruction of the mellifluous intonations of ancient Greek and Latin and their replacement by the dull and nasal consonants which Emperor Julian had compared to the croaking of frogs. As prose replaced poetry the civic culture of its speakers likewise became prosaic, Rousseau claims, and thereafter, in the final chapter of his *Essai*, entitled 'Rapport des langues aux gouvernemens', he argues that languages which have come to be separated from music are inimical to freedom.

No earlier sketch of that chapter figures in *Du principe de la mélodie*, but the political implications which Rousseau draws directly from his account of the corruption of music and language in the manuscript I uncovered and transcribed[19] point to a thematic unity of his philosophy which embraces disciplines that his specialist interpreters must bridge if they are to grasp his meaning correctly. It was Rousseau's belief that a prosaic rhetoric inspires servile manners and that speech made hollow by its lack of tone and rhythm also makes for hollow men. The languages of modern Europe are little more than the ineffectual chatter of persons who just murmur feebly to one another, with voices that lack inflection and therefore spirit and passion as well, he argued. As our speech has succumbed to the loss of its musical traits, so has it been deprived of its original vigour and clarity and become instead little more than the faint mutterings of individuals who have no strength of character or purpose. In the form they have currently adopted in commercial society, the vocal intonations which had once expressed our pleasures, Rousseau explains, have been reconstituted as the terms that denote our trades. Whereas the languages

---

[19] In R. Wokler, 'Rameau, Rousseau and the *Essai sur l'origine des langues*', *Studies on Voltaire and the Eighteenth Century*, CXVII (1974), pp. 179–238. Working independently, Marie-Élisabeth Duchez incorporated a transcription of the same text in her '*Principe de la mélodie* et *Origine des langues*: Un brouillon inédit de Rousseau sur l'origine de la mélodie', *Revue de musicologie*, 60 (1974), pp. 33–86. The material we each transcribed from Ms R 60 of the Bibliothèque de la Ville de Neuchâtel now figures in Vol. 5 of the Pléiade edition of the *Œuvres complètes de Rousseau*, published in 1995 and edited by Duchez, as *L'Origine de la mélodie*. The only complete transcription of Ms R 60 can be found as an appendix to my Oxford DPhil dissertation, published as *Rousseau on Society, Politics, Music and Language* (New York, 1987), pp. 435–501.

of passion had been superseded by the languages of need — that is, *aimez-moi* had been replaced by *aidez-moi* — now all that we say to one another is *donnez de l'argent*. Any attentive reader of the *Contrat social* will recognize the same critique of commercial society in Book III, chapter fifteen, with the same expression — *donnez de l'argent* — there rendered as the principal medium of commercial society's discourse.

To my mind, Rousseau's philosophy of music forms a no less integral feature of his political theory than does the same subject in the *Republic* of Plato, and yet, despite the fact that the text had been recorded more than seventy years ago,[20] and despite other evidence known to scholars that it had originally been drafted as a fragment of the *Discours sur l'inégalité* and was then withdrawn because of its length,[21] *Du principe de la mélodie* had never been seriously studied before, largely on account of its also including more technical treatments of music in reply to Rameau's objections to the articles on music Rousseau had prepared for Diderot's *Encyclopédie*. Rousseau's philosophy of music, which forms much the largest single subject aside from his correspondence in the quite massive Neuchâtel archive, has only in the past twenty years or so received the editorial notice it merits, simply because a certain (albeit modest) command of musical notation and musical theory is indispensable for that task, and Rousseau's literary and political editors have been unable or unwilling to acquire a sufficient mastery of the subject to deal with it in a scholarly way. But it lies at the heart of both Rousseau's life and his writings as a whole, and I believe that there can be no persuasive interpretation of his political philosophy which ignores it.

Let me add one other point here about what might be regarded as solely aesthetic and acoustical reflections in the context of Rousseau's political and social philosophy. In recounting what he takes to be the decay of Western music in its divorce from the inflected languages of antiquity, Rousseau as I read him just adds a correlative perspective to his account of civilization as mankind's

---

[20] By Théophile Dufour in his posthumously published *Recherches bibliographiques sur les œuvres imprimées de Rousseau* (Paris, 1925), II, pp. 179–80, where the text is described as a '3e cahier' in connection with Rousseau's *Examen de deux principes*, under its former classification number 7877.

[21] According to Rousseau's own 'Project de préface' (Neuchâtel Ms R 91) designed to introduce a collection of three of his works in one volume. For an account of the genesis of the *Essai sur l'origine des langues* in the light of *Du principe de la mélodie*, see especially ch. 5 of Wokler, *Rousseau on Society, Politics, Music and Language*, pp. 294–326. The significance of the manuscript for an understanding of both the *Discours sur l'inégalité* and the *Essai sur l'origine des langues* is considered at length by Charles Porset in ' "L'inquiétante étrangeté" de l'*Essai sur l'origine des langues*: Rousseau et ses exégètes', *Studies on Voltaire and the Eighteenth Century*, 151–5 (1976), pp. 1715–58, and by R. Wokler in '*L'Essai sur l'origine des langues* en tant que fragment du *Discours sur l'inégalité*: Rousseau et ses "mauvais" interprètes', in *Rousseau et Voltaire en 1978*, ed. M. Launay (Geneva, 1981), pp. 145–69.

progressive enslavement to institutions which purport to make it free. That proposition is indeed implied by his manuscript testimony to the effect that *Du principe de la mélodie* once formed a fragment of the *Discours sur l'inégalité*. What, indeed, are our moral relations as Rousseau conceived them but calculations of intervals in scales whose harmonies may take the form of dominant and subdominant modes? The prevailing social divisions between persons have their counterpoint in the divisions of their octaves, the enthralments of instrumental music are matched by those of instrumental politics, and the subjugation of peoples is achieved in no small measure by their masters' conjugation of verbs and their manipulation of language in general.

When Rousseau takes issue with the notion of the *basse fondamentale* of Rameau, in particular, his style of cross-examination seems to me remarkably akin to that of John Plamenatz on Hobbes.[22] Rousseau's method of interrogating not only Rameau but also Locke, Diderot, Buffon, Condillac and Helvétius, as well of course as his most formidable adversary, Hobbes, distills from their writings what he regards as profound, disposes of what he holds to be mistaken, inconsistent or naïve, relocates their arguments in specific contexts to show that they do not hold universally, if at all, identifying them as peculiar perspectives bred of a particular time and set of circumstances, wrongly extrapolated in his view, to human nature in general. His main complaint against other luminaries bears a striking resemblance to the allegations of decontextualized anachronism so often made by advocates of the new history, except that in order to grasp this charge one must first contextualize it philosophically, with respect not just to the immediate circumstances of its composition in connection with Rameau's notion of the *basse fondamentale*, but also a whole tradition of speculation, across a variety of disciplines, which Rousseau takes to task as if confronting contemporary adversaries. His charges are quintessentially those adopted by Plamenatz, and indeed, if I dare say so, Macpherson, as well. Supposing that in order to break the hermeneutic circle, we must somehow at least attempt to enter the minds of past authors and not just reveal the strategies of their published works, why must we handicap what is already an undeniably, perhaps insuperably, difficult task, by excluding from our focus of interpretation the very devices which those authors themselves employed to understand their own precursors?

It was by way of Rousseau's *Discours sur l'inégalité*, whose few surviving manuscript fragments I have been assembling throughout almost the whole of my professional life, that I was initially drawn to Lord Monboddo's papers and

---

[22] See John Plamenatz, *Man and Society* (London, revised edn., 1992), I, ch. 5, pp. 172–215.

[23] Some of the papers pertaining to Monboddo in public and private archives which I have managed to photocopy over the years, including his correspondence with Lord Lyttelton which once formed part of the Hagley MSS in the Birmingham Reference Library, have been dispersed and may now be difficult to trace. Such material informs,

correspondence on the origins of language and on the humanity of apes lodged in collections in Edinburgh, Cambridge, Birmingham and elsewhere.[23] Monboddo was one of the eighteenth century's greatest admirers of this text, though he also took issue with it and, in the course of attempting to refine his own anthropological speculations on the origins of language so as to correct Rousseau even while acknowledging his debt, he recast the first edition of his own work *On the Origin and Progress of Language* along lines, illuminated by his manuscripts, which turn on his correspondence with commentators and the availability of sources to which he had access in the Advocates' Library in Edinburgh. In recounting these matters I felt inclined to follow the trajectory of Monboddo's and indeed Rousseau's own speculations on the humanity of orang-utans in the direction of twentieth-century scientific experiments on the teaching of languages to apes. Did I breach some sacred principle of the division of labour in moving from eighteenth-century speculation and experiments to contemporary research on what strikes me as precisely the same questions as were at issue in the Enlightenment? In investigating recent palæoanthropological findings and studies of the sublaryngeal vocal tract was I just moving out of my depth? Why should DNA hybridization studies in genetics pass without any comment from those who are convinced that they can trace these biological formulations of Scottish conjectural history to their source? One of the most striking features of the European Enlightenment was the interdisciplinary character of its philosophy, its lack of impermeable boundaries within its maps of knowledge, its denial of esoterically privileged information to any hegemonic castes. Manuscripts may have that character too. They demand public scrutiny. They invite their interpreters to investigate their meanings and pursue their intimations wherever they might lead, *sans parti pris*.

Lack of attention to manuscripts sometimes accounts for major flaws in the interpretation of an author's published work. Consider the example of one of the pre-eminent political theorists of America since the Second World War who, with profound sophistication, showed how it was possible to contribute directly to our subject through the translation of classic texts, including Plato's *Republic* and Rousseau's *Lettre à d'Alembert sur les spectacles* and *Emile*. Both in his introduction and notes to Rousseau's greatest masterpiece Allan Bloom rightly remarks that *Emile* was conceived in large measure as a reply to Locke's *Thoughts concerning Education*, and since Rousseau's stance is so plainly defined by way of objections to Locke, he contends that a deep understanding of Rousseau presupposes some knowledge of Locke's teaching.[24] That is undeniably true. Such understanding also presupposes some familiarity with

---

for instance, my essay, 'From Apes to Races in the Scottish Enlightenment: Kames and Monboddo on the History of Man', *Science and Philosophy in the Scottish Enlightenment*, ed. Peter Jones (Edinburgh, 1989), pp. 145–68.

[24] See Rousseau, *Emile*, ed. and trans. Allan Bloom (New York, 1979), Notes, preface, n. 4, p. 481.

Helvétius, however, whom Bloom neglects to mention. There are at least four surviving manuscripts of *Emile*, as well as a number of fragments, and I do not suggest that it is the responsibility of a translator to collate them. But even if Bloom had deemed it unnecessary to leave the shores of Lake Michigan for a visit to Paris and especially Geneva to inspect Rousseau's papers, he ought at least to have read the first draft of *Emile*, known as the *Manuscrit Favre*, published in the same volume of Rousseau's *Œuvres complètes* from which his translation is drawn, and then consulted the excellent notes to the text by John Spink, as well as the more comprehensive annotation by Pierre Burgelin to the final version of *Emile*.

In offering his readers a guide to Rousseau's meaning, Bloom ought above all to have paid some attention to the wonderfully majestic collation and edition of the manuscripts of the 'Profession de foi du vicaire Savoyard' and the equally splendid three-volume study of *La Religion de Rousseau* prepared by much the most distinguished Rousseau scholar of his generation, Pierre-Maurice Masson,[25] killed on the Front in the First World War, whose profoundly moving final letters to his wife and to his publishers with respect to editorial matters, incidentally, have survived. If Bloom had managed a few supplementary hours of essential reading, he would have found that in *Emile* Rousseau addresses passages from Helvétius's *De l'esprit* and in his original draft refers to it; and either through Masson's or Burgelin's editorial notes, Bloom might also have had his attention drawn to a letter drafted in September 1762, and to a passage of the *Lettres de la montagne* of 1764, in which Rousseau claims that he had originally intended to attack this already celebrated work but had then suppressed his criticism in order to dissociate himself from the muckrakers which *De l'esprit* had stirred immediately on its publication in 1758.[26]

Much of Rousseau's argument in his 'Profession de foi du vicaire Savoyard' in the fourth book of *Emile* forms a proof of the existence of God by way of refuting the central thesis of Helvétius's work — that is, the contention that human intelligence springs from sensory experience and that our judgments are therefore no more than sensations. Because our senses are passive, our impressions of the objects that excite them cannot spontaneously give rise to our judgments of the relation between objects, he argues in his 'Profession de foi' in reply to Helvétius. Judgment is a matter of interpretation, which therefore

[25] See Masson's Rousseau, *La 'Profession de foi du vicaire savoyard'*, édition critique, d'après les Manuscrits de Genève, Neuchâtel et Paris, avec une introduction et un commentaire historiques (Fribourg and Paris, 1914), and *La Religion de Rousseau* (Paris, 2nd edn., 1916).

[26] See Rousseau, *Emile (Manuscrit Favre)* in Vol. 4 of the Pléiade edition of his *Œuvres complètes* (Paris, 1969), pp. 218–19 and 1283; Rousseau to Jean-Antoine Comparet, around 10 September 1762, in the *Correspondance complète de Rousseau* (Geneva and Oxford, 1965–98), Leigh 2147, Vol. 13, pp. 37 and 43; and Rousseau, *Lettres de la montagne*, Première Lettre, in his *Œuvres complètes*, Vol. 3 (Paris, 1964), pp. 693 and 1585.

requires human agency, pointing to intelligence and a will, which cannot have sprung from our bodily parts or matter alone, but must stem from an intelligence outside us, and hence, according to Rousseau, from God who is the ultimate author of our spirituality.

The educational doctrine of *Emile* as a whole, moreover, refutes a second principle articulated by Helvétius but equally ignored by Bloom, that is, the claim that *l'éducation peut tout*, challenged by Rousseau not only in *Emile* but also in the *Nouvelle Héloïse*, in a long passage to which Bloom never refers, where, through his fictional protagonist, Saint-Preux, he objects to this notion because it gives rise to the dangerous pretensions of tutors who suppose themselves licensed to mould pupils in any way that they choose.[27] Bloom would have been well-advised to take some heed of Rousseau's challenge to Helvétius. He of course has not overlooked Rousseau's insistence throughout the text upon the difficult art of governing without precepts and of doing everything by doing nothing. But in failing to notice that Rousseau's argument forms a challenge as much to Helvétius as to Locke, he misses half the point. For Rousseau's whole philosophy of education, as he puts it in *Emile*, is at bottom purely negative.[28] It sets aside all the books and lessons by which children's tutors might otherwise indoctrinate their pupils, shaping them before their time in the image of adults, rather than allowing their education to proceed endogenously out of their own curiosity and first-hand experience as they mature. That programme of negative education stands at the opposite end of a spectrum from one which at its other extreme embraces the claim that *l'éducation peut tout* as a practical conclusion of the argument that judgment springs directly from sensation. Some easily accessible information about the manuscript background of *Emile* would have served Bloom well in the fulfilment of an undertaking he set for himself of both translating and interpreting Rousseau's text.

A little further reflection on this subject, moreover, should soon show that Rousseau's challenges to Locke and Helvétius form parts of much the same argument — that is, a response to what Rousseau took to be dangers inherent in contemporary materialism. This point, which I should like to develop by way of some final remarks on Locke, underpins my contention that some of our new historians of political thought have circumscribed their subject in too narrowly political a way, excluding from their range of interests themes that once figured very near the heart of political argument but are not now accorded that status in more rigorous interpretations of its appropriate contexts. If I may here speak on behalf of intellectual historians of the Enlightenment more generally, there seems to me something rather odd about Locke scholarship as it is currently practised in certain quarters — by which I do not mean at all the meticulous

---

[27] See Rousseau, *La Nouvelle Héloïse*, Cinquième Partie, Lettre 3, *Œuvres complètes*, Vol. 2 (Paris, 1964), pp. 563–5 and 1672–3.

[28] See Rousseau, *Emile*, Livre II, *Œuvres complètes*, Vol. 4, pp. 323–4.

concentration of a number of scholars upon the political landscape of the world which Locke inhabited but rather such enthusiasm as is displayed by those who first offer us very close readings of the *Second Treatise* and then transpose its themes on natural law, labour or property to contemporary philosophical discourse informed by Ludwig Wittgenstein, Robert Nozick, Gerry Cohen, Michel Foucault and other modern luminaries.[29] Historians who with one hand point the way to a redemptive truth which corrects philosophical error ought not, with the other hand, to throw dust in their readers' eyes.

However subtly addressed, some of the questions at issue in these discussions seem to me desultory, feeding upon each other rather than drawing succor from Locke. Where, I wonder, do Locke's other writings figure in the scholarship now so earnestly addressed to the *Second Treatise*, and where, with respect to the new history, should one turn for guidance in identifying the influence throughout the eighteenth century of a thinker pre-eminently regarded at the time as godfather of the whole Enlightenment? Philosophically minded postmodernists may be excused for forgetting the French Revolution and the nineteenth century in order to hold an Enlightenment Project of their own invention responsible for the most sinister crises of modernity, but are historians of ideas entitled to skip stages as well? Allowing that most interpreters of the *Second Treatise* in the eighteenth century were best acquainted with it through the passages cited by Jean Barbeyrac in his annotations to Pufendorf's *De jure naturæ et gentium*, Locke's work was undoubtedly then known and read first-hand as well. But by contrast with his *Letter concerning Toleration*, *Thoughts concerning Education* or especially the *Essay concerning Human Understanding* his principal contribution to political thought cannot by any means be said to have had a wide circulation, and it is mainly to these other texts and not the *Second Treatise* that most Enlightenment commentaries on Locke were addressed. I shall conclude with just one, albeit a centrally important, example.

In the course of a long controversy about the nature of the human intellect to which Descartes, Spinoza, Leibniz, Cudworth and many other philosophers had already contributed, Locke observed, in the fourth book of his *Essay concerning Human Understanding*, that it was at least conceivable that God should add or, rather, 'superadd', to matter a faculty of thinking, thereby animating insensate particles with the power of thought. A few pages later, he stressed that it was impossible for matter of itself ever to give rise to thought, thus combating the chief contention of materialists, chiefly Spinozists, of his own day, who asserted what he denied.[30] But Locke's proposition that through God's will matter might be made to think occasioned numerous rebuttals from theologians and philosophers of the early eighteenth century, most of whom associated this claim with

---

[29] I have here in mind Tully's *Locke in Contexts*.

[30] See Locke's *Essay concerning Human Understanding*, Book IV, ch. 3, § 6, and Book IV, ch. 10, § 10.

Locke's further suggestion, in the same section of his work, that the truths of morality and religion do not depend upon the immateriality of the soul.

Such questions were to lay at the heart of the dispute between Anthony Collins and Samuel Clarke in the first decade of the eighteenth century, with which some greater familiarity by modern philosophers might have led to our being spared its reconfiguration as a 1960s debate on methodological individualism, whose central points had been virtually exhausted two hundred and fifty years earlier. Hartley, Reid and Priestly, in turn, pursued certain ramifications of Locke's argument about thinking matter several steps further. In France, Voltaire commented upon it in his *Lettres philosophiques* of 1734, and French materialists throughout the mid-eighteenth century, including Maupertuis, La Mettrie, Diderot and d'Holbach drew inspiration from it, some stressing what would now be termed its *physicalist* and others its *physiological* or organic implications. In his *Traité des sensations* of 1754, Condillac attempted to construct a theory of the formation of human intelligence from pure sensory experience, while in the article 'Évidence' published in the sixth volume of the *Encyclopédie* in 1756, Quesnay (most probably) attempted to show that sensation gives rise to judgment, and then two years later in *De l'esprit* Helvétius put forward the same thesis, rejected by Rousseau in *Emile*.

But this eighteenth-century debate as to whether our judgments might spring from sensation did not end with Rousseau and Helvétius. Through Helvétius especially it was taken up again by Bentham and then above all by James Mill, whose whole philosophy of education, as it was the great misfortune of his son to experience first-hand, was essentially Helvétian in character and ultimately Lockeian in origin. To my mind, it is the eighteenth-century debates about sensationalism, and the implications of that doctrine for the philosophy of education as pursued above all by the utilitarians and Philosophic Radicals of the nineteenth century, which point most comprehensively to Locke's influence upon Enlightenment political and social thought. Here is the Locke whom the philosophes of the eighteenth century knew best. But I suspect that it is because these arguments appear to be drawn from another discourse, which according to the contextualist canons of our new histories of political thought is not fundamentally political in focus, that they have been largely ignored by Locke's most recent political interpreters and have been left instead to be explored by historians of philosophy, theology and science.[31] More's the pity.[32]

Robert Wokler   UNIVERSITY OF EXETER

[31] Particularly by John Yolton in *Thinking Matter: Materialism in Eighteenth-Century Britain* (Minneapolis, c. 1983) and in *Locke and French Materialism* (Oxford, 1991).

[32] This essay is distilled from a paper I prepared for the Oxford Political Thought Conference at New College in 1994 and draws a few fragments from other writings, including my 'Past Master' *Rousseau*, first published by the Oxford University Press in 1995. I am grateful to Quentin Skinner for bringing Schuhmann's work on Hobbes's *Short Tract* to my attention, and to Janet Coleman for her comments on an earlier draft of the essay and for her forbearance.

ENLIGHTENMENT AND COUNTER-ENLIGHTENMENT, REVOLUTION AND COUNTER-REVOLUTION; A EUROSCEPTICAL ENQUIRY

J.G.A. Pocock*

Abstract: As part of a programme of disintegrating and re-assembling the concept or concepts of 'Europe', there is offered (1) a revision of Franco Venturi's exceptionalist account of England's place in Enlightenment, (2) an alternative to Isaiah Berlin's account of the movement through Enlightenment to historicism. The objective is to enhance the British and English role in European intellectual history, while showing that we must rewrite the concept of 'Europe' in order to do so. There persists the 'Eurosceptical enquiry' whether 'Europe' is interested in history at all.

His eye ranging from John Mair and the late scholastics to Jeremy Bentham and the Philosophic Radicals, the author of several essays showing early modern Scots active in the Parisian, Catholic and Imperial worlds to which they fared forth, J.H. Burns has unchallengeable credentials as a scholar at once Scottish, British and European. The present essay is written from a standpoint 'Eurosceptical' in the proper sense that it is sceptical about Europe; uncertain, that is, what the term means or how it is being employed, and disposed to suspect that its indeterminacy is being deliberately exploited with hegemonic intentions. To write history which critically explores the meaning of 'Europe' is to oppose oneself to this hegemony where it may be intended, but may at the same time do a service to 'Europe' by supplying it with a better history than is achieved by leaving it indeterminate. If as a result we find that there are several 'Europes', or ways of using the term, this too may do service to those trying to integrate Europe, by drawing attention to the problems they face; though it is fair to add that the standpoint of the essay does not necessarily entail commitment to that project, and that scepticism leaves open the question whether it deserves to succeed.

As a Scot — indeed a London Scot — Burns is interested in British history as well as European. If, however, we look at the ways in which these two terms are associated and exploited in the discourse — we might almost say the cant — of present fashion, we find them used with destructive intent; to destroy historic political structures, and melt them down into something new and indeterminate, seems to be a 'European' enterprise, in which what remains of the Marxist Left joins for reasons of its own. Thus, a 'British history' in which a number of

*   History Department, Johns Hopkins University, Baltimore, MD 21218, USA.

histories shall be exhibited as interacting becomes a merely anti-English device for predicting the dissolution of the United Kingdom; but no sooner has this prediction been set in place than we are informed that a 'British' perspective is not enough, and something called 'European' must take its place. In pursuit of this enterprise, whatever may be its aims, first English and then British history is condemned, and targeted for demolition, as 'exceptionalist';[1] there is to be a 'European' norm, situated everywhere and nowhere rather than somewhere, from which neither 'British' history nor presumably that of any other 'nation state' is permitted to stand aside in any narrative of its own making. The history of 'Europe' in this sense, however, is not being written, and it is doubtful whether there is any intention to do so; the rhetoric aims more at the destruction of histories than at their reconstruction.

In this essay I shall explore some problems set up by the concept of exceptionalism, and attempt to resolve them, having in my eye the works of two great historians, in no way guilty of the vulgarisms I have just identified, whom we have lost in recent years. In the first place it is to be premised that the problem with any exceptionalism is less the exception which it alleges than the rule which it establishes. Any culture is likely to have a history of its own; the error is that of treating it as a departure from a set of norms shared by others; but this error is as likely to be committed by the critic of exceptionalism as by those at whom he aims the charge. Early in the sequence of great writings that constitute his *Settecento Riformatore*,[2] Franco Venturi was led to pronounce the exceptionalist thesis that 'in England the rhythm was different'.[3] The rule he here established was that Enlightenment entailed the presence of *philosophes*, and it led him to the following syllogism: Edward Gibbon was a great Enlightened figure, but there were no *philosophes* in England, and therefore Gibbon must have been a solitary exile in his own country. Venturi further proposed that the great figures of Scottish Enlightenment were *philosophes* in the European sense, and this has been used by Scottish proponents of disunion to argue that Scotland has been both Enlightened and European whereas England has been neither; exceptionalism is a weapon as double-edged as the claymore.

That there was a cosmopolitan — i.e. largely but not wholly French — movement of *philosophes*, and that it was not represented in England, are propositions that need not be doubted. But Venturi's formulation did not address the questions of in what ways Gibbon was English and — more aggressively — whether there was something English about his brand of Enlightenment.

---

[1] See, e.g. David Armitage, 'Greater Britain: A Useful Category of Historical Analysis?', *American Historical Review* (forthcoming).

[2] Franco Venturi, *Settecento Riformatore* (Turin, Vol. I, 1969; II, 1976; III, 1979; IV (1 and 2), 1984; V (1), 1987). English translation of Vols. III and IV, R. Burr Litchfield, *The End of the Old Regime in Europe* (3 vols., Princeton, 1989–91).

[3] Franco Venturi, *Utopia and Reform in the Enlightenment* (Cambridge, 1971), pp. 132–4.

There has since occurred a redrawing of the map of Enlightenment which displays its origins in a diversity of Protestant cultures; Enlightenment in England was Latitudinarian, in Scotland it was Moderate, and was propounded by clerics and conformist laymen with such energy as to suggest a reason why *philosophes* did not occur though their kinds of unbelief often did. There was a conservative Enlightenment which was often Socinian, a radical Enlightenment which was often Spinozist, and the two British Enlightenments interacted with others located in the recently Calvinist and persistently Lutheran cultures of Protestant Europe.[4] As for Gibbon, he was drawn to Parisian Enlightenment, but there are important moments in his life at which he turned away from the *Encyclopédie* of the *philosophes* and the dining tables of the *gens de lettres*, to become a man with two homelands — London and the south of England, Lausanne and the Pays de Vaud — and the author of a history of the Roman empire which increasingly became a history of the Christian church, written from a standpoint where the concerns of Anglican, Gallican and Huguenot clerics merged with those of deist and sceptical philosophers.[5] To Europeanize his Englishness is at the same time to Anglicize his Europe; and his early criticisms of the *Encyclopédie*, and his preference for history over philosophy, seem to point towards his instantly Burkean response to the French Revolution when he heard of it (which was before he heard of Burke's *Reflections on . . . that event*).[6]

It is important at this point that Burke was an Enlightened and European thinker, who saw the French Revolution and the partitions of Poland as spelling the end of Enlightened Europe and its fall into a condition resembling religious warfare.[7] The great works of Enlightenment historiography, with which the

[4] Margaret C. Jacob, *The Radical Enlightenment: Pantheists, Freemasons and Republicans* (London, 1981); J.G.A. Pocock, 'Clergy and Commerce; The Conservative Enlightenment in England', in *L'Età dei Lumi: studi storica sul settecento europeo in onore di Franco Venturi*, ed. R. Ajello *et al.* (Naples, 1985); Richard B. Sher, *Church and University in the Scottish Enlightenment: The Moderate literati of Edinburgh* (Princeton, 1985); John Gascoigne, *Cambridge in the Age of the Enlightenment: Science, Religion and Politics from the Restoration to the French Revolution* (Cambridge, 1989) and *Joseph Banks and the English Enlightenment: Useful Knowledge and Polite Culture* (Cambridge, 1994); Peter Harrison, *'Religion' and the Religious in the English Enlightenment* (Cambridge, 1990); B.W. Young, *Religion and Enlightenment in Eighteenth-Century England: Theological Debate from Locke to Burke* (Oxford, 1998).

[5] J.G.A. Pocock, *Barbarism and Religion: Enlightened History and Gibbon's Decline and Fall of the Roman Empire. Vol. I: The Enlightenments of Edward Gibbon* (Cambridge, 1999).

[6] *The Letters of Edward Gibbon*, ed. J.E. Norton (London, 1956), Vol. 3, pp. 161,167–8, 176, 183–5, 216 (on Burke), 227, 229–30, 257–8.

[7] See in particular Burke's *Letters on a Regicide Peace*; J.G.A. Pocock, *Virtue, Commerce and History* (Cambridge, 1985), pp. 208–10; and *The French Revolution and the Creation of Modern Political Culture*, Vol. 3, ed. Francois Furet and Mona Ozouf (Oxford, 1989), pp. 31–5, 42–3.

Decline and Fall must be associated although it departs from them, all record the emergence from medieval and post-Reformation conditions of a 'Europe' of stable sovereign states, connected to form a 'confederacy' or 'republic' by patterns of *jus gentium* and *raison d'état*, commerce, manners and enlightenment.[8] The culminating point to which these histories look is the monarchy of Louis XIV, followed by the treaty of Utrecht in which Britain and France emerge as the dominant forms of monarchical civility. The first 'Europe' in the modern sense was as much an Anglo-French condominium as its present successor is a Franco-German; its cultural politics were conceived as the reconciliation of liberty with politeness; and the 'cosmopolitan' historiography it produced dealt primarily with the formation of the French and English monarchies out of the conditions following the papal overthrow of the Hohenstaufen. Italian and Netherlandish cities were allowed a culturally if not a politically important role, but Enlightened historians had little to say about the historic formation of the Germanic body, the Hapsburg lands or the Polish commonwealth. These cultures produced their own historians and their own Enlightenments, and there were West European historians who looked beyond Spain to America or beyond Russia to China and Japan; but the exemplary narratives of the Enlightened cosmopolis related late Roman history followed by French and English (the latter best written by Scots). This gave rise to a pattern of world history into which Amerindians, and with greater difficulty Indians, found themselves written, as 'savages' or as 'orientals'.[9]

We have reached a point at which we can confront an Enlightenment looking west with an Enlightenment looking east, deeper into the European peninsula. It is reasonable, in this perspective, to speak of a 'Utrecht Enlightenment', dateable between 1713 and 1789, with its own utopia and historical telos: a 'Europe' of French manners and English liberty, in which sovereign civil societies were associated in a pattern of treaties and commerce, able to restrain the disruptive forces of religion and conduct their own wars within the disciplines of *jus gentium* and European civility. This utopia did not last, and by the end of his life Burke was lamenting the destruction of Europe by forces including a revolutionary spirit, at once profoundly anti-religious and a new religion, which had returned Europe to the condition of spiritual warfare from which Enlightened civil society had been designed as an escape. We may trace the destruction of Utrecht further back, to the decades in which the great Enlightened histories were being written. The war of 1756–63 enlarged conflict beyond the limits within which the Utrecht order was effective. Anglo-French rivalry exploded beyond Europe and the Spanish succession, to become a contest for empire in North America, India and the global ocean; and there

---

[8] Pocock, *The Enlightenments of Edward Gibbon*, chs. 1, 3.
[9] Pocock, *Barbarism and Religion, Vol. II: Narratives of Civil Government* (Cambridge, forthcoming).

broke out a coincident struggle for hegemony between Austria, Prussia and Russia in that trans-Elbian Europe of which cis-Alpine and Paduan Enlightenment knew so little and had so little to say.[10] A number of consequences may now be entered upon the historical scenario; one of them those partitions of Poland which Burke considered a disaster for Europe on the same scale as the French Revolution. The British handling of the Seven Years War and its aftermath left the Hanoverian kingdom diplomatically isolated and without a European ally when the revolution in the American colonies led to a renewal of war between the maritime empires. Though the colonies giving access to the Mississippi valley were lost, empire survived in Canada and the Caribbean, India and the ocean, and Britain remained insulated as a maritime super-power from the revolutionary consequences into which the debts resulting from the American war plunged the states of Europe. The Dutch *ancien régime* collapsed in 1787, the French in 1789; but though revolution had been feared and may have threatened in 1780–83 — the years of the Yorkshire Association, the Irish Volunteers and the Gordon Riots — the British state survived Franco Venturi's *prima crisi* and *caduta dell'Ancien Régime*,[11] leaving it useful both to affirm and to deny that it was an *ancien régime* at all. Profound changes, social, structural and ideological, of course ensued, and the half-century following the American war presents a British equivalent of Reinhart Koselleck's *Sattelzeit*.[12] This is a historical context in which to view the work and significance of Jeremy Bentham, and to make him a pivotal figure is to stress the differences between what was happening in the European islands and the experiences in which revolution and counter-revolution were engulfing the peninsula and the heartlands. When differences occur it is useless to condemn them as exceptionalisms.

This essay will not attempt to establish a relationship between Bentham's work and its historical context.[13] Better than Paine or Godwin with whom Venturi sought to bracket him, Bentham indeed fits into the role of a British *philosophe*, in search of new principles on which society might be constructed, and offering himself to government and public as the engineer of that reconstruction. But his background was more Tory than Whig; he took part in drafting the government's reply to the American Declaration of Independence; he looked on the rights of man as nonsense on stilts; and one context in which to view his very un-Christian thinking is that affirmation of Christian utilitarian-

---

[10] Larry Wolff, *Inventing Eastern Europe: The Map of Civilisation on the Mind of the Enlightenment* (Stanford, 1994).

[11] The subtitles of Vols. III and IV of Venturi's *Settecento Riformatore*.

[12] For this concept, as central to Koselleck's *Begriffsgeschichte*, see Melvin Richter, *The History of Political and Social Concepts: A Critical Introduction* (New York, 1995), pp. 36–8.

[13] Professor Burns will recollect a seminar at the Folger Shakespeare Library, when he remarked that it was his duty to persuade me that Bentham was a human being, and I replied that I should be glad to be convinced that he was not a monster from inner space.

ism which forms part of the abandonment of neo-classical whiggish thinking
that begins after 1780. William Paley, and after him Adam Smith, were the
philosophes of the post-revolutionary order.[14] This essay is concerned more
with historiography than with philosophy, and aims to use the former genre in
establishing the British role in the intellectual history of Revolutionary Europe.
From Venturi — but still with Gibbon in mind — I turn to the second figure
whose thought I desire to use, and at the same time comment on, in establishing
this scenario.

Isaiah Berlin — English, Russian and Jewish, and in that sense a great
European — propounded a pattern of Enlightenment and Counter-
Enlightenment, Revolution and Counter-Revolution, from which this essay
derives much of its title.[15] He did not originate it, since the entire literature of
German historicism lies behind it, but he employed it in establishing a scenario
of Enlightenment originating in France and travelling eastward, undergoing as
it went transformations whose shock waves were felt all the way back to its
points of origin. The aim of this essay is not to challenge Berlin's narrative, but
to enquire whether the same or some other narrative is needed when we pursue
the history of Enlightenment and Revolution westward into the Atlantic islands.
In the beginning — we may simplify Berlin's narrative as running — there was
the heavenly city of the eighteenth-century philosophers: the creed of a uniform,
unchanging and rational human nature, from which the *philosophes* hoped to
draw law-based explanations of all historical phenomena. It is possible to
narrate a journey from this premise, leading both to the utopian progressivism
of Condorcet and to the intellectual terrorism of the Jacobins who pursued him
to his death; at which point the classical Enlightenment appears radically
divided against itself. Far eastward in Germany, however, there was occurring
a Counter-Enlightenment, to be particularly associated with the name of Herder,
in which the moral will of human groups constantly embodied and created itself
in acts rather poetic than philosophical, leading to the creation of cultures,
nations and states, so that human nature existed not as a uniformly operating
substance but as a series of self-performative acts, constituting a history.[16] This
was to an important extent an anti-colonial ideology, representing first the
rebellion of the German imagination against French cultural hegemony and

[14] For the idea of a counter-revolutionary turn, in response to the American rather
than the French revolution, see Ch. 8 of *The Varieties of British Political Thought,
1500–1800*, ed. J.G.A. Pocock, Gordon J. Schochet and Lois G. Schwoerer (Cambridge,
1993); Eliga H. Gould, 'American Independence and Britain's Counter-Revolution',
Past and Present, 154 (1997), pp. 107–41.

[15] Several of Berlin's key writings on this theme — 'The Counter-Enlightenment'
(1980), 'Herder and the Enlightenment' (1976), 'The Hedgehog and the Fox' (1978) —
are collected in Isaiah Berlin, ed. Henry Hardy and Roger Hausheer, *The Proper Study
of Mankind* (London, 1997; New York, 1998).

[16] See further Isaiah Berlin, *Vico and Herder: Two Studies in the History of Ideas*
(London, 1976) and *Against the Current: Essays in the History of Ideas* (London, 1979).

later that of the Russian imagination against German hegemony: the hegemony in each case being perceived as that of a rational state form over creative and poetic powers which it repressed. French hegemony was experienced first as that of the Enlightened *ancien régime*, later as that of the far more aggressive and immediate revolutionary Empire; and Counter-Enlightenment became Counter-Revolution when it was an instrument in the creation of powerful combinations of state, *Volk* and nation which met the Revolution and threw it back — historical forms as new and revolutionary as those which they countered.

Are there comparable phenomena to be found in the western approaches to Enlightened Europe? The belief in a uniform human nature is certainly there; it was a premise of both jurisprudence and philosophy, whether the reasons which led to knowledge of it were Platonic or Lockean. But in the writings of David Hume, it consists of little more than a collection of benchmarks from which we set out in search of the bewildering diversity of the historical phenomena that arise from it, while in the stadial theories of Adam Smith and his colleagues human nature is shown reorganizing, developing and even transforming itself as it passes through the four stages of history, so that antique man or the contemporary savage are almost impossible for moderns to understand. If there are laws of human nature — John Millar said that Smith was a Newton where Montesquieu had been a Bacon[17] — they guide us in the labyrinth of history, but do not reduce it to the mere map of their workings; for narrative remains paramount, and in the narrative of historical action humans are led by the mysteries of the human heart to behave in ways we would not have expected of them. Scottish conjectural history was, almost by definition, never quite reducible to civil history or civil history to it, and Adam Smith and Hugh Blair, when functioning as literary critics, insisted that it should not be, as it easily might distract the reader from following the narrative. 'The science of the legislator'[18] functioned in the context of history as we found it, and never reduced history to itself.

If we take Edward Gibbon as a leading or indicative figure in Anglo-Scottish Enlightened thought — he had few if any disciples, and the image of him as a solitary need not be altogether abandoned — we find his first work, the *Essai sur l'Etude de la Littérature*, begun when he was twenty-one and published in 1762, to be a critique of d'Alembert's *Discours Préliminaire à l'Encyclopédie*, of which 'immense compilation' he never formed a high opinion.[19] He was

[17] John Millar, *Historical View of the English Government* (London, 1818), Vol. II, pp. 429–30, n.

[18] Knud Haakonssen, *The Science of a Legislator: The Natural Jurisprudence of David Hume and Adam Smith* (Cambridge, 1981).

[19] The *Essai sur l'Etude de la Littérature* is to be found in *The Miscellaneous Works of Edward Gibbon*, ed. Lord Sheffield (London, 1814), Vol. IV, pp. 1–94. A modern edition is desirable. For Gibbon on the *Encyclopédie* see *Edward Gibbon: The History*

offended — his word is 'provoked'[20] — by d'Alembert's apparently rigorous separation between the faculties of reason and memory, from which it seemed to follow that the philosophy erected by the former was inherently superior to the history dependent on the latter, and that a natural history of the human mind was preferable to the civil history of its actual but accidental experience. Gibbon replied that the study of history entailed all the faculties of the mind, in particular those of 'the imagination and the judgment', and that the phenomena of history were similarly produced by the interaction between them, so that the historian needed the critical capacity to interpret human artefacts. History might be the search for causes; there might be laws underlying it, like Dangeau's laws of probability underlying the fall of the dice; but the historian's supreme pleasure was the ironic observation of the paradoxes of human behaviour.

One would hesitate before calling Edmund Burke an ironist, but there is a perceptible connection between Gibbon's youthful insistence that the complexity of history is always paramount and his Burkean response to the French Revolution when he heard of it in Lausanne nearly thirty years later. Here we have a mindset, post-Calvinist and increasingly Anglo-Hanoverian, which defended history against philosophy and ended up counter-revolutionary — in the sense that it was instinctively opposed to revolution, not that it set up one kind of revolution against another. By 'Counter-Enlightenment', are we to mean one brand of Enlightenment in opposition to another, or a fixed antipathy to Enlightenment in some final sense of the term? Gibbon's defence of history, and his practice of it in association with other historians, went on within Enlightenment, no less than did the philosophy he criticized in d'Alembert (who was nearer to agreeing with him than we may suppose). This may seem to link him with Counter-Enlightenment in the former sense rather than the latter, but does not mean that he was ever obliged to re-invent Enlightenment in a Counter-Revolutionary sense, as may have been the case with some leaders of German thinking; nor is there any way of linking him, or Burke, with the neo-Catholicism of de Maistre. Burke looked back to a Europe of piety and manners, not of faith; both he and Gibbon were overtaken by the Evangelical wave which is the true English Counter-Revolution.

Gibbon advocated history against philosophy, but the historical discipline which he practised and defended was learned and clerical, a product of *l'étude de la littérature* and *des belles lettres*; of the huge wealth of texts and scholarship, ancient, medieval and Renaissance, which in d'Alembert's view had divorced the progress of the mind in Europe from what it would have been in nature. Gibbon joined with those — clerics, humanists, jurists, philosophers — who inhabited this document-based history, and situated himself in a rooted and

---

of the Decline and Fall of the Roman Empire, ed. David Womersley (London, 1994), Vol. I, p. 765 (ch. XX, n. 130, the concluding footnote).

[20] *Edward Gibbon: Memoirs of My Life*, ed. Georges A. Bonnard (New York, 1969), p. 99.

continuing *république des lettres*. In so doing, he separated himself (knowingly) from the *philosophes* and *gens des lettres* who would be perceived as having something to do with Revolution, and at the same time (quite unknowingly) from the forerunners of Isaiah Berlin's Counter-Enlightenment and Counter-Revolution. His visit to Paris in 1763, when he worried about the provinciality of his Lausannais-English French but moved freely enough in Parisian culture to decide that in the end he did not belong to it, may usefully be contrasted with the visit in 1769 paid by Johann Gottfried Herder,[21] who found that his ear for spoken French did not permit him to follow what was going on in salon conversation, and returned to his *Heimat* to continue the discovery of the *Volk*, their self-creation in custom and song, and a vision of history as the autonomy of all self-creative endeavour. In this contrast the westward and eastward movements of Enlightenment and Counter-Enlightenment are made visible. Gibbon departed in search of erudition, a history already in place, deposited in the great archive of European and Roman-Mediterranean literature, and undergoing scrutiny by a scholarship already possessed of a past. Herder departed in search of what he was to describe as 'yet another philosophy of history', an invention of invention to be undertaken on altogether new grounds. Gibbon went in search of history, we may say, Herder of historicism; and the politics of the matter is that both were rejecting the cultural primacy of Paris and its enterprises, and preparing the way for rejections of the Revolution, when its consequences were known, as different as Burke's from Fichte's.

Gibbon's turn towards history was not a retreat into Englishness — the erudition with which he aligned himself was cosmopolitan — though it did entail a decision to cease thinking in French and write a great history in great English; but it led to a Burkean conclusion, the instant decision of the ruling structures of the Atlantic archipelago to have nothing to do with the French Revolution from the moment of its outbreak. In military terms, insular Europe was able to maintain this posture, and thus keep its interactions with the revolutionary idea down to a minimum; in peninsular Europe, however, and in the heartlands beyond it, invasion and occupation by the revolutionary empire — intellectually fertile as its Soviet successor was not — compelled the most complex responses by political structures, theories of state, and even (a product characteristic of the era) philosophies of history. As a result, the intellectual history of peninsular and heartland Europe came to be dominated by the grand themes of revolution and counter-revolution, Enlightenment and Counter- Enlightenment; and the grand theme of Isaiah Berlin's writings — the movement from enlightened rationalism to romantic historicism and the triumph of the moral will — came to dominate this picture while being included in it, though in fact it has been a global force reaching beyond Europe and

[21] See Anthony J. La Vopa, 'Herder's *Publikum*: Language, Print and Sociability in Eighteenth-Century Germany', *Eighteenth-Century Studies*, XXIX(1) (1995), pp. 5–24.

Russia into the colonial and post-colonial history of the planet. Europe and Russia being marginal to one another, the history of the former in the era of revolution and counter-revolution came to be largely a Franco-German history, consisting of Napoleonic intrusion and Prussian response, with the great philosophers of idealism playing their part — for Burke's perception that the powers of the mind were seeking control of history was all too accurate.

In insular Europe and the Atlantic archipelago — where, to use Venturi's words, the rhythm was already different — no such intimate dialectic between opposites occurred, in the absence of occupation and liberation; and the possibility of a British exceptionalism grew much stronger for the lack of such an experience. The Napoleonic episode obliged the dialectic between revolutionary empire and romantic nationalism to become the definition of European history, while the British, spared that experience by the distant line of storm-beaten ships, saw no need of a general or philosophical history of Europe to explain themselves to themselves, or of a historicist idealism to explain the primacy of their own will (while they had one). Burke had not been an English exceptionalist, but equally was not the man to write a comprehensive history of that Europe with which he was so much concerned; after him, however, the English were more concerned to study their own history to understand why there had not been a British revolution than to study that of Europe to explain what had happened there. By the middle of the next century they had returned to the history of their autonomous structures, and Macaulay was using 1642 and 1688 to explain why they had not had a 1789 and would not have an 1848 — a problem and a solution to which we still adhere. But this left the history of 'Europe' to define itself in French and German terms which had nothing to say to, or of, them. An essentialism confronted an exceptionalism; both were spurious, but remained unresolved.

This is to speak of the philosophical historiography of post-revolutionary Europe in mainly Franco-German terms; an approach so far from needing justification that we must remind ourselves that it is not the only one. An alternative, closer to eighteenth-century predilections, took shape in and beyond that Lausanne where Gibbon had lived at the beginning and end of his productive life: that great enterprise in Franco-Swiss and Franco-Protestant historiography begun by Germaine de Staël and Benjamin Constant[22] and continued by François Guizot and (perhaps) Alexis de Tocqueville. This we might almost call the Enlightened Restoration; it was in so many ways a review and transformation of the account of European history constructed by the great narrators of the eighteenth century. Theirs as we saw had been an Atlantic Europe, produced by the encounter between France and the maritime powers over the Spanish succession. It was of course de Staël who saw that Germany, no less

---

[22] For recent work on this subject, see Bianca Fontana, *Benjamin Constant and the Post-Revolutionary Mind* (Cambridge, 1991); Martin Thom, *Republics, Nations and Tribes* (London, 1995).

than England, needed to be drawn more fully into the self-image of Enlightened Europe; but to perceive a problem is not immediately to resolve or annul it, and Guizot's magisterial *History of Civilisation in Europe* — of which we have recently been reminded by Larry Siedentop's edition[23] — is still a history, like Voltaire's or Robertson's, of the monarchies, confederations and churches shaped out of Western feudal society, one more Frankish than Austrasian, in which post-Hohenstaufen and Lutheran Germany plays a visible but still marginal role. It concludes where the Utrecht Enlightenment began, with a confrontation between England and France, and this is where we find Guizot organizing the history of Europe as (in the fullest sense) a history of ideas. He distinguishes European culture into its Roman, Christian and barbaric components, medieval political culture into its monarchical, noble and urban components, at every point according to the idea of each (if Guizot had an English equivalent it would have to be Coleridge) and at the climax of his lectures he explains that the structure of the French kingdom has been such that each component exists independently of and at tension with the others, so that its idea has been able to develop and exert its energies to the full. In England, by contrast, the several principles have from the start been associated and even mixed with each other, so that the structure of the English mind in historic action has been inherently more pragmatic than idealist.[24] I have not noticed that Guizot applies this analysis to German history, or to Spanish, or to Dutch.

Now in this comparison of French and English cultures we are plainly to recognize Gibbon's encounter with d'Alembert, when he complained that French philosophy divided the faculties of the mind with hegemonic and anti-historical consequences, and himself sought with Burkean consequences to re-associate them in the study of history. We are also to hear the voice of Burke, proclaiming that in the revolutionary regression the energies of the French mind have destructively liberated themselves from the civilizing disciplines of society and history, as has not happened in England and ought not to have happened in the civility of Europe. Guizot stands in an interesting relation to his own analysis. On the one hand he is visibly in sympathy with the qualities he ascribes to the English; he is in a sense reversing the analysis of Hume, in which English liberty was to be moderated by the civility of France (though Hume would have regarded the history of the idea with extreme scepticism).[25] In his later work, Guizot embarked to his credit on the study of revolution in

---

[23] Larry Siedentop, *François Guizot: The History of Civilization in Europe* (London, 1997).

[24] *Guizot*, ed. Siedentop, pp. 228–31.

[25] For the background to Hume on France and England, see particularly Nicholas Phillipson, *Hume* (London, 1989); *Political Discourse in Early Modern Britain*, ed. Nicholas Phillipson and Quentin Skinner (Cambridge, 1993), Chs. 14–16; and Phillipson in *The Varieties of British Political Thought, 1500–1800*, ed. Pocock, Schochet and Schwoerer, pp. 240–5.

seventeenth-century England, though whether he succeeded in regarding that as a European rather than a national phenomenon I will not enquire; perhaps he had the sense to consider national peculiarity as itself a product of history, instead of seeking to deny its existence. On the other hand, however — in opposition to all of this — his final conclusion is that the hegemony of the idea, released into Europe by the special structure of French history, has made the French people and their collective mind the unchallengeable rulers and shapers of the history of Europe — a conclusion, by the way, with which the very different intelligence of Joseph de Maistre concurred.[26] It is the idea which reigns, and France is the cradle of the idea. Other cultures, as we know all too well, were to make the same claim for themselves; but Gibbon, Burke and Guizot join in furnishing an explanation why Britain would not be among them. It had not been the business of English or Scottish Enlightenment to release the creative and destructive energies of the mind, but to contain them within society and history, as all Enlightenments had once sought to contain the energies of religion. If Revolution and Counter-Revolution meant that only a history of such energies could narrate and explain the history of Europe, then the British had no wish to write such a history, or to be part of it.

Coleridge's *On the Constitution of Church and State According to the Idea of Each* does indeed organize an ideal English history, in which the energies of landed inheritance, commercial enterprise and reflective intelligence are distinguished and each is provided with its idea.[27] His purpose, however, is consonant with Guizot's, that of showing the three ideas as participant in a mixed constitution — not unlike that of *His Majesty's Answer to the Nineteen Propositions of Parliament*, written on the eve of civil war two centuries before[28] — so that no one of them will break up the fountains of the great deep[29] by escaping from its association with the others. In executing this purpose, however, Coleridge does not employ like Guizot a restated Enlightenment history of western Europe, but falls back on the problems whose resolution or persistence furnish the classic themes of English history. Having himself travelled from the revolutionary fringes of Rational Dissent in the 1790s to a position deeply if idiosyncratically Anglican forty years on, Coleridge addresses yet again the question of the ecclesiology of the Church of England as by law established;

[26] *Guizot*, ed. Siedentop, pp. 231–45; Joseph de Maistre, *Considerations on France*, ed. Richard A. Lebrun (Cambridge, 1994), pp. 9, 21–2.

[27] John Morrow, *Coleridge's Political Thought: Property, Morality and the Limits of Traditional Discourse* (London, 1990); *Coleridge's Writings on Political Society*, ed. John Morrow (Princeton, 1991), pp. 152–220.

[28] Michael J. Mendle, *Dangerous Positions: Mixed Government, the Estates of the Realm, and the Answer to the XIX Propositions* (Alabama, 1985); C.C. Weston and J.R. Greenberg, *Subjects and Sovereigns: The Grand Controversy over Legal Sovereignty in Stuart England* (Cambridge, 1981).

[29] Edmund Burke, *Reflections on the Revolution in France*, ed. J.G.A. Pocock (Indianapolis, 1987), p. 51.

but he uses it to address the problem, at once Enlightened and Counter-Enlightened, of ensuring that the English critical intellect does not move beyond Dissent to assume the character of Venturi's *philosophes* or Burke's revolutionaries. In proposing that the energies of the mind and the clerisy which executes them be constituted as a National Church endowed out of the nation's material substance, he delineates the alliance (very much a structure of class) which was to keep Anglo-British letters and learning the preserve of an independently contributing mandarinate, an Establishment embracing its own Dissent, until it was torn down by that belated bourgeois revolutionary Margaret Thatcher, bent on subjecting the National Church to the powers of state and market. The point for our purposes, however, is that Coleridge locates the history of the idea in England's dialectic with itself, less in Kant's or Hegel's debate with French Enlightenment and Revolution than in a tradition of Cambridge Platonism submerged by Locke and Newton at the time of the revolution of 1688 and now re-emerging.[30] After forty years of Revolution and Empire, Counter-Revolution and Restoration, English history was to explain itself by itself, not by constructing a history of Europe that would include itself.

We have reached a point from which it is possible to begin explaining the zero-sum relation which has arisen between English–British history and the history of what has been allowed to term itself 'Europe': the great antagonisms between Enlightenment and Counter-Enlightenment, revolution and state, France and Germany in peninsular Europe, Germany and Russia in its heartland. This history did not explain England to itself, and there have been those — evidently including John Stuart Mill[31] — who have thought English history parochial in consequence; to which it may be replied that history has no single centre and is not divided into metropolises and peripheries. Because of this sea-borne division between insular and peninsular Europe, however, there can be said to have arisen a division between histories, one of which has been allowed to represent itself as the history of the whole; while that of England, not explained by the histories of the peninsular sub-continent, did not in the nineteenth or twentieth centuries discover a larger context in which to include itself (there is no obligation to discover such a context, but it can aid self-understanding). Attempts to construct British history in an oceanic and imperial setting shipwrecked on the immoveable obstacle of the United States, the great anti-self to Hanoverian and Victorian Britain; Seeley's attempt at a pan-British history became a history of the Anglo-American relationship, in which the

---

[30] Morrow, *Coleridge's Political Thought*, pp. 158–9, 163–4.

[31] Stefan Collini, Donald Winch and John Burrow, *That Noble Science of Politics: A Study in Nineteenth-Century Intellectual History* (Cambridge, 1983), p. 144; J.W. Burrow, *Whigs and Liberals: Continuity and Change in English Political Thought* (Oxford, 1988), *passim*.

history of the neo-Britains or colonies of settlement did not find a shaping role.[32] The British state and its empire became caught up in the appalling wars and revolutions of a Franco-German-Russian 'Europe', whose history it did not explain and which did not explain it to itself. As this 'Europe' seeks to end its wars by reconstituting itself as a Franco-German consortium and local embodiment of the global market, it legitimately demands that Britain join in this enterprise, but demands less legitimately that British history be rewritten in what are imperatively, and therefore imprecisely, insisted upon as 'European' terms. It is partly for the paradoxical reason that this history is seen as lying outside Franco-German history that the demand implies that it shall cease being a self-explanatory 'British' history; but the 'European' project is sufficiently part of a larger project of globalization to ensure that the same demand is served on all constituent parties. Autonomous histories are assumed to be the histories of 'nation states', and 'nation states' are assumed to be no longer meaningful and to have no meaningful pasts.

'British history' is in fact that of a plurality of 'nations', which may or may not have been durably associated in a single or plural state form. Confronted with a multi-national state, the post-modern political mind seeks first to dissolve it into its constituent nations, after which it pronounces that 'the nation state' is obsolete; from which we may infer that its true aim is the demolition of the state, and that 'nation' is the name of a mere decoy duck. At this point, what has been termed 'the new British history' takes on a significant character. It has taken shape as a project of recounting the problematic history of nation- and state-formation in insular Europe, otherwise termed 'the Atlantic archipelago', as a plural history in which several nations come into being, take on political forms, and are or are not durably associated in a unitary state or association of states. The term 'British' is both an adjective which may conveniently denote the enterprise of unification or association, and a means of indicating the possibility that a larger nationality may have emerged at some points of this process. Here, confusingly, the British Old Left has re-asserted itself, seeking to use 'the new British history' as a means to 'the break-up of Britain' and the reconstitution of its components as quasi-autonomous regions of the new European (no longer Soviet) empire;[33] we observe the pursuit of the old doomed Marxist strategy of pushing the capitalist revolution to its final triumph in the hope that a socialist revolution will ensue. We may leave this strategy to its fate,

---

[32] Deborah Wormell, *Sir John Seeley and the Uses of History* (Cambridge, 1980); Eliga H. Gould, 'A Virtual Nation: Greater Britain and the British Implications of the American Revolution', *American Historical Review* (forthcoming).

[33] Tom Nairn, *The Breakup of Britain* (London, 1981); Tom Nairn, *Faces of Nationalism: Janus Revisited* (London, 1997). Cf. Raphael Samuel, *Island Stories: Unravelling Britain: Theatres of Memory, Volume II*, ed. Alison Light with Sally Alexander and Gareth Stedman Jones (London, 1998). See also Thom, *Republics, Nations and Tribes*.

and consider 'British history' in the context of the historiography of Europe: that is, as a means of enlarging the last-named context beyond the eastward-facing dialectic of Revolution and Counter-Revolution with which this enquiry has been concerned.

The successful American revolution of 1776–83 and the failed Irish revolution of 1798 will appear in this narrative as leading to the Union of Britain and Ireland in 1800; the momentous step by which the Hanoverian regime secured itself against the crisis of European revolution, but ensured its own transformation when Catholic Emancipation in 1829 brought on the end of the 'long eighteenth century' in English and British history. The last Age of Union — in the periodization of that history which is emerging — ends in 1921, with the Irish revolution that brings about the only major transformation of a state form to occur in Western Europe as a consequence of the First World War. Processes going on as these words are being written include the statecraft by which a sovereign United Kingdom and Irish Republic ally themselves to impose a de facto condominium on the six counties of Northern Ireland, and the experiments in devolution which may reconstitute the United Kingdom as a more confederal structure. These are acts of sovereignty which may, or equally may not, point towards the abdication of sovereignty in face of the post-political and post-democratic demands of Europeanization and globalization. One need not predict the outcome, but need only define the problem, in order to point out that the history of insular Europe is still going on, and that the doctrine that these islands are part of Europe entails a re-writing and pluralization of the history to be termed European: one in which the history of Revolution and Counter-Revolution loses nothing by finding itself in company with other histories. If Britain is to be a component of 'Europe', there must be a 'Europe' whose history can be written as partly of British making, in which process 'Britain' can be perceived as making itself. It does not appear, in the light of such perceptions as Isaiah Berlin's, that peninsular and heartland 'Europe' meet these specifications. The history of the Atlantic archipelago steps forward as an alternative possibility; that some want it written as a means to the breakup of Britain and the winding up of its history increases the Eurosceptic's doubts as to what the 'European' enterprise is meant to achieve. A European Britain should entail a British Europe. If such a history cannot be the history of 'Europe' as an entity, the conclusion may be drawn that 'Europe' is not an entity, but a convergence of histories; not their sum but their product, neither their extinction nor their transcendence.

J.G.A. Pocock   THE JOHNS HOPKINS UNIVERSITY

VIRTUOUS COMMERCE AND FREE THEOLOGY: POLITICAL ECONOMY AND THE DISSENTING ACADEMIES 1750–1800

Gregory Claeys*

Abstract: Eighteenth-century Dissenting Academies provided a liberal education oriented towards practical and commercial subjects, and began the earliest sustained development of political economy teaching in Britain. Leading tutors, like Joseph Priestley and Richard Price, as well as students like William Godwin, were however divided on key issues such as luxury, and the degree to which machinery and the division of labour could be extended without harming the labouring classes.

Throughout much of the eighteenth century the great universities of England blithely ignored the commercial revolution around them. The case was rather different in the Dissenting academies of this period, where those unable to subscribe to the Thirty-Nine Article religious test of the Church of England could attain both a high educational standard and the sort of practical training denied them elsewhere. Here their teachers, often educated in Scotland, Holland or elsewhere abroad, were often the finest minds of each generation of Dissenters, as well as, in the eighteenth century, the leading liberal or Rational Dissenters of the nation. Keen to acknowledge theological controversy, they also acknowledged the demands and ambition of the aspiring middle classes, who were chiefly the students at these institutions, as well as the importance of commerce to the prosperity of the Dissenting cause generally.

By the 1760s the Dissenting tutors possessed a unique vantage point on the influence of commercial development upon society and manners derived from their own proximity to the commercial classes, their liberal and reforming outlook on politics, and their devotion to religious freedom. Unhampered by traditional curricular requirements, they adapted their own interests only to the expectations of the parents of their pupils, who for the most part demanded only the most modern and practical approach possible. They thus compensated for their small numbers and insufficient funding with a rigour, breadth and enthusiasm which profoundly impressed generations of Dissenting as well as Anglican students. These went on to make considerable contributions to virtually every area of eighteenth- and nineteenth-century life, and included writers like Oliver Goldsmith and Daniel Defoe, engineers and manufacturers like the iron

* Department of History, Royal Holloway, University of London, Egham, Surrey TW20 0EX, UK.

masters John and William Wilkinson, the mathematician and pamphleteer
Richard Price, the scientist and theologian Joseph Priestley, the economist and
divine Thomas Malthus, and many others.

The products of the academies thus became the most influential section of
the rising Dissenting middle class, whose economic power was considerable
by the end of the century. Nor were they unaware of what they conceived to be
their special social mission. As the tutor John Aikin put it in 1790, the Dissenters belonged 'to the most virtuous, the most enlightened, the most independent
part of the community, the *middle class*. If this nation is ever to improve, or
even if it is to retain, the freedom it possesses, to this class alone must it be
indebted for the blessing.'[1] But the ideal of the academies was never to create
a merely mercantile middle class. As Thomas Barnes put it at the opening of
Manchester Academy in 1786, the provision of a taste for letters to those
intended for a commercial life would 'highly improve and finish the mercantile
character', saving them from the 'low debasing pleasures' to which merchants
were exposed, providing students with 'sweet entertainment and consolation in
retirement, and in old age', and generally rendering them 'more amiable, more
useful, more happy'.[2]

Despite their achievements the Dissenters have been greatly neglected. Far
too little is known even about such major and cohesive groups as the Unitarians,
whose theology verged upon deism, and who came to make one of the most
prominent Dissenting contributions to British intellectual life.[3] Little has been
written about the educational system of Dissent and the causes of its comparatively great influence.[4] Any investigation of the subject is hampered by a variety
of problems, however. Many academies were ephemeral establishments lasting
only a few years, often closing their doors when tutors moved or died, changing
their location and names as demand dictated, and leaving few records of
curricula, lectures or even the names of tutors themselves. Despite such obstacles, it is possible to obtain some picture of how the academies grappled with

[1] John Aikin, *An Address to the Dissidents of England on Their Late Defeat* (London,
1790), p. 18.
[2] Thomas Barnes, *A Discourse Delivered at the Commencement of the Manchester
Academy* (Warrington, 1786), pp. 23–4.
[3] On Dissent see generally Michael Watts, *The Dissenters. Vol. 1: From the Reformation to the French Revolution* (Oxford, 1978). Also useful is John Wilkes, 'The
Transformation of Dissent: a Review of the Change from the Seventeenth to the
Eighteenth Centuries', in *The Dissenting Tradition*, ed. C.R. Cole and M.E. Moody
(Athens, 1975), pp. 108–22. The standard study of Dissenting social theory in this period
remains Anthony Lincoln, *Some Political and Social Ideas of English Dissent 1763–1800*
(Cambridge, 1938).
[4] The chief texts are: Irene Parker, *Dissenting Academies in England* (Cambridge,
1914); H. McLachlan, *English Education under the Test Acts. Being the History of the
Nonconformist Academies* (Manchester, 1931); J.W. Ashley Smith, *The Birth of Modern
Education. The Contribution of the Dissenting Academies 1660–1800* (London, 1954).

the problems of theorizing the evolution of commercial society. The views of the most prominent Dissenting economic writers who also taught at academies — Richard Price and Joseph Priestley — were published, in the latter case directly from lecture notes. Some of the teachings of other tutors like Andrew Kippis, Abraham Rees, Gilbert Wakefield and William Frend, as well as the economic ideas of their students, can also be reconstructed to some degree in order to fill out this picture. Before examining these and situating them in the wider debate on commerce in the second half of the eighteenth century, however, let us first briefly consider the background and social history of the academies themselves.

I
The Academies

The evolution of a system of separate schools for Dissenters in the late seventeenth and early eighteenth centuries resulted primarily from Restoration efforts to curb the intellectual opportunities of the Puritans, especially through the Act of Uniformity (1662) and the Five Mile Act (1665). The former required all schoolmasters in public or private schools to declare their support for the established liturgy, and to apply for a teaching licence from the leading cleric in the diocese. The latter strictly forbade Nonconformists (as the Dissenters were usually called until the mid-nineteenth century) to teach at all under penalty of a £40 fine. The immediate effect of this legislation was to provoke the resignation of some 2000 rectors and vicars, but among its principal objects was the exclusion of the Dissenters from Oxford and Cambridge. At the former students were required to subscribe to the Thirty-Nine Articles upon entry and to take the Oath of Supremacy, while at Cambridge most degrees could only be received upon declaration of membership of the Church of England.

Dissenters who sought higher education for their sons thenceforth had the choice of sending them to Scotland, the Netherlands or elsewhere abroad, or of establishing their own institutions of instruction. The latter became possible largely because existing legislation was not rigidly enforced. At least twenty and perhaps as many as one hundred and fifty ejected ministers and schoolmasters opened schools of one type or another. An Act of Toleration eased the situation, though failing to clarify fully the status of such schools. But in only one important case, that of Philip Doddridge at Northampton Academy in 1733, was a prosecution brought for teaching without a licence, and here Doddridge emerged victorious. By 1690 at least twenty-three academies existed, the majority of which were conducted by former Fellows or Tutors from Oxford and Cambridge, who often attempted to continue a classically-based system of education, using the same texts as the universities and teaching in Latin until well into the eighteenth century.[5] For a time, at least, the academies prospered.

---

[5] On the origins of the academies see e.g. Parker, *Dissenting Academies*, pp. 45–123.

Dissenters refused to allow their sons to be forced to conform at the Universities, the quality of teaching remained exceptionally high (Anglicans were soon being sent to learn there). At least half of the academies were open to those who sought some other career besides the clerical (of the three hundred and three students educated at the largest academy, Richard Frankland's, only one hundred and ten became pastors).[6]

By the end of the eighteenth century at least seventy academies had been established. Most did not last longer than twenty years, and often considerably less. By no means all of the academies were as progressive as those later associated with the Rational Dissent of Price and Priestley. One established by John Hubbard (1692–1743) and continued by Zephania Marryat (1685–1754), for example, was so strictly Calvinist that Priestley refused to attend it, going instead to the more liberal Northampton Academy run by Doddridge, where Moravian and antinomian principles had secured some hold. Others no doubt changed their character as they did their location. Frankland's Academy, for example, moved six times between 1669 and 1698, Doolittle's five times between 1672 and 1707. As a general trend the evangelicals throughout the eighteenth century attempted to restrict the academies to the training of ministers, particularly after the spread of Arianism (the belief that Christ was not wholly divine even if possessed of the divine Logos) and the even more militant Unitarianism of Priestley and Thomas Belsham (in which the separate existence of souls was altogether denied). Nonetheless the more liberal academies, such as Warrington, Manchester, Hackney and Exeter, still continued to attract students, though this became more difficult after a large number of new private schools were opened when the Dissenters were finally given the legal right to teach in 1779. Some eighteenth-century sects nonetheless still continued to maintain their own academies for as long as possible, with the Welsh Calvinists, for example, established at Abergavenny in 1754, and the Baptist Academy being kept afloat at Bristol thanks to the fund-raising efforts of the Educational Society. For some time, in fact, a Baptist university in Bristol, for law, medicine and theology, was seriously considered.[7]

A typical academy in the late seventeenth century had one tutor and twenty or thirty students, while those in the following century tended to be larger. As at the universities, students entered at a fairly young age; Defoe was fourteen on his admission to Newington Green. The course was usually four years, and included general classical knowledge, though the emphasis was often upon

[6] Watts, *The Dissenters*, pp. 264, 367; Nicholas Hans, *New Trends in Education in the Eighteenth Century* (London, 1951), p. 58; Parker, *Dissenting Academies*, pp. 48–9.

[7] Hans, *New Trends in Education*, pp. 55–6; McLachlan, *English Education*, pp. 18–19, 4–5; *The Correspondence and Diary of Philip Doddridge* (5 vols., London, 1829), Vol. 5, pp. 78–9; Thomas Rees, *History of Protestant Nonconformity in Wales* (London, 1883), p. 387; Graham Hughes, *With Freedom Fired: The Story of Robert Robinson, Cambridge Nonconformist* (London, 1955), pp. 75, 92.

theology. Defoe for example learned geography, history, 'politics as a science', mathematics, logic and natural philosophy. At other academies, such as Sheriffhales, students could concentrate on theology, law or medicine. This curriculum was gradually expanded during the eighteenth century, with a greater emphasis given to both natural science and secular subjects generally.

Northampton is a good example, since of the approximately thirty-four academies in existence in the first half of the eighteenth century, more is known about Northampton than any other. Here, around 1720, were taught geometry, algebra, Hebrew, geography, French, Latin, divinity, mechanics, hydrostatics, physics, anatomy, astronomy, English essays (Bacon, Addison and Steele were the models), history, logic and rhetoric. Geography, history, ethics and metaphysics were on some accounts not generally taught in the early academies, though on occasion they were certainly covered by private reading. According to David Bogue and James Bennett, the early nineteenth-century Dissenting historians, the ordinary seventeenth-century course did include logic and moral philosophy (Epictetus, Pufendorf and Marcus Antoninus were named) among other subjects. By what is often referred to as the third and final period (1750–1800) of the academies, secular subjects became more prevalent. Some civil law and history (chiefly of England and of Non-Conformity) were being taught at Kibworth in the 1720s. Commercial law was included in Joshua Oldfield's course at Hoxton Square in the early 1700s. Lectures on civil government and the British constitution were included at Kibworth, at Daventry Academy (1752–89), and at Northampton (re-opened between 1789 and 1798) under John Horsey, while Andrew Kippis lectured on the general principles of law and government at Hackney College (1786–96).[8]

The introduction of commerce into the curriculum at Dissenting academies during the eighteenth century was in part prepared by the popularity of numerous small, non-sectarian commercial academies which catered to the needs of merchants' sons and others interested in a practical commercial education. But their pupils also included the well-to-do and more literate. Founded in 1717 as a commercial school, the Soho Academy, for example, included among its pupils John Horne Tooke and Edmund Burke's son Richard. The course of commercial studies was often organized around a single text, such as N. Magens' *The Universal Merchant*, translated by the Dissenter William Horsey, which covered commerce, banking, credit, trade, bullion and coinage. Recourse was no doubt also frequent to works like the later *The Dictionary of Merchandize and Nomenclature in All Languages* (1803), intended for merchants and counting-house libraries. Some tutors also wrote their own text-

---

[8] Parker, *Dissenting Academies*, pp. 54–79; David Bogue and James Bennett, *History of Dissenters. From the Revolution of 1688, to the Year 1808* (4 vols., London, 1808), Vol. 2, pp. 79–81, Vol. 4, pp. 302–8; J. Ashley Smith, *The Birth of Modern Education*, p. 125; McLachlan, *English Education*, pp. 157, 160–1, 167, 247–8.

books. Thomas Mortimer, for example, instructed five pupils aged sixteen or older at his house for one hundred guineas annually, and published *The Elements of Commerce, Politics and Finances . . . Designed as a Supplement to the Education of British Youth After They Quit the Public Universities or Private Academies for his students*. On the whole, however, their concern was to teach the practical side of commerce rather than to offer any theoretical exposition of its principles. Islington Academy in 1766 taught merchants' accounting and similar subjects requisite to form the 'gentleman, scholar and man of business', while the Mercantile School, Glasgow, the City Commercial School, London, the Commercial and Mathematical School, Salford, and the Mount Pleasant School, Liverpool, were among many similar institutions offering commercial subjects in the 1790s. Complaints were nonetheless widespread that no proper institution existed for the education of British merchants. At one point a form of educational 'counting house' or mercantile university was also briefly proposed by the commercial writer Malachy Postlethwayt, who sought to begin a two-year course of studies which included foreign exchange, writing, accounting, funds and stocks, custom practices, modern languages, geography as well as the general principles of trade. This idea was also taken up by Defoe. Some political economy was taught rather later in other forms of private academy (for example at Bath in the 1790s). But this was probably comparatively unusual. More commonly the curriculum was restricted to those aspects of mathematics, geography, navigation, statistics, coinage and other sciences which had a commercial application, as well as the more direct study of commerce and trade. Where more theoretical concerns are evident (especially after mid-century) the works of Sir James Steuart appear to have been used to some extent.[9]

The most important of the Dissenting academies to take commercial subjects seriously lent its location the pleasing title of 'The Athens of the North'. Warrington Academy (1757–86) had the largest proportion of students 'intended for a life of Business and Commerce' (twenty-five percent, or a total of ninety-eight, between 1757 and 1783). At least a third of these were Anglicans, and the student body came from as far away as America and the West Indies. For the commercial course the normal period of studies was shortened to three years, and broadened to include such subjects as 'manufactures, traffick, coins'.

[9] Hans, *New Trends in Education*, pp. 87–93, 79–80; Thomas Mortimer, *The Elements of Commerce* (London, 1772), p. i; Malachy Postlethwayt, *The Merchant's Public Counting House: or, New Mercantile Institution: Wherein is Shewn, The Necessity of Young Merchants Being Bred to Trade with Greater Advantages Than They Usually Are* (London, 1750), pp. 3, 15–57. For similar eighteenth-century texts on mercantile education, see *The Tradesman's Director, or the London and County Shopkeeper's Useful Companion* (London, 1756) and William Markham, *A General Introduction to Trade and Business* (London, 1738). Defoe's scheme for a university was outlined in *Augusta Triumphans: or, the Way to Make London the Most Flourishing City in the Universe* (London, 1728).

Many of the best-known, and the most liberal, Dissenters of the eighteenth century taught at Warrington. Dr John Aikin, Doddridge's first pupil at Kibworth and a graduate of Aberdeen, became a tutor there in 1761 and introduced political philosophy and political economy into his lectures on jurisprudence. Joseph Priestley was among the staff between 1761 and 1767, while the Rev. William Enfield (1741–97) lectured on commerce after 1770 (he was tutor until 1783 and a major contributor to Dissenting periodicals). Jacob Bright also taught commerce here between 1763 and 1783. Elsewhere similar types of lectures were developed in the final decades of the eighteenth century. At Manchester Academy Thomas Barnes (1746–1810) taught the history and principles of commerce, commercial laws and regulations, and commercial ethics (including oaths, contracts and commutative justice). At Hackney Richard Price lectured on a variety of related subjects, while Exeter Academy (founded in 1760) followed the example of Warrington by introducing commerce into its curriculum (and one account lists over a quarter of its students as interested in commerce and trade). Most academies seem to have taught commercial subjects over several years, with the ages fifteen to seventeen being recommended as the optimum period for commencing the subject.[10]

Throughout the eighteenth century the academies thus broadened their curricula, especially by the inclusion of more modern languages, natural sciences, history and commerce. All of these subjects still tended to be more closely linked than they would be by the nineteenth century. Priestley, for example, esteemed chemistry as a prerequisite for commercial geography and as a subject necessary for the citizens of a state engaged in competition for world trade. His pioneering development of history also reflected his interest in politics. Many subjects remained intimately connected with theology, with the Baptist leader Robert Robinson agreeing with Priestley, for example, in viewing history as a demonstration of divine Providence, which 'jointly with the works of nature . . . leads us to the knowledge of His perfection and will'.[11]

How far this curricular expansion reflected developments elsewhere is difficult to determine. Of the increasing Scottish influence on the academies during the eighteenth century there is no doubt. Through sources like the Presbyterian Fund (founded in 1690) and Dr Williams' Trust (1706), Dissenting congregations could send promising students to Scotland as well as the Continent, and in the early period in particular students ventured as far afield as Leiden, Utrecht and Halle. After the middle of the eighteenth century, when English became the common language of instruction at the academies, Scottish universities still

[10] McLachlan, *English Education*, pp. 209–13; Ashley Smith, *The Birth of Modern Education*, pp. 160–78; H. McLachlan, *Warrington Academy* (London, 1943), pp. 17–19; Parker, *Dissenting Academies*, p. 121; J.B. Florian, *An Essay on an Analytical Course of Studies* (London, 1796), pp. 72–3.

[11] Ashley Smith, *The Birth of Modern Education*, p. 157; McLachlan, *English Education*, p. 35; Hughes, *With Freedom Fired*, p. 94.

received an increasing number of Dissenting students, many of whom later became tutors in academies (Samuel Benion, John Seddon, John Aikin, Robert Hall, among others). At the University of Glasgow, the main centre of Dissenting attendance in Scotland, Francis Hutcheson had begun teaching in English, while the ethics of Hutcheson and theology of Leechman were of no small influence on later tutors (it was Leechman who gave the D.D. degree to John Taylor, the first head of Warrington Academy, the year before his appointment as tutor). A similar influence seems evident in various fields of natural science.[12]

II
Tutors and Teaching

Though Joseph Priestley and Richard Price were certainly the best-known Dissenting tutors of their time, and are therefore discussed in much greater detail below, others also taught political economy or touched upon commercial topics. The surviving records unfortunately tell us very little about their teaching or ideas about commerce.

A partial exception to this lamentable deficiency of materials from which to generalize is that of James Burgh (1714–75), who was born in Perthshire, educated at St Andrews, and was a cousin of William Robertson the historian. Burgh set up an academy at Stoke Newington in 1747 and remained there until 1771, retiring to concentrate on his chief work, the widely acclaimed *Political Disquisitions* (1774–5). We will see that the degree to which they embraced the ethos of commercial society was one of the central divisions in Dissenting social and political thought. One theme which ran through Burgh's many works was the destructive consequences of the diffusion of luxury, a topic about which many Dissenters could wax enthusiastic despite the presence of many commercial entrepreneurs amongst them. In his first publication, written in honour of the suppression of the 1745 rebellion, Burgh noted that it was 'obvious to every Eye, that LUXURY and IRRELIGION, which are inseparable companions, are the characteristic Vices of the Age, and that our degenerate Times and corrupt

[12] McLachlan, *English Education*, pp. 29–34. A list of British Dissenting tutors and authors who were awarded degrees at Scottish Universities in the eighteenth century is provided in Hans, *New Trends in Education*, p. 247, while those students who used Dr Williams' scholarships to attend Glasgow are listed in Olive Griffiths, *Religion and Learning. A Study in English Presbyterian Thought from the Bartholemew Ejections (1662) to the Foundation of the Unitarian Movement* (Cambridge, 1935), pp. 181–2. Some of these connections are explored in Peter Jones, 'The Scottish Professoriate and the Polite Academy, 1720–46', in *Wealth and Virtue: the Shaping of Political Economy in the Scottish Enlightenment*, ed. Istvan Hont and Michael Ignatieff (Cambridge, 1983), pp. 89–117, and Peter Jones, 'The Polite Academy and the Presbyterians, 1720–1770', in *New Perspectives on the Politics and Culture of Early Modern Scotland*, ed. John Dwyer, Roger Mason and Alexander Murdoch (Edinburgh, 1982), pp. 156–78.

Nation have the Unhappiness of being singular in this respect'. As Price would later do, he singled out the metropolis as demonstrating that 'the trading part of the Nation' had committed itself to luxurious profusion, and where there was to be found 'little else than Scenes of Wantonness, Pleasure, and Extravagance'. No small part of Burgh's outrage was doubtless derived from a puritan rejection of ostentation. Where only a few years before were found 'decent Citizens dressed in a Garb, plain, uniform, and fit for business', he emphasized, could now be seen 'a motley Race of *English* Traders burlesqued into *French* Dancing-Masters; their Cloaths bepatched with Lace, their hands unfitted for Business for being muffled up in Cambrick to the Fingers Ends. and their Feet crippled by Wooden-heeled Shoes of some Inches high'. The great successes of the rebels of 1745, who had come within a hundred miles of London, were also for Burgh partly accounted for by the depradations of luxury, which had rendered the British 'so enervated and effeminate, that if they happen to be destitute of an Army trained to War and Hardship, they are before an enemy as a Flock of Sheep before Wolves'.[13]

Like many other Dissenters, Burgh's views led him to champion a life of prudence, self-sufficiency and moderation. Emphasizing in his *Thoughts on Education* (1747) that the only value of wealth was in 'being applied to the purchase of the necessaries and conveniences of life, and to the relief of the indigent', Burgh measured the value of a fresh egg against that of a Brazilian diamond and found the latter wanting, 'because the first will save the life of a human creature from famine, but the latter is not capable of being applied to any sort of use, besides pleasing the eye'. Only the conveniences of life were therefore to be sought, for more than this was 'absolutely useless and indeed troublesome'. The lifestyle of the aristocracy in particular was also singled out for criticism in Burgh's *The Dignity of Human Nature* (1764), which was probably his ethics lectures at Stoke Newington. Here, as earlier, he condemned (like many Dissenters) the wickedness of the theatre and the noise and distraction of balls and masquerades, cautioning young shopkeepers from attempting to emulate such manners. Virtually all academies seem to have included business ethics in their course for students of commerce, and Burgh counselled the young merchant not to over-trade, cheat, lie, or succomb to greed. He also addressed a few comments to the subject of taxation, arguing that '[w]hatever tends to the increase of luxury and extravagance ought to be laid under severe restraints, and heavy taxes; as in general all taxes ought to fall on the luxury and superfluity of life, while industry and frugality escape free'. Amongst the more interesting aspects of this text, too, is the fact that it presents us with virtually the only reading list for a commercial education in use at a mid-eighteenth-century academy. On the subjects of trade and commerce Burgh

---

[13] *Dictionary of National Biography*, Vol. 3 (1908), p. 322; [James Burgh], *Britain's Remembrancer* (London, 4th edn., 1745), pp. 8, 14–15, 20. On Burgh see Carla Hay, *James Burgh. Spokesman for Reform in Hanoverian England* (Washington DC, 1979).

recommended Postlethwaite's *Dictionary of Trade and Commerce*, Joshua Gee's *The British Merchant*, Davenant on trade and revenues, Locke on trade and coin, Sir Josiah Child on trade, Uztariz's *Theory of Trade and Commerce*, *The Universal Library of Trade and Commerce*, *The Merchant's Map of Commerce* and the *Lex Mercatoria Rediviva*, and various works by Josiah Tucker, Edward Oldenburgh, 'Lockyers' and 'Stevens'.[14]

The effects of luxury on the British system of government was one of the main themes which Burgh carried over into the *Political Disquisitions*, which was widely circulated in the American colonies as well as in Britain. A particular concern here was the overwhelming power of the aristocracy, whose influence Burgh argued could only be countered by the representation of merchants or 'property' in general in parliament. Under the existing system of representation, luxury clearly helped the aristocracy, since '[e]very man, in proportion to his degeneracy into luxury, becomes more and more obnoxious to bribery and corruption. He finds wants and desires before unknown; and these wants and desires being *artificial* merely are all without *bounds* and *limits*.' Wealth, he admitted, did not '*necessarily* enervate a people, unless there be a relaxation of discipline, and degeneration of manners'. In practice, however, sumptuary laws might help to counter the effects of luxury (such as a heavy tax on saddle horses and carriages). Strongly commending the view of his 'worthy friend', Adam Ferguson, whose *Essay on the History of Civil Society* (1767) had inveighed at length against the effects of luxury on public virtue, Burgh agreed that luxury was 'the parent of wants, and want begets in the minds of men disobedience and desire of change'. What was required instead was emulation of those like the Quakers, whose frugality and industry proved the effects of an early and sufficient education against vice. In this judgment Burgh's preferences were shared by a vast number of his fellow Dissenters.[15]

Two other tutors of importance were Andrew Kippis (1725–95) and Abraham Rees (1743–1825), both of whom served together first at Hoxton and later,

---

[14] [James Burgh], *Thoughts on Education* (London, 1747), pp. 16–17; James Burgh, *The Dignity of Human Nature* (London, 1764), pp. 35, 37, 40, 133, 153–5. Uztariz's text was the *Theorica y practica de comercio y de marina* (Madrid, 1724, 1742, 1757) (see Earl J. Hamilton, 'The Mercantilism of Geronimo de Uztariz: A Reexamination', in *Economics, Sociology and the Modern World*, ed. Norman Himes (Cambridge, MA, 1935), pp. 111–29). Gee was also the author of *The Trade and Navigation of Great Britain Considered* (London, 1729), Postlethwaite of *Britain's Commercial Interest Explained and Improved* (2 vols., London, 1757), among other works, Edward Oldenburgh of *A Calculation of Foreign Exchanges as Transacted on the Royal Exchange of London* (London, 1792). 'Lockyers' is possibly John Lockyer, author of *An Account of Trade in India* (London, 1711), while 'Stevens' may be Capt. John Stevens, who wrote *The Royal Treasury of England; or, an Historical Account of All Taxes* (London, 1725).

[15] James Burgh, *Political Disquisitions* (3 vols., London, 1774–5), Vol. 1, pp. 54, 134, 276, 278–486; Vol. 2, p. 37; Vol. 3, pp. 60–1, 4, 64, 194, 201.

having resigned when they became Unitarians, at Hackney. Kippis was the son of a Nottingham silk-hosier and studied for five years under Doddridge at Northampton, joining the Coward Academy (named after a wealthy West Indian merchant) at Hoxton in 1763, and receiving the D.D. from Edinburgh on the unsolicited advice of Robertson. The author of an unpublished life of Sir James Steuart, Kippis seems to have been generally disposed to the extension of commerce, arguing in 1783, for example, that Britain should take advantage of the ending of the war in America to gain a large share of her commerce as well as more of that of France. If ports at home were opened, Britain and Ireland could become 'a magazine between the old and new worlds, between the north and south of Europe'. Instead of returning to the 'idea of narrow monopoly', therefore, Britons should trust their commerce 'to the greatness of our capital, the superior skill of our manufacturers, and the singular advantages of our insular situation'. Duties should thus be shifted from articles of 'active trade' to luxury goods or those intended for home consumption alone, though Kippis warned of the potential effects of any unpaid national debt.[16]

Kippis was also alert to the effects of greed and affluence on the population. Though liberal in his views of the poor, having castigated Mandeville for wanting to 'keep the inferior orders of people in a state of absolute ignorance', Kippis did not believe that Providence intended 'to gratify the whole of our wishes, or to place us in those circumstances of splendour, rank, and wealth which our vanity, pride, or folly might desire'. The bulk of mankind, instead, must rather occupy the lower stations, devote themselves to labour, and possess only the common supplies and conveniences of existence', which in any case was 'sufficient to the purposes of real happiness'.[17]

Also well known in Dissenting circles was the son of a Glamorganshire Nonconformist minister, Abraham Rees, who was educated at Coward's Academy, Wellclose Square, London, entering in 1759, and in 1761 becoming assistant tutor in mathematics and natural philosophy. He accompanied the academy when it moved to Hoxton in 1762, remaining as resident tutor until 1785, when he became tutor in Hebrew and mathematics at Hackney (1786–96). Pastor of a Southwark Presbyterian congregation from 1774, he moved to the Old Jewry in 1783 and remained there until his death. He also received the D.D. from Edinburgh in 1775, and wrote the greater part of the thirty-nine volume *New Cyclopaedia of the Arts, Sciences, and Literature*. Rees had no direct

---

[16] Arthur D. Morris, *Hoxton Square and the Hoxton Academies* (London, 1957), pp. 8–9; *Dictionary of National Biography*, Vol. 11 (1909), pp. 195–7; [Andrew Kippis], *Considerations on the Provisional Treaty with America, and the Preliminary Articles of Peace with France and Spain* (London, 1783), pp. 33, 108, 145–7.

[17] Andrew Kippis, *A Sermon Preached at the Old Jewry, on Wednesday the 26th of April, 1786, on the Occasion of a New Academical Institution among Protestant Dissenters, for the Education of Their Ministers and Youth* (London, 1786), p. 13; Andrew Kippis, *Sermons on Practical Subjects* (London, 1791), pp. 124–5, 312.

concern with commercial or historical topics, but scattered amongst his sermons is some evidence of his views in this area. Strongly reliant upon Providential intentions, Rees included an unequal distribution of wealth in this life amongst these, finding this 'the wisest and the best' plan for mankind. Providence offered much opportunity for the 'exercise of the virtues and duties which could have no place in a state of more equal distribution'. Thus it helped to 'try the temper and improve the character', to 'inculcate a lesson of mutual dependence and obligation', and to strengthen the bonds of society, uniting men to one another 'by means of their wants and their mutual services', and helping to cultivate the powerful instincts and affections of human nature. Against the effects of affluence, particularly 'imaginary wants and ungoverned passions', Rees believed that religion could act to form a barrier against the abuse of prosperity, showing how 'to enjoy it with sobriety and moderation'. In a sermon entitled 'Abundance not Essential to the Most Important Purposes of Life', he warned of the peculiar pains, afflictions and evils attendant on affluence, allowing only the use of wealth in the cause of religion and virtue as a means of justifying a superior position and ensuring that new demands of rank, family, fashion, splendour and pleasure did not destroy liberality and benevolence. Thus the excesses of commercial society could be regulated without the need to revert to an earlier mode of subsistence.[18]

If Kippis and Rees could include among their illustrious students William Godwin and William Hazlitt, it is a matter of some interest to know how much influence Gilbert Wakefield (1756–1801) had upon one of his students, who was to become one of the foremost political economists of the day: Thomas Robert Malthus. The son of a Nottingham minister, Wakefield followed his father to Jesus College, Cambridge, on a scholarship, remaining four years and becoming a classics fellow of the College in 1776. Ordained deacon in 1778, he soon embraced Unitarianism, resigned his curacy, and married in the following year. Classical tutor at Warrington from 1779 until its dissolution in 1783, he taught privately for a time, then joined Hackney in 1790, though resigning after only a year over disagreements with the system of education and of public worship. His political opinions grew steadily more radical, however (though he was the author of a well-known critique of Paine's *Age of Reason*), and when Wakefield contended that the poor and labouring classes would lose nothing by a French invasion, and that he himself would then be found 'at his post among the illustrious dead', he was imprisoned for seditious libel, and died of typhus fever six months after his release. Young Malthus studied with him not only at Warrington but at Wakefield's house in Nottinghamshire, where for some time he was evidently the sole pupil, before following his tutor to Jesus College in late 1784. Whether Malthus gained some of his later hostility to manufactures from Wakefield cannot be established, though the latter was far more an

---

[18] *Dictionary of National Biography*, Vol. 16 (1909), pp. 840–1; Abraham Rees, *Practical Sermons* (London, 2nd edn., 1812), Vol. 2, pp. 353, 315–16, Vol. 1, pp. 396–7.

egalitarian than ever Malthus was. It would be tempting to read an agrarian bias
back into Wakefield's views in the 1780s. (His library included Harrington,
More and Burgh but also Hume and Davenant.) But even if this is probable,
further evidence is still necessary before it can be safely asserted.[19]

Another Warrington tutor was William Enfield (1741–97), who taught belles-
lettres and served as rector at the Academy from 1770 to 1783. The son of poor
parents, Enfield was educated at Daventry under Caleb Ashworth on a scholarship, but gained the Doctor of Laws degree from Edinburgh in 1774. Enfield
taught commercial subjects at Warrington, though whether these involved
political economy proper or only 'Social Duties of the Commercial Kind' (as
a section of his *Principles of Mental and Moral Philosophy* was entitled) is not
known. In the latter case his emphasis would have been, as in lectures at other
academies and his more practical sermons, on the need for justice, honesty,
fairness and impartiality in all business dealings. We know at least that he was
generally well-disposed to Smithian principles, for in a review of the *Wealth of
Nations* he noted that it was 'on the whole more satisfactory, and rests on better
grounds' than previous works. Elsewhere Enfield also enumerated the 'ad-
vances in sciences and arts' and 'extensive spread of a liberal spirit and candid
manners' as being amongst the signs of a 'gradual progress of human nature
towards perfection', noting that in this process it had been the introduction of
commerce which 'gave the lower classes of the people consequence with the
nobles, and raised them to a spirit of independence'. This agreed with similar
analyses by Hume and Smith. Like the latter, too, Enfield held the settlement
of 1688 as responsible for much of the commercial prosperity of the eighteenth
century, and saw liberty generally as 'the parent of industry, the nurse of science
and arts, and the inspiring soul of enterprize'. In a review of Priestley's
'Lectures', too, he expressed particular satisfaction with its position on the
National Debt (though disagreeing with Priestley's views on religious establishments).[20]

Even less is known about two other tutors who touched upon commercial
subjects in their lectures. In his remaining manuscript lectures on government
and the British constitution, John Horsey, who taught at Northampton in the

[19] *Dictionary of National Biography*, Vol. 20 (1909), pp. 452–5; Patricia James,
Population Malthus. His Life and Times (London, 1979), pp. 16–25; Gilbert Wakefield,
Memoirs of the Life of Gilbert Wakefield (2 vols., London, 1804), Vol. 1, pp. 333–54;
Gilbert Wakefield, *A Sermon Preached at Richmond in Surrey on July 29th 1784*
(London, 1784), p. 16; Gilbert Wakefield, *A Letter to William Wilberforce* (London,
1797), pp. 30, 64.
[20] *Dictionary of National Biography*, Vol. 6 (1908), pp. 787–8; Lucy Aikin, *Memoirs
of John Aikin* (2 vols., London, 1823), Vol. 1, pp. 293–310; William Enfield, *Principles
of Moral and Mental Philosophy* (London, 1809), pp. 239–42; William Enfield, *Sermons
on Practical Subjects* (3 vols., 1798), Vol. 1, p. 206; *Monthly Review*, 54 (1776),
pp. 299–300; William Enfield, *A Sermon on the Centennial Commemoration of the
Revolution* (London, 1788), pp. 3, 13; *Monthly Review* (January 1798). pp. 5–8.

1790s, took much from Blackstone, and included a discussion of labour as the foundation of property and all value (including rent) with some reference to Locke. With citations from Grotius as well as Locke, Horsey also vindicated the inequalities of commercial society, denying that there was necessarily any equality of property in the state of nature 'though there is an equality of dominion', adding that it was 'not desireable that there should [be], because there are several offices in life which are necessary to be performed for hire [and] a difference in ingenuity and industry will naturally occasion a proportionate difference in property'. Similar views were probably held by Horsey's predecessor at Northampton, Thomas Belsham, who taught civil government and the British constitution to second-year students from 1781 to 1789. At the successor college to Warrington, Manchester Academy (1786–1803), commerce lectures were also given by Thomas Barnes (1746–1810), who received an Edinburgh D.D. degree in 1784 and had been trained at Warrington under John Aikin and Joseph Priestley. Barnes was chiefly a tutor of Hebrew, Metaphysics, Ethics and Theology, but also covered the history and principles of commerce, the commercial laws and regulations of different states, and commercial ethics, including oaths, contracts, and commutative justice. He was also noteworthy as the anonymous author of *Thoughts on the Use of Machines, in the Cotton Manufacture* (of which 5000 copies were printed and dispensed in 1780), one of the first defences of the 'new trade', its market and customers, wherein Barnes conceded that local difficulties might be experienced by some when machinery was first introduced. On some accounts Manchester Academy succeeded where Warrington had failed because of the former's slightly more conservative bias. It eventually became the present Manchester College, Oxford, established as a training ground for Unitarian ministers.[21]

III
Joseph Priestley and Richard Price

Joseph Priestley (1733–1804) was one of the best-loved as well as most calumnied of eighteenth-century Dissenters. An internationally respected scientist, philosopher and theologian, his enthusiasm for the French revolution led a mob to destroy his house, library and scientific laboratory, and eventually resulted in his being driven into American exile. A tutor at two of the leading academies of the period, Warrington (1761–7) and Hackney (1791–4), Priestley

---

[21] Dr Williams' Library, MS. 69.3, John Horsey, 'Five Lectures on Government', p. 3; [Thomas Barnes], *Thoughts on the Use of Machines, in the Cotton Manufacture* (Manchester, 1780), pp. 8–9, 13, 19; Barnes, *A Discourse Delivered at the Commencement of the Manchester Academy*, appendix, p. 4; McLachlan, *English Education*, pp. 161–2, 256–7; Ashley Smith, *The Birth of Modern Education*, p. 169; *Collecteana Relating to Manchester and Its Neighbourhood*, ed. John Harland (Manchester, 1867), pp. 232–42.

was like many of his colleagues also educated in a Dissenting institution. Born near Leeds, he attended Northampton Academy shortly after it had moved to Daventry, remaining there from 1751 to 1755. Here his principal tutor was Caleb Ashworth (1722–75), though the educational methods of the academy were still dominated by the ideas of Philip Doddridge (1702–51), chief tutor from 1729–51, whose widely-emulated lectures remained the chief course of study. These covered a broad area which included civil government, the law of nations, ethics (Grotius, Pufendorf, Cumberland and Hutcheson were among the leading texts), and included a strong measure of Hartley's associationist psychology. The latter in particular was to prove of lasting influence on the young Priestley, for he developed out of it his own idea of human perfectibility, which in turn underlay parts of his theory of commerce.[22]

Priestley's own education was probably fairly typical of a mid-eighteenth-century academy. Under Doddridge, Northampton Academy usually had between thirty and fifty students. Fees in the 1730s were approximately £16 per annum, with a further £4 for tuition. On entry students paid one guinea for a 'closet', but brought their own pair of sheets and candles, and put out their own washing. Discipline could be moderately strict; Doddridge expected all boarding students to be present for family prayers at 6:10 a.m., or to forfeit a penny fine in their absence (how much was raised in this way is not recorded). The intellectual atmosphere under Ashworth was doubtless similar to that under Doddridge. Following the introduction of teaching in English several generations earlier, Latin had fallen by the wayside, and Priestley later complained that though he found time to read ten pages of Greek daily with another student, there were no compositions or orations in Latin. What the college seemed to specialize in, instead, was theological controversy, with students and tutors evenly and keenly divided on such questions as liberty versus necessity, or the sleep of the soul.[23]

After his graduation, Priestley moved as tutor to Warrington (which had opened with three students in 1757) in September 1761, and remained six years. His salary was £100 per annum plus a house, and a further £15 annually for boarders, the total sum of which he found insufficient to support his family, which helped to provoke his resignation. His responsibilities were considerable. He began as tutor of languages and belles-lettres, and taught amongst other subjects Latin, Greek, French, Italian, the theory of languages and universal

[22] Ashley Smith, *The Birth of Modern Education*, pp. 148–9; Philip Doddridge, *The Works of the Rev. Philip Doddridge* (10 vols., Leeds, 1804), Vol. 4, pp. 414–51; *Dictionary of National Biography*, Vol. 16 (1909), pp. 357–76. Priestley's views are summarized in Lincoln, *Some Social and Political Ideas of English Dissent*, pp. 151–81. A more recent study is Jack Fruchtman, *The Apocalyptic Politics of Richard Price and Joseph Priestley* (Philadelphia, 1983).

[23] Parker, *Dissenting Academies*, pp. 78–9; Ashley Smith, *The Birth of Modern Education*, pp. 148–9.

grammar, oratory and philosophical criticism, and civil law. Moreover, Priestley also substantially widened the curriculum at Warrington, and began what some have praised as the first modern teaching of history at the university level. This development came about because, as Priestley wrote in 1766, most of the pupils were 'young men designed for situations in civil and active life', especially the learned professions, with about a quarter enrolled in business and commercial subjects. Such interests, Priestley conceived, demanded the enlargement of their minds to 'give them liberal views of many important subjects', such as poor law reform.[24]

Priestley's historical lectures became perhaps his best known contribution to the Dissenting curriculum. The theme of liberty predominated throughout both their political and commercial sections, which were first written in 1761 but not published until 1785, by which time Priestley had both read and become acquainted with Adam Smith. But a predilection for liberty certainly predated the publication of the *Wealth of Nations*. An early idea of Priestley's had been that 'the more liberty is given to every thing which is in a state of growth the more perfect it will become, and when it is grown to its full size, the more amply will it repay its wise parent for the indulgence it gave in its infant state'. 'Liberty of commerce' was also invested with a considerable variety of both political and economic meanings. In the narrower, more economic sense, it meant adherence to such trading maxims as the idea that 'everything will find its value'. As a general principle, it entailed relying upon the calculated consequences of self-interest, and the notion that '[i]ndividuals, when left to themselves, are in general sufficiently provident, and will daily better their circumstances; and as it may be presumed that, in consequence of giving constant attention to their interest, they will understand it, it is seldom wise in governors to pretend to direct them'. Legislative interference in trade thus had for Priestley rarely been advantageous. The only partial exception he cited was the Navigation Acts, which restricted imports to those commodities produced by the exporting nation, but which were largely beneficial to the country (Holland) against which they were directed. The real advantages of free commerce, however, lay in other consequences besides the prospect of economic improvement. Trade acquainted mankind with one another, expanded the mind, and inevitably induced a desire for peace with other nations. It also had important political ramifications. Despotism limited exchange in the first instance, but once commercial expansion was underway and the connections and interests of individuals had become increasingly complicated, the actions of government took on a similar character, and became correspondingly more

---

[24] Parker, *Dissenting Academies*, pp. 105–7, 114–19; Henry Bright, 'A Historical Sketch of Warrington Academy', *Transactions of the Historic Society of Lancashire and Cheshire*, 11 (1858–9), p. 15; Ashley Smith, *The Birth of Modern Education*, p. 243; J. Priestley, *Memoirs of Dr. Joseph Priestley* (London, 1904), p. 31; Bogue and Bennett, *History of Dissenters*, Vol. 2, pp. 304–5; McLachlan, *Warrington Academy*, p. 56.

dangerous because of their complexity. Thus Priestley thought the functions of government should be as limited as possible. His chief model here after the late 1770s was the American constitution, which in his view was designed to leave each individual secure in the enjoyment of his natural rights. Some collective tasks such as education and public works should be undertaken, but not more. No doubt Priestley also had the experience of Dissent strongly in mind here, for the prototype of harmful intervention was the enforcement of a religious creed upon all citizens. Theological freedom was thus a general model for all liberty, not a special case of its application.[25]

Like Smith, Priestley did not intend his notion of free commerce to entail a specific or restricted defence of the merchant class. The gain of the merchant was not always that of the nation, for example where the import of foreign goods decreased the consumption of domestic manufactures, though Priestley warned that if 'merchants importing foreign goods can sell those cheaper than the manufactures can be bought at home, it is an indication that it is not for the interest of the nation at large to encourage such manufactures'. Nor was commerce to be given preference over agriculture, 'the only stable foundation of most of the improvements in social life'. The earth was the source of both animal life and of those raw materials from which manufactures were produced, and if its produce could not feed the nation, 'their very subsistence must necessarily be precarious'. But agriculture alone would not ensure the perfection of farming, since 'the desire of procuring mere subsistence, without any view to superfluity' was not always an adequate motive to production. Greater encouragement instead would come from exciting 'other kinds of industry, affording a ready market for the exchange of corn for commodities'. A large agricultural surplus in turn would keep wages in manufacturing low. This purpose could be served by public granaries, such as Sir James Steuart had proposed. But a flourishing state of commerce might have the same effect because merchants would supply corn whenever a dearth threatened. Citing Postlethwayt, Priestley therefore emphasized that the interests of trade and agriculture were reciprocal, and that if trade were to be increased, the amount of land under cultivation should also be augmented, and more waste lands enclosed.[26]

Like Smith, Priestley also stressed the benefits of home consumption, believing that 'neither agriculture nor trade can flourish where the general ease does not begin with the class of labourers'. With many mid-eighteenth-century

[25] J. Priestley, *An Essay on a Course of Liberal Education for Civil and Active Life* (London, 1765), pp. 9, 32–3, 142, 167; J. Priestley, 'Lectures on History and General Policy', in *The Works of Joseph Priestley* (25 vols., London, 1803) (hereafter *Works*), Vol. 24, pp. 113, 305, 321, 316, 233, 229, 255. A brief account of Priestley's economic ideas is given in Chuhei Sugiyama, 'The Economic Thought of Joseph Priestley', *Enlightenment and Dissent*, 3 (1984), pp. 78–89.

[26] Priestley, 'Lectures', pp. 329, 300–2.

writers, however, he took a relatively harsh view of the maintenance of labourers through the poor laws. Statesmen ought to consider the plight of the poor, but here as in other areas there was 'great danger of their attempting too much, and thereby encumbering themselves without remedying the evil'. The great evil here was the problem of removing the motivation to labour through such support. Eventually, though, Priestley did consider some form of mandatory social insurance for the poor as the best means of replacing the poor laws.[27]

Though he can certainly be classed among the optimists in his views on social progress, Priestley's attitude towards commercial society was not entirely unambiguous. Like many other republican liberal writers of the period, he especially feared the long-term political consequences of commerce, and repeatedly emphasized that '[v]irtue and public spirit are the necessary supports of all republican governments'. The spirit of commerce, however, was undoubtedly a threat to the virtues required in a republic, and Priestley warned of the need for 'the extreme caution of all wise legislators to keep luxury out of them, and to preserve as great an equality in the riches and the power of all the members of the state as possible'. The Roman, Florentine and Athenian constitutions, he considered, had all been ruined in this fashion, and it was evident that commerce, 'which never fails to introduce luxury and inequality into men's circumstances', did not 'perfectly suit with the true spirit of a commonwealth'. But this did not induce Priestley, like Burgh, to prefer an essentially agricultural economy, or to propose sumptuary laws to restrict the diffusion of luxury. Instead he came, like Hume, to conceive of the progress of manners as a counterweight to the dangers of luxury, and of the passage from barbarism to refinement as not only underlying the evolution of 'a regular form of government', but as constituting a genuine and marked improvement over the virtues of the ancient republics.[28]

Despite his political concerns Priestley's attitude towards luxury was therefore relatively optimistic. Generally speaking the more conveniences an individual possessed, the more he or she was able 'to enjoy life, and make themselves and others happy', and given his utilitarianism this was of some importance to Priestley. Some danger of course arose from extravagance, but Priestley clearly rejected the puritan condemnation of personal adornments, conceding instead their economic advantages. As long as luxuries did not actually weaken the physical constitution, gratifying a 'taste for mere *ornament* in dress, equipage, etc' could 'do no real harm. Wants of this kind, more than all our other wants, promote industry, and are a most effectual means of circulating wealth.' It was not true that 'living in luxury tends to make men effeminate and cowardly', because 'more spirit and courage may be expected from a man who has had good nourishment, and who has something to defend,

---

[27] *Ibid.*, pp. 239–40, 271; *Works*, Vol. 25, pp. 314–19.
[28] Priestley, 'Lectures', pp. 338–9.

than from one who is almost starved, and who has little or nothing to fight for'.[29]

Commercial society also met with Priestley's approbation on other grounds. He clearly agreed with Hume's conception of the refinement of manners and the improvement of modern over ancient morals, stressing that more advanced societies lacked 'that treachery and cruelty which characterise almost all un-civilised and barbarous states', and commonly possessed 'a higher and juster sense of honour, and a greater humanity of temper'. What for Priestley lent the moderns such an advantage over the ancients was that they had begun to attain 'true *politeness*', defined as 'the art of seeming to be habitually influenced by those virtues and good dispostions of mind which most contribute to the ease and the pleasure of those we converse with'. The essence of politeness or 'refined good breeding' was that it required individuals to 'preserve the appear-ance of sentiments quite contrary to those they are naturally inclined to'. Thus was tempered the Dissenting concern with sincerity as the cardinal virtue. For despite Priestley's perfectibilism, he was inclined to believe that mankind was naturally 'selfish, sensual, haughty, overbearing, and savage', while society obliged all to maintain 'a spirit of moderation, humanity, and condescension'. To eradicate such deeply-rooted vices was impossible. What was necessary instead was to 'learn the art of preserving the appearance of virtue', for if this were 'habitual and uniform', it would have 'nearly the same effect in society; though the virtues themselves would enable a person to contribute to the happiness of others with far less pain and mortification to himself'. Politeness was consequently the compromise which commercial society entered into with virtue. But this was less likely to develop in republics, where the struggle for self-advancement tended to undermine an attitude of demeanor to others, than in monarchies, where all the members of a state were far more dependent upon each other, and 'in which all appearance of selfishness, and every unsociable disposition, entirely vanishes, and every one seems to have no other object than the ease and pleasure of others'. Arising in renaissance Florence, politeness had been brought to perfection by the French, for whom '*l'art de vivre*', the art of society and conversation, had become the most agreeable of activities. Here, in particular, it was the treatment of women by men which marked the progress of politeness, and which served for Priestley as the single most important standard for judging its achievements. By such means alone, then, the progress of commercial society would hinder further corruption.[30]

In his lectures Priestley next turned to the means by which wealth was produced and disseminated. Probably following Smith, he agreed that labour was 'the only original source of wealth', but added that since society had formulated rules of inheritance, some were exempted from labour and could

[29] *Ibid.*, pp. 339–42.
[30] *Ibid.*, pp. 343–6.

live upon rents or the profits of trade. Magistrates, teachers, physicians, lawyers
provided services, they were not themselves productive labourers but rather
'servants', who tended as a class to increase with the gross produce of society.
But this did not necessarily result in a greater burden upon the poor. On the
question of the price of goods in relation to the various classes, Priestley
followed Steuart in seeing the regulation of necessaries as a function of the
buying power of the common people, with competition or demand adjusting
prices. Nor was the amount of specie in circulation vital in this respect. An
occasional rise in the value of money might be advantageous, but the devalu-
ation of currency by a nation to pay its debts more cheaply Priestley condemned,
again following Steuart. Moreover, provided industry and population continued
to expand he felt there was no need to worry, as the 'mercantilists' had done,
about the flow of specie out of the country and the resulting imbalance of trade.
If anything, too much money was harmful insofar as it raised the wages of
labour and checked the growth of manufactures. Efficient industrial nations did
tend to accumulate money more quickly. But to prohibit the export of coin was
worse than useless, since it merely raised prices at home and made all manufactures less competitive. The general flow of money into a country had the
effect of raising demand for both agricultural and manufacturing produce and
increasing production itself, while the process of currency depletion did the
reverse, discouraging the provision of commodities as well as improvement and
the growth of population generally.[31]

Like most other eighteenth-century political economists, Priestley believed
that an increasing population was in fact a crucial indicator of national progress.
This in turn depended on the provision of plenty and the accessibility of an easy
subsistence. But it was not desirable that any country grow so large as to be
unable to feed itself. Since manufactures and trade tended to centralize the
population, they became dangerous at the point at which provisions were
required from abroad. New agricultural machinery also inhibited population
growth insofar as it made less labour necessary on farms, but was beneficial if
'the produce of the lands, thus easily reaped, be disposed of to purchase
superfluities at home; especially if those superfluities consist not of eatables:
for then the lands yield their full produce in the necessaries of life, and all who
subsist upon them live within the country'. Provided with more manufactures,
farmers would be induced to raise more crops, the sale of which would further
promote manufactures and employment in them. It was possible, Priestley
acknowledged, for manufactures to be sold abroad and for population to increase accordingly, but not probably desirable. The idea of a fully developed
international division of labour, or of Britain as the 'workshop of the world',
had not yet developed, and would not here have been accepted.[32]

---

[31] *Ibid.*, pp. 329–32.
[32] *Ibid.*, pp. 370–4.

The next branch of political economy which concerned Priestley was taxa-tion. His principal aim here was to condemn heavy taxes which raised the price of labour and manufactures and even destroyed industry altogether. Preference ought to be given to taxes on consumption rather than possession, for reasons of simplicity, and correspondingly Priestley rejected the taxation of manufac-tures, opting instead for raising revenue from the property acquired by the manufacturers themselves. He rejected the Physiocratic proposition that all taxes should fall upon the land since its net produce was the only real wealth of the country, arguing instead that the burden should be shared in proportion to their property. Luxury goods and imported commodities were especially recommended for heavy imposts, provided this did not serve the interests of only a narrow section of the community.[33]

Finally, Priestley briefly considered the problem of public credit and the national debt. Following Steuart, he conceded that the advantage of such a funding system was that it made large sums of money available to the state in emergencies. If the taxation required to repay this were moderate, such loans might indeed be acceptable (as Paine would later argue). But this was not the case in Britain, and since the debt was increasing, its effects might in fact 'be fatal' in the long run. This would be true, for example, if foreigners came to possess the greater share of the funds. But there were great dangers in being 'tributary' to Britons too. Citing Hume and Smith, Priestley warned that the national debt might result in 'the gradual diminution of the power of the state, in consequence of the increase of taxes, which discourage industry and make it difficult to vend their manufactures abroad'. Only a sinking fund could remedy this, but Priestley was sceptical that such measures would be effectively applied, especially since the state was far too prone to 'the expensive folly of going to war'. Such habits could only be curbed, in turn, by a diminution of aristocratic and monarchic corruption.[34]

Widely circulated, these lectures were Priestley's chief contribution to the curricula of the academies. Published in 1785, they were delivered again at the New College at Hackney from 1791 to 1794, where Priestley found refuge during the early years of the French Revolution. He did not write again on political economy, but there is little reason to suspect that his general faith in the diffusion of commerce was anything but reinforced by the Revolution, which he experienced as a strongly providential direction of human events.[35]

Of less import for the evolution of teaching methods in the academies, but as well known in the country at large and among the Dissenters in particular, were the statistical calculations and economic proposals of Priestley's close

[33] *Ibid.*, pp. 403–9.

[34] *Ibid.*, pp. 409–15.

[35] Priestley, *Memoirs*, pp. 81–2; J. Priestley, *Letters to the Right Hon. Edmund Burke Occasioned by His Reflections on the Revolution in France* (Birmingham, 3rd edn., 1791), p. 150.

friend Richard Price, who was tutor for a time at the Hackney Academy, and was another leading Rational Dissenter. The latter was born in 1723 at Llangei-nor, Glamorganshire, the son of a strict Presbyterian teacher and minister. Educated at a succession of academies until 1744, he became the house chaplain to a wealthy Stoke Newington businessman. Financially independent through several inheritances, Price settled as minister at Newington Green in 1758, remaining there for nearly thirty years and from 1770 to 1791 also preaching at the Gravel Pit Chapel, Hackney. A philosopher as well as mathematician, Price published *A Review of the Principal Questions in Morals* (1758), became a member of the Royal Society, and frequented from about 1770 onwards such institutions as the Whig Club, where he met Franklin, Priestley, other Dissent-ing ministers like Andrew Kippis, and political writers like James Burgh. From about 1770 he became concerned with theories of insurance and financial reform, and these were among the topics he taught at the Unitarian New College, Hackney, where he moved in the spring of 1787. For a time he also offered instruction in ethics, mathematics, astronomy and natural philosophy. But he did not remain long at the post, and the college closed as a result of financial difficulties incurred by an overly rapid building programme in 1796.[36]

Positioned in the household of a prominent Dissenting financier, and with many businessmen in his congregation, it is not surprising that Price came to take an interest in financial affairs and economic problems. Among his earliest and most enduring interests was the calculation of old age and sickness insur-ance, and he is often regarded as one of the founders of the modern conception of welfare for his work in this area. Price's *Observations on Reversionary Payments* (1771) attempted to establish the correct method for calculating savings which would later be returned in pension form. This was set, however, in the wider context of the general well-being of society. His calculations of life expectancy in an early paper for the Royal Society induced Price to examine the causes of variation in population, and to link these to the wider question of the nature of commercial society. However, he came quickly to condemn the rapid growth of urban centres as one of the chief sources of national decline.

---

[36] John Williams, *Memoirs of the Late Rev. Thomas Belsham* (London, 1833), pp. 447–8. On Price's life and educational background see: *Dictionary of National Biography*, Vol. 16 (1909), pp. 334–7; Rees, *History of Protestant Nonconformity in Wales*, pp. 312–417; H.P. Roberts, 'Nonconformist Academies in Wales', *Transactions of the Honourable Society of Cymmrodorion* (1928–9), pp. 1–98; and the biographies of Roland Thomas, *Richard Price, Philosopher and Apostle of Liberty* (Oxford, 1924), Carl Cone, *Torchbearer of Freedom. The Influence of Richard Price on Eighteeenth Century Thought* (Lexington, 1952), and D.O. Thomas, *The Honest Mind. The Thought and Work of Richard Price* (Oxford, 1977). There is also useful information on Price's relation to Hackney in 'Richard Price's Journal for the Period 25 March 1787 to 6 February 1791', *National Library of Wales Journal*, 21, ed. D.O. Thomas and Beryl Thomas (1980), pp. 366–413.

This was in part because of their effects upon the price of agricultural goods. The more London in particular grew, 'the fewer hands must be left for agriculture; and, consequently, the less must be the plenty and the higher the price of all the means of subsistence'. But there were other grounds for Price's rejection of cities. Moderate towns had their advantages, but great towns were mere 'nursuries of debauchery and voluptuousness', and as such great checks on population. Elsewhere Price calculated that the rate of deaths in Manchester was twice as high as that in the adjacent countryside, the chief reasons for this being 'the luxury and irregular modes of life which prevail in the towns', and 'the foulness of the air'. Such views echoed his preference for 'the simplicity and innocence of a life agreeable to nature', and he clearly aligned himself with those country party critics who argued that most of 'that black catalogue of diseases which ravage human life', was 'the off-spring of the tenderness, the luxury, and the corruptions introduced by the vices and false refinements of civil society'.[37]

Price's treatment of commercial progress thus resulted from his worries about the physical decline of the population. For the most part he was convinced, like many other eighteenth-century writers, and not a few (like Cobbett) fifty years later, that the population of England had been declining for some time. Calculating the number of houses in London largely on the basis of house and window duties for example (Cobbett would later count empty church pews), Price reached the conclusion in 1779 that the population of Britain had fallen by some twenty-five percent since 1688. Despite the fact that the labouring people were 'the chief strength and security of every state . . . for, from cottages our navies and armies are supplied', one and a half million people at least had been lost since the Glorious Revolution, including 200,000 in the last eleven years. Given such a trend, the nation could scarcely be expected to survive another century. The chief cause of these losses, Price felt, was the luxury induced by commerce itself, which only appeared to add to the national wealth and power while secretly destroying both. Another important cause of depopulation was the vast increase in taxation required for both political corruption and military adventures, because this raised the cost of living. Also relevant was the increasing concentration of agriculture, which proceeded rapidly throughout the eight-

---

[37] R. Price, 'Observations on the Expectations of Lives, the Increase of Mankind, the Influence of Great Towns on Population, and Particularly the State of London with Respect to Healthfulness and Number of Inhabitants', Royal Society *Philosophical Transactions*, Vol. 59 (1769), pp. 118–19; R. Price, 'Observations on the Difference between the Duration of Human Life in Towns and in Country Parishes and Villages', *Philosophical Transactions*, Vol. 65, part 1 (1775), pp. 424, 428; R. Price, *Observations on Reversionary Payments* (2nd edn., London, 1772), pp. 275–6. See D.O. Thomas, 'Richard Price and the Population Controversy', *Price-Priestley Newsletter*, 4 (1980), pp. 43–62.

eenth century, and where once again an apparent economic advantage only disguised a greater long-term evil.[38]

For Price, one main source of the increased taxation of the eighteenth century also simultaneously threatened the political liberties of the country: the national debt. From the early 1770s onwards he offered calculations for the successful re-establishment of a Sinking Fund from which the debt might be repaid, and there is some evidence that Pitt among others paid some heed to his ideas. But the political element in his views was no less important than the economic. If the government had the capacity to ruin the public funds, fund-holders themselves might be driven to loyalty, acquiescence and servility. Foreign enemies as well might induce economic collapse by merely threatening an expensive war. Quoting Hume, Price emphasized that either the nation could end the system of public credit, or the latter would destroy the former. In 1785 he similarly warned the infant United States to redeem its war debts and remain free of public credit. Price's later American writings also recommended that the new nation aim at the ideal between the savage and refined states, avoiding the commercial and aristocratic extremes to which Britain had been led, and maintaining instead 'an independent and hardy yeomanry, all nearly on a level, trained to arms, instructed in their rights, clothed in home-spun, of simple manners, strangers to luxury, drawing plenty from the ground, and that plenty gathered easily by the hand of industry and giving rise to early marriages'. For Britain, therefore, a partial reversal of the progress of commerce and industry was necessary. Here we can see how much less a partisan of commercial society Price was compared to Priestley. Agriculture was to be promoted, some part of the inhabitants of the towns driven back into the countryside, regulations established for preserving the lives of infants, and luxury, celibacy, and the engrossing of farms to be discouraged. Taxes were to be lightened and the national debt attacked root and branch. But, Price confessed, there was evidence that such proposals were 'crying in vain', because '[c]orruption and follies of the worst sort have, I am afraid, taken too deep root among us'. At the opening of Hackney in 1787, he insisted that it was man's nature to have no limits to his knowlege and capacity for improvement. This optimism also suffused his famous address to the Revolution Society, which provoked Burke's *Reflections*. Yet economically, and as a moralist, Price remained pessimistic in the last years before his death in 1791.[39]

[38] R. Price, *An Essay on the Present State of the Population* (London, 1779), pp. 277–80; Price, *Observations on Reversionary Payments*, pp. 361–5; R. Price, *An Appeal to the Public, on the Subject of the National Debt* (London, 1772), p. 45.

[39] Price, *Observations on Reversionary Payments*, pp. 161, 364–5; R. Price, *Observations on the Nature of Civil Liberty, the Principles of Government, and the Justice and Policy of the War with America* (London, 4th edn., 1776), pp. 111–28; R. Price, *Additional Observations on the Nature and Value of Civil Liberty, and the War with America* (London, 1777), pp. 89–147; *Richard Price and the Ethical Foundations of the American*

IV
Students and Academic Debates

Having considered the tutors, what can be said about the students at Dissenting academies which can help to reconstruct the content and intention of the commercial education to which they were exposed? Almost the only direct evidence of this type which remains are the manuscript notes of the Literary Society at Northampton in the 1780s, and the subsequent student journal named the 'Academical Repository', which appeared sporadically at the Academy between 1785 and 1796. The Literary Society, which with several tutors comprised some twenty members, debated such topics as whether the state of nature or that of civilization was more productive of happiness (both sides appear to have been supported in the debate). A month later, in early May 1780, a further debate considered the question of whether the institutions of Solon at Athens or those of Lycurgus at Sparta had been more conducive to the happiness of the state, with several members of the Society supporting Lycurgus' prohibition of luxury. Yet in the chief economical piece written for the journal, the anonymous 'Observations on Luxury' which appeared in April 1786, luxury was defended as a source of diligence and industry, with the author claiming that manufacturing in the towns drained the countryside only of superfluous hands, and deriding the diatribes of moralists and divines against the growth of pride and sensuality. The social benefits of such commerce instead were held to more than outweigh the dangers involved, since property was circulated, inventiveness and talent aroused, and a greater sense of equality nurtured. On the whole, however, it is difficult to judge how far such a Priestleyan vindication of commerce found support here or elsewhere.[40]

Another possible source for such speculation lies in the published writings of those students of academies who went on to write on economic topics. The Rev. David Williams (1738–1816), who studied for the ministry at Carmarthen Academy from 1753 to 1757, for example, later gave a series of lectures on the political principles of Montesquieu which also paid homage to the 'profound Historian of the Wealth of Nations', recommending that every monarch study Smith for at least half an hour daily. Against Montesquieu, Williams condemned the Spartan model of government and the introduction of any kind of agrarian equality into refined and cultivated societies. Following a line of argument derived from Steuart, Williams agreed that there was 'hardly any cause [which] would more effectually or speedily destroy an industrious nation, than a power, left to every man, to enjoy the fruits of his industry' (he later

---

Revolution, ed. Bernard Peach (Durham, 1979), pp. 185–7, 208–12; R. Price, *The Evidence for a Future Period of Improvement in the State of Mankind* (London, 1787), p. 12; R. Price, *A Discourse on the Love of Our Country* (London, 1789), pp. 29–30.

[40] Dr Williams' Library, MS. 69.7, April 5, 1780, May 9, 1780; MS. 69.8, April 1786, pp. 272–9.

planned a course of lectures on Steuart's *Political Economy*, again demonstrating Steuart's considerable influence in the eighteenth century). If profits generally were too high, Williams thought, the costs of labour and commodities would rise steeply, destroying British commerce in foreign markets. Taxation was thus ultimately beneficial to industry. Williams also attacked the emerging social division of labour in commercial society, conceiving still more critically than Smith that the greater part of the community became degraded 'into unconscious parts of general machines . . . below the condition of brutes' as a result of the peculiar despotism of modern mercantile governments, who were motivated more by the pursuit of wealth than the love of liberty. The real problem of luxury, then, was essentially political in nature. Great wealth was harmful if the people were 'reduced to slavery, civil or commercial, by mechanic and habitual dependence on taskmasters'. But luxury need not be ruinous 'in states wisely constituted', or dedicated to liberty. Elsewhere Williams conceded that the poor were 'ever miserable, in proportion to the number of those idle and vicious persons, with which they are unhappily loaded.' The law of nature dictated that 'those only . . . can be confined wholly to labour, who are incapable of improving themselves in their knowledge, virtues and pleasures'. If a society was constituted upon just and natural principles no amount of wealth, then, could harm it. In fact the greater its quantity, the greater would be the happiness of the inhabitants, while commodities acquired from other states meant less work was available at home. Wealth and luxury thus only ruined a nation when they were 'obtained by fraud, injustice, oppression, or any kind of vice'.[41]

Far more conspicuous in his condemnation of luxury (at least in his youth) was William Godwin (1756–1834), whose *Enquiry Concerning Political Justice* (1793) agitated the minds of middle-class youth like no other text in the revolutionary period. What attitudes towards commerce Godwin derived from the Sandemanian Baptist views with which he was raised (which strongly emphasized the duty to share property with the poor), what was impressed upon him during his education under Kippis and Rees at Hoxton between 1773 and 1778, and what additional conclusions he reached in early manhood from reading and thought, cannot be easily separated. There is no doubt of his early hostility towards the political corruption of Walpole, or concern that the ruling passion of the English in the eighteenth century had become the desire for accumulation.[42] In an early novel, Godwin portrayed the idyllic life and virtues of uncorrupted shepherds for whom the temptations of luxury were non-

---

[41] *Dictionary of National Biography*, Vol. 21 (1909), pp. 390–3; David Williams, *Lectures on Political Principles* (London, 1789), preface, pp. 53, 245–51, 83–6; David Williams, *Lectures on the Universal Principles and Duties of Religion and Morality* (London, 1779), pp. 83–4, 157–9, 161, 177.

[42] W. Godwin, *The History of the Life of William Pitt, Earl of Chatham* (Dublin, 1783), pp. 7, 12.

existent, though he also inserted a passage on the marvels of an iron plough able to improve agriculture forty-fold.[43] A sense of ambiguity about commerce, in fact, pervaded Godwin's early writings and can be traced throughout his life. In an anonymously published history of recent Dutch political developments, Godwin acknowledged that the spirit of commerce preponderated over all other considerations in Holland, but added that '[i]f selfishness be inimical to some of the virtues, it is favourable and auspicious to others', in this case especially political freedom. Deeply opposed to despotism and friendly towards the Foxite Whigs, Godwin also accepted the generally Smithian biases of this circle, writing in 1785 that '[i]t must be granted indeed that commerce never stands on so noble and fair a basis, as when it is made as free as the air we breathe, and every species of manufacture and exchange is committed whole and unmutilated to the hands of industry' (which was a euphemistic plea for a sharp reduction in taxation, places and pensions). In various sections of *Political Justice*, Godwin hinted at the possible future development of a simple, just and egalitarian society where independence and virtue would largely supplant inequality, luxury and commercial exchange. This was the most egalitarian vision penned by any Dissenter in this period. But Godwin's plea for simplicity of manners was tempered by the mid-1790s by his committment to the cause of cultural progress. The idea of a 'state of high civilisation' in which access to all forms of pleasure and culture was extended to all thus increasingly became his goal.[44]

Many others amongst those who were enthusiastic Godwinians in the 1790s seem to have shared both this initial desire for primitive virtue and a subsequent devotion to the redeeming qualities of culture (and the Pantisocrats Wordsworth, Coleridge and Southey could be included here). This may have been true for the essayist and literary critic William Hazlitt, a Hackney student between 1793 and 1795, the prime years of Godwin's reputation. Hazlitt later adopted a moderate view of the problem of the spirit of trade in Britain, hoping that the latter 'with all her high hopes, and called to a far different destiny, may *ever* share the fate of Holland', remaining a radical opponent of Malthus (arguing that '[a]ll authors but Mr. Malthus seem agreed that luxury has been fatal to the spirit of liberty'), and warning in later years of the dangers of 'Effeminacy of Character' and of the need for radical political reform.[45] Still

[43] W. Godwin, *Imogen, A Pastoral Romance*, ed. J. Marken, *Bulletin of the New York Public Library*, 67 (1963), pp. 20, 197.

[44] [W. Godwin], *History of the Internal Affairs of the United Provinces* (London, 1787), p. 24; W. Godwin, *Uncollected Writings*, ed. J. Marken and B. Pollin (Gainesville, FL, 1968), p. 53; W. Godwin, *Enquiry Concerning Political Justice* (Harmondsworth, 1976), p. 75.

[45] McLachlan, *English Education*, p. 248; [William Hazlitt], *Free Thoughts on Public Affairs: or, Advice to a Patriot* (London, 1806), pp. 38–9, 44; [William Hazlitt], *A Reply to the Essay on Population by the Rev. T.R. Malthus* (London, 1807), p. 202;

other products of the academies, however, modelled their concerns upon the calmer, more statistical and investigative methods of Price, like Thomas Percival, a friend of Price's, and the first student to enroll when Warrington opened in 1757. Percival was greatly concerned with the rising death rate in the cities, and furnished some statistics on this to Price. His schemes for the police and regulation of health in Manchester in the 1790s resulted in the establishment of a local Board of Health in 1796. As the first President of the Manchester Literary and Philosophical Society (whose members at this time included the young Robert Owen), he read papers on such subjects as the 'Principles and Limits of Taxation'. He was also largely instrumental in the founding of the Manchester Academy in 1786, which was later to have a close if unofficial relationship with the Literary and Philosophical Society.[46]

Not all of the Dissenters who made important contributions to economic debates at the end of the century had attended academies. William Frend (1757–1841), for example, began at the King's School, Canterbury, and became a Fellow of Jesus College, Cambridge, in 1781. The zealousness of his conversion to Unitarianism cost him this office in 1788, but he was afterwards the author of a number of pamphlets on political, religious and economical subjects, as well as for twenty years an actuary. His economic interventions included a discussion of the war as the principal cause of the high price of bread, a condemnation of the effects of the increasing circulation of paper money on provision costs, and a longer work which attacked the abuse of the national debt 'in the hands of the monied interest', and aimed to simplify the system of taxation by making it exactly proportionate to the ability to pay. As a leading Unitarian, too, Frend doubtless contributed to the formation of that brand of liberal Unitarian social thought diffused through the *Monthly Repository* (1806–38), which while it was enthusiastic about the progressive extension of commerce also defended the rights of the poor and expressed some sympathy for co-operation as well as for Owenite schemes of social reform.[47]

William Hazlitt, *Table-Talk; or, Original Essays* (London, 1821), Vol. 2, pp. 199–216; William Hazlitt, *Political Essays, with Sketches of Public Characters* (London, 1822), pp. 256–64 (see also H.W. Stephenson, *William Hazlitt and Hackney College* (London, 1930)).

[46] Thomas Percival, *The Works, Literary, Moral and Philosophical of Thomas Percival* (2 vols., London, 1807), Vol. 1, pp. cxxiii, cxcix, Vol. 2, pp. 229–85; McLachlan, *Warrington Academy*, pp. 104, 115–17.

[47] William Frend, *Scarcity of Bread. A Plan for Reducing the High Price of This Article* (London, 1795), pp. 2–3; William Frend, *The Effects of Paper Money on the Price of Provisions* (London, 1801), pp. 11–12, 25–6; William Frend, *The Principles of Taxation; or, Contribution According to Means* (London, 1804), pp. 12, 40; William Frend, *The National Debt in its True Colours; With Plans for Its Extinction by Honest Means* (London, 1817). For the economic views of the Unitarians see e.g. *Monthly Repository*, Vol. 1 (1806), p. 325; Vol. 16 (1821), pp. 88–101. On the later period see in

Conclusion

The Dissenting academies ceased to be of much importance after the last decade of the eighteenth century for several reasons. In the more liberal academies indiscipline seems to have been something of a problem from the 1770s onwards. Drunkenness and practical jokes appear to have contributed to the downfall of Warrington Academy in 1786, when its subscriptions fell below a manageable level, while pedagogical and theological differences prevented it from merging with the more successful Daventry Academy. Hackney was ridden with scandals of various types, from Wakefield denying the need for public worship to the students entertaining Thomas Paine at a republican dinner at the College in 1792. The radical good will which many leading Dissenting tutors had shown to the rebellious colonies and then the new government of America caused far less backlash, in fact, than that excited by anti-Jacobinism from 1794 onwards. On the positive side, the interests of the Dissenters were admirably served by the foundation, especially for the teaching of medicine and law, of 'the godless institution of Gower Street', London University, in 1828 and the freedom from religious tests which distinguished it from Oxford and Cambridge.[48] (At Coward College, the eventual successor to Daventry Academy, students in 1833 attended the arts courses at University College, receiving only their theological training elsewhere.) The effects of the academies upon education generally in this period were no doubt great; the infant school movement was developed by David Williams, while the first prototype of the later mechanics' institute movement was founded in Birmingham in conjunction with Priestley's church, calling itself first the 'Sunday Society' and later the 'Birmingham Brotherly Society'. But once a recognized course of university studies was available to them, no separate stream of education was required for Dissenters pursuing a secular vocation. In addition, leading Dissenting families by the mid-nineteenth century were not averse to sending their sons to Oxford or Cambridge as a means of integrating themselves more successfully into élite culture. The great role which the Dissenters played in eighteenth- and early nineteenth-century industry and commerce was by this means not a powerful modernizing element in British life after the 1840s. For instead of going on to create a progressive commercial class, many Dissenters aimed instead — like many industrialists — to emulate the ideals and lifestyle of the gentry, which was clearly incommensurable, either with further professionalization or, more specifically, with any too rigid adherence to the social teachings of classical political economy.[49]

particular C.M. Elliott, 'The Political Economy of English Dissent 1780–1840', in *The Industrial Revolution*, ed. R.M. Hartwell (Oxford, 1970), pp. 144–66.

[48] Negley Harte, *The University of London 1836–1986* (London, 1986), pp. 52, 64.

[49] McLachlan, *Warrington Academy*, pp. 101–2; Watts, *The Dissenters*, pp. 488–9; Hans, *New Trends in Education*, pp. 209–12; Raymond Holt, *The Unitarian Contribution to Social Progress* (London, 1952), p. 267.

Through examining the available evidence about the views on commerce of the tutors in these academies as well as, more briefly, those of some of their more famous students, we can see that even within the considerable limitations imposed by the lack of evidence there are traces of consistency in the teachings of the various academies. Much of what was taught in the commercial courses — we can recall again, for example, William Enfield's lectures at Warrington — had less to do with formulating the laws by which the economy worked than with ensuring that those who engaged in commercial activities recognized Christian constraints upon their behaviour. But if commercial ethics did predominate, the teaching of political economy proper, at a period when the definition of the art and science had not yet been rigorously circumscribed, did occur in a number of important cases. In the most prominent of these examined here, the lectures and writings of Joseph Priestley and Richard Price, a coalescence of views clearly occurred around such issues as the national debt, the need for a reasonable but neither equal nor grossly unequal distribution of property, the effects of corruption upon the political system, and the desirability of a considerable measure of parliamentary reform along the lines of radical Whig reform proposals. In their conception of commercial development, however, there is a distinct variation of emphasis in the writings of Priestley and Price, and evidence exists as we have seen of a more general split along these lines among Dissenting tutors and students. Priestley was far more positive in his evaluation of the results of luxury and the refinement of manners than Price, whose more mercantilistic concern for the effects of luxury upon population in particular led him to be more suspicious not only of cities but of the extension of luxury generally. There is no reason not to suspect that this evidences a much wider difficulty which many Dissenters had in reconciling their religious beliefs and traditions with their intimate involvement in commerce.

Despite this difference in emphasis, there is little doubt that both Priestley and Price were generally 'liberal' in their attitude towards state interference in trade and commerce, both through their experience of state interference in the religious sphere, and because they were convinced of the economic advantages of free trade. In this sense the close Scottish connection with many of the academies probably was conducive to the relatively quick acceptance of Smithian political economy by many Dissenters. The deep involvement of the Dissenters in trade as well as their antagonism towards the aristocratic, Anglican regime facilitated their vindication of most of what commercial, urban society had introduced. On the whole the Dissenting tutors were sceptical about the superior virtues of rural society, attacking, as John Aikin did, the idea of the supposed superiority of manners there.[50] Some tutors, like Richard Price, did retain a more republican perspective. But Price simply had many more

---

[50] John Aikin, *Letters from a Father to His Son* (2 vols., London, 1806), Vol. 2, pp. 197–216.

reservations about the ultimate price to be paid for economic freedom, both in Britain and the new United States. Price was in this sense far more within the tradition of Country Party emphasis upon the virtues of an agricultural society than Priestley, who fought free of many of his early biases of this type. But both were on the whole still staunch defenders of the middle and commercial classes, and largely identified their interests with those of the whole community.

But the split between these two great political and religious leaders of Dissent (who also disagreed strongly on the question of liberty and necessity, with Priestley taking the latter side) was also symptomatic of a deeper breach within Dissent during this period. Whatever relationship puritanism had in fact had to capitalism in the sixteenth and seventeenth centuries, Dissent in the eighteenth century underwent a gradual but marked process of secularization, of weakening of religious belief (such as produced Unitarianism) and of integration into a more latitudinarian society. In this process the Dissenters' involvement in commerce played an important role, for the great Quaker, Baptist, Unitarian and other Dissenting families which gained fortunes in commerce and industry after 1700 found that social recognition usually occurred here, where mere religious virtue had failed to produce results. But it would not be unfair to say that in many Dissenting families there was a relatively constant tension between accounting and conscience, acquisition and salvation, investment and the pious distribution of alms to the poor.

In this sense it was not only the ethical demands of Dissent which stood in the way of a whole-hearted embracing of commercial society, but also the presuppositions of an older form of political oeconomy. The central emphasis given to population by both Price and Priestley as well as to national self-sufficiency (a problem on which Priestley vacillated as we have seen) was that of those forms of seventeenth-century economic thought often termed 'mercantilism', for which the ultimate prosperity of the state lay in the strength of its population, both because this ensured more producers and since the military capacity of the nation rested upon its population. The shift to a central concern with wealth as the object of economic science did not occur until after Malthus had come to see population growth as akin to original sin. Price and Priestley thus shared the presumptions of Tucker, Steuart and Smith on the need for an expanding population and for home consumption as a significant portion of economic activity. It is difficult to say how far the vast majority of Dissenters would have agreed with Price and Priestley on such points, although recent evidence suggests that their own congregations were generally much more conservative than both, not to mention other congregations.[51] But this at least reinforces the conclusion that there was not a single 'political economy of British Dissent' taught at the academies during the eighteenth century, but rather

---

[51] See John Seed, 'Gentlemen Dissenters: the Social and Political Meanings of Rational Dissent in the 1770s and 1780s', *Historical Journal*, 28 (1985), pp. 299–325.

an often conflict-ridden account of how commerce and morality might be reconciled in a progressive state of society.

Appendix I
Commerce Students at Manchester Academy, 1786–97

Year	Total New Students	New Students in Commerce
1786	8	2
1787	17	11
1788	7	6
1789	13	3
1790	7	7
1791	14	9
1792	14	6
1793	10	7
1794	15	12
1795	5	4
1796	14	9
1797	11	10

(*Source*: *Roll of Students Entered at Manchester Academy, 1786–1803* (Manchester, 1868)).

Gregory Claeys   UNIVERSITY OF LONDON

CRIME, PUNISHMENT AND LIBERTY

F. Rosen* [1]

Abstract: This essay considers the relationship between crime, punishment and individual liberty in three main thinkers of the Enlightenment: Montesquieu, Beccaria and Bentham. It examines the development of the idea of a proportion between crime and punishment and challenges the view that the eighteenth-century Enlightenment was engaged in the creation of a new form of oppression through a system of rational punishment which was intended to replace that of the medieval period.

In recent decades some social historians, partly under the influence of the French philosopher, Michel Foucault, have viewed the major thinkers of the European Enlightenment as being engaged in the replacement of one system of tyranny and terror with a worse one.[2] These writers have rejected the received opinion, that the eighteenth-century Enlightenment sought to introduce the values of humanity and rationality into a penology characterized by medieval superstition and brutality.[3] They have argued that Enlightenment ideas about punishment used rationality to oppress those unfortunate enough to be caught up in the system: they were subjected to a new regime, centred around hard and often useless labour, solitary confinement past the point of madness, and the penitentiary system. This penology, they believe, was a system more closely related to the emerging capitalism of the eighteenth century, but was nonetheless as oppressive as the one it succeeded.

I want to challenge this view by looking again at the intellectual framework in which the new ideas developed. My challenge will be an indirect one: I want to show that however the prisons and punishments of nineteenth-century

* Bentham Project, University College London, Gower Street, London, WC1E 6BT.

[1] This paper draws on research for my essay, 'Utilitarianism and the Reform of the Criminal Law' to be published in *The Cambridge History of Eighteenth-Century Political Thought*, ed. R. Wokler and M. Goldie, forthcoming from Cambridge University Press.

[2] See, for example, M. Foucault, *Surveiller et punir: Naissance de la prison* (Paris, 1975), translated as *Discipline and Punish: The Birth of the Prison* (London, 1977); D. Hay, 'Property, Authority and the Criminal Law', in *Albion's Fatal Tree, Crime and Society in Eighteenth-Century England*, ed. D. Hay, P. Linebaugh, C. Winslow, J. Rule and E.P. Thompson (London, 1977); M. Ignatieff, *A Just Measure of Pain: The Penitentiary in the Industrial Revolution 1750–1850* (New York, 1978); and M. Ignatieff, 'State, Civil Society and Total Institution: A Critique of Recent Social Histories of Punishment', in *Legality, Ideology, and The State*, ed. D. Sugarman (London, 1983).

[3] This traditional view may be seen in the monumental work by L. Radzinowicz, *A History of English Criminal Law* (5 vols., London, 1948–86).

Europe and the United States developed,[4] the ideas and ideals of the main
writers of the eighteenth century were directed at bringing the idea of liberty to
bear on the problem of crime and punishment.

I shall concentrate on three thinkers: Montesquieu (1689–1755), Beccaria
(1735–94) and Bentham (1748–1832). Their main achievement was to devise
a system of punishment which sought to protect the individual within society,
prevent the criminal from committing crime, deter others from doing the same,
and protect the liberty of the criminal. In incorporating the idea of liberty, they
called for a proportion between crimes and punishments which formed the
intellectual framework for these other ideas. My object is to explore this
framework to see how so improbable an idea as liberty became the key characteristic of this exercise of state power. I shall not claim to have dismissed the
charge that Enlightenment penology was oppressive behind a *facade* of liberty.
But I shall argue that the so-called 'facade' was in fact the foundation of the
structure and the idea of liberty is firmly embedded in that foundation.

Those familiar with the considerable philosophical literature on punishment
may be surprised that my approach will appear to ignore some of the main terms
and categories of this material. By approaching punishment through the main
writers of the Enlightenment I have shifted the argument away from the familiar
ground on which battles have been fought in the twentieth century between
utilitarians and retributivists. In part, I consider (perhaps wrongly) the more
recent debate to have been resolved largely in favour of the utilitarians, or at
least in favour of a theory which has utilitarianism at its foundation.[5] For
example, a main concept of some retributivists, that a person who does wrong
should suffer in proportion to his or her wrong-doing, can be absorbed as a
secondary principle into utilitarian thought without requiring the rejection of
utilitarianism as providing the ultimate justifying aim of punishment.[6] The
argument of some retributivists that utilitarianism allows for the punishment of
the innocent will be seen to be inapplicable to a writer like Bentham because
he holds that there should be a proportion between crimes and punishments and
hence there should be no punishment without a crime.[7] Nevertheless, there still
remain some practical issues on which those who see punishment as concerned

---

[4] As David Garland has pointed out, Foucault has tended to see Bentham's ideas, for
example, as reflecting modern penal practice when they were in fact set forth as ideals
to aim at. See D. Garland, *Punishment and Modern Society* (Oxford, 1990), p. 163.

[5] See, for example, H.L.A. Hart, *Punishment and Responsibility, Essays in the
Philosophy of Law* (Oxford, 1968); Ted Honderich, *Punishment, The Supposed Justifi-
cations* (Harmondsworth, 1984); and C.L. Ten, *Crime, Guilt, and Punishment, A Philosophical Introduction* (Oxford, 1987).

[6] See J. Rawls, 'Two Concepts of Rules', *Philosophical Review*, LXIV (1955), and
the 1968 postscript to C.W.K. Mundle, 'Punishment and Desert', *Philosophical Quarterly*, IV (1954), both of which appear in *The Philosophy of Punishment*, ed. H.B. Acton
(London, 1969), pp. 81–2, 103–14.

[7] But see Ten, *Crime, Guilt, and Punishment*, pp. 13–37, 67 ff.

with retaliation and those who emphasize deterrence disagree. These will be considered in the concluding section of the paper.

I

Montesquieu was the first major writer to place the reform of the criminal law on the agenda of the Enlightenment. One way in which he did so was to call for a proportion between crimes and punishments. In Book VI of *The Spirit of the Laws* (1748) he wrote that 'it is essential for penalties to be harmonious among themselves, because it is essential that the greater crime be avoided rather than the lesser one'.[8] To punish robbery and murder with the same penalty (as was common in Europe) obviously encouraged the robber to commit murder, and Montesquieu praised the English practice of transportation to America for robbers (though not for murderers) as a way of distinguishing between crimes. But he did not explain at this point how punishments could be 'harmonious among themselves' beyond various examples where the lesser punishment was or was not provided as an encouragement to the reduction of crime. However, he returned to the theme of proportion in Book XII of *The Spirit of the Laws* where the discussion was developed within the context of his account of political liberty.[9]

By political liberty Montesquieu meant the security of the individual so that life and property are not threatened either by others or by the state itself. One instrument by which security can be realized is punishment or the threat of punishment of those who would injure other members of society. In linking crime, punishment and liberty, Montesquieu wrote:

> It is the triumph of liberty when criminal laws draw each penalty from the particular nature of the crime. All arbitrariness ends; the penalty does not ensue from the legislator's capriciousness but from the nature of the thing, and man does not do violence to man.[10]

Montesquieu was not initially concerned here (as he was in Book VI) with how penalties harmonized with different crimes (e.g. murder and robbery), but he turned to examine the different sorts of offences to which punishment should be attached. He began by distinguishing four sorts of crimes: (1) against religion; (2) against mores; (3) against tranquillity; and (4) against the security of citizens. In crimes against religion such as sacrilege, witchcraft, etc. Mon-

---

[8] Montesquieu, *The Spirit of the Laws* (hereafter *SL*), VI.16. Translations are taken from Montesquieu, *The Spirit of the Laws*, ed. A. Cohler, B. Miller and H. Stone (Cambridge, 1989).

[9] Discussions of liberty in Montesquieu have tended to emphasize constitutional liberty and the separation of powers and have ignored the material in Book XII. See, for example, R. Shackleton, *Montesquieu, A Critical Biography* (London, 1961), pp. 284–301.

[10] *SL*, XII.4.

tesquieu knew that traditional penalties in many societies, and especially in France, were horrendous. He simply rejected most of these so-called offences insofar as they did not violate individual liberty. As crimes, they had the lowest and not the highest priority. The same argument was applied to the second category of crimes against public mores. In this category he tended to include mainly sexual offences. He distinguished between sexual crimes, such as rape or kidnapping which threatened individual security, and those which were more simply based on the pursuit of pleasure. For the latter, he suggested a number of mild penalties and argued that such offences were based less on wickedness than on 'forgetting or despising oneself'.[11] In the third category were crimes against tranquillity by which he meant public order offences which did not threaten the security of other individuals. Here again, no great penalties were proposed. These were reserved for the final category of crimes against security, where the idea of proportion entered at still another level. For these offences, punishment was needed and Montesquieu conceived of it as 'a kind of retaliation'. The punishment 'is derived from the nature of the thing and is drawn from reason and from the sources of good and evil'.[12]

Despite these vague phrases, Montesquieu clearly sought to proportion punishment to the severity of the offence (in terms of the violation of individual security) with death envisaged as the appropriate punishment for murder, and lesser penalties for lesser crimes. He believed that offences against property should not be punished as severely as those against persons, and while he could conceive of some capital offences involving the theft of property, he thought that loss of goods for those who had them and corporal punishment for those who did not were preferable.[13]

What was significant in Montesquieu's analysis was the way in which the idea of liberty as individual security formed the basis of his examination of proportion in the relationship between crimes and punishments. Proportion was no longer a formal idea suggested in the traditional phrase depicting justice as 'to each his due'. The basis of 'his due' was to be calculated in terms of individual security with those acts which posed the greatest threat to security to receive the greatest punishment. Montesquieu developed his idea in skilful assaults on existing offences such as magic, heresy and homosexuality ('the crimes against nature').[14] From his point of view these often capital offences were virtually dismissed as not being crimes at all.

He criticized at length the crime of high treason for its vagueness[15] and for the tendency to include within the offence a variety of actions including forgery and counterfeiting.[16] Even worse was the extension of the offence of high treason to thought, speech and writing, which he rejected as not being crimes,

---

[11] *Ibid.*
[12] *Ibid.*
[13] *Ibid.*

[14] *SL*, XII.5–6.
[15] *SL*, XII.7.
[16] *SL*, XII.8.

except when part of the preparation of an actual criminal act.[17] 'How, then, can one make speech a crime of high treason? Wherever this law is established, not only is there no longer liberty, there is not even its shadow.'[18]

As we are the beneficiaries of many of the ideas set out by Montesquieu and eventually adopted throughout the world, it is perhaps difficult to appreciate the novelty of his approach. He went further than an opposition to severe penalties and to punishment based more on religious enthusiasm than on actual injuries to individuals. Although offences against religion were in decline in some countries (especially Britain), severe penalties were not. In Britain, for example, more than one hundred and sixty different offences were subject to the death penalty, and this number was actually increasing. Every British schoolboy can still provide the gory details of what is involved in being hanged, drawn and quartered, the traditional punishment for high treason; other punishments, especially flogging and a kind of perpetual imprisonment in chains and fetters were no less horrific, even if less dramatic. In response, Montesquieu called for a careful definition of offences based on the idea of individual liberty as security; he sought to proportion punishments to the severity of the threat to security; he attempted to link punishment to the nature of the crime itself (as a kind of 'retaliation'); and he called attention to the link between customs, mores and forms of government on the one hand and crime and punishment on the other in order to encourage a more varied approach to criminality which placed considerable emphasis on prevention rather than strictly on punishment.

II

Cesare Beccaria's celebrated work, *On Crimes and Punishments*, was published in 1764, sixteen years after Montesquieu's *Spirit of the Laws*. In many respects it is a very different work and one which employed a different methodology. If Montesquieu's approach was 'satirical, witty, urbane, irreverent',[19] Beccaria introduced into his arguments for the first time, according to Bentham, 'the precision and clearness and incontestableness of mathematical calculations'.[20] This 'mathematical' approach was combined with a passionate attack, especially in the chapters on torture and the death penalty, on the cruelty and folly of the criminal law and its enforcement in Europe.[21]

---

[17] *SL*, XII.9–13, 16.

[18] *SL*, XII.12.

[19] M. Cranston, *Philosophers and Pamphleteers, Political Theorists of the Enlightenment* (Oxford, 1986), p. 9.

[20] J. Bentham, *The Works of Jeremy Bentham*, ed. J. Bowring (11 vols., Edinburgh, 1838–43), Vol. III, pp. 286–7. See H.L.A. Hart, *Essays on Bentham, Studies in Jurisprudence and Political Theory* (Oxford, 1982), p. 40.

[21] See C. Beccaria, *On Crimes and Punishments*, trans. D. Young (Indianapolis, 1986), pp. 29–33, 48–53.

Like Montesquieu, Beccaria took the theme of individual liberty as the basis of his treatise, though he followed Rousseau in employing the doctrine of the social contract. To escape from a state of war, where liberty had ceased to have value, free and equal individuals sacrifice part of their liberty to establish peace and security.[22] The portion of liberty which was given up is used by the sovereign to defend the liberty of members and the bond of society itself, and punishment plays a key role in this defence. Punishments are then seen as providing motives for individuals to prevent their acting so as to cause anarchy and chaos.

Beccaria agreed with Montesquieu that every punishment which was not based on the absolute necessity to defend the security of members of society was tyrannical, and this limited power of punishment was the sole, legitimate use of that liberty which was given up by individuals to the sovereign. 'All punishments that exceed what is necessary to preserve this bond', he wrote, 'are unjust by their very nature.'[23]

On a number of themes, Beccaria restated Montesquieu's position and then built on it. For example, he favoured mild rather than severe punishments and used several arguments already developed by Montesquieu such as the importance of encouraging criminals to choose the lesser crime and the diminishing value of severe penalties, which, when generally accepted, no longer deterred. But Beccaria stressed, in addition, the importance of the certainty of punishment as opposed to its severity. To the argument that the prospect of severe punishment deterred crime, he replied that 'crimes are more effectually prevented by the *certainty*, than the *severity* of punishment'. 'The certainty of a small punishment', he continued, 'will make a stronger impression, than the fear of one more severe, if attended with the hopes of escaping . . .'.[24] Beccaria applied a utilitarian calculation which led him to conclude that the expectation of pain to follow the crime from immediate apprehension, trial and punishment would be sufficient to prevent crime and would enable the legislator to avoid the use of severe punishments.

Like Montesquieu, he believed that 'there must be a proportion between crimes and punishments',[25] but he also did not work out such a proportion with any precision. He conceived of a scale of crimes with those that threatened the bond of society itself at the top and the smallest injustice to the individual at the bottom. Punishments would then be ranked to match the crimes. Such a

---

[22] See *ibid.*, Ch. 2, pp. 8–9.

[23] *Ibid.*, p. 9.

[24] This much-quoted passage in the eighteenth century is taken from the 1767 English translation of Beccaria's work which was based on André Morellet's French version of 1766. See *An Essay on Crimes and Punishments; Translated from the Italian with a Commentary, Attributed to Mons. De Voltaire, Translated from the French* (London, 1767), p. 98.

[25] Beccaria, *On Crimes and Punishments*, p. 14.

scale, once established with scientific precision, could even be used to provide a common measure to assess the degrees of liberty and slavery, and humanity and cruelty in various nations.[26] The stage of civilization achieved by various states could be assessed by the various punishments they employed.

Beccaria provided few clues as to how any precise relationship between crimes and punishments might be established. The object of having mild punishments, applied with certainty, based on a clearly defined code and serving to prevent crime, would go part of the way towards establishing the guiding principles of such a scale. But both Beccaria and Montesquieu did little to develop such ideas as proportional punishments or even the idea of using mild punishments to prevent crime. What was perhaps more important was their use of these concepts to *exclude* other and more traditional means of approaching crime and punishment. They strongly opposed the intermingling of the ideas of crime and sin, and reserved for the former a narrow definition and a minimal range of punishments. As for the latter, sinful acts were not necessarily considered crimes at all.

In his treatise Beccaria covered a wide range of topics. He was eloquent in rejecting the cruelties of excessive punishments currently employed and especially common punishments for sodomy, infanticide, bankruptcy, so-called crimes against religion such as heresy, sorcery and witchcraft, and crimes against property. He was also eloquent in his opposition to the death penalty, for which he could find virtually no justification except for extreme necessity where a powerful figure in the state actually threatened it with destruction. Such times of threatened anarchy would, however, be rare.

III

Approximately a dozen years after Beccaria's treatise was written, Jeremy Bentham, who was born in the very year that Montesquieu's *Spirit of the Laws* was published, began to develop a theory of punishment. Although he was greatly indebted to these earlier thinkers, he found that they had done little more than set an agenda. With regard to the much-discussed proportion between crimes and punishments, he noted:

> Establish a proportion between crimes and punishments, has been said by Montesquieu, Beccaria, and many others. The maxim is, without doubt, a good one; but whilst it is thus confined to general terms, it must be confessed it is more oracular than instructive.[27]

Bentham fully accepted the assumptions regarding liberty which had been built into the idea of a proportion between crimes and punishments. The object was to protect all members of society, the law abiding as well as the offending. This protection, or security, was enhanced when individuals were free to act as

---

[26] *Ibid.*, p. 15.
[27] Bentham, *Works*, ed. Bowring, Vol. I, p. 399.

they pleased so long as they caused no harm or injury to other assignable individuals. When acts did cause harm, the penalties should be no more than necessary to prevent the offender from committing the crime, and should always encourage the offender either not to commit it, or to do even less injury than otherwise might be done.

Bentham constructed what Etienne Dumont, whose publication of these writings in 1802 made Bentham famous throughout the world, called the 'logical apparatus': 'the scaffold which ought to be taken down when the building is erected'.[28] With respect to proportion, he presented a series of rules which should guide the lawmaker in the construction of an actual penal code. Once the code was drafted, the rules would no longer be necessary, except, as Dumont put it, as 'a machine for thought — *organum cogitativum*'.[29]

The very idea of a penal or criminal code, though widely advocated in Continental Europe, met considerable opposition in a country like Britain where a combination of statute and common law had made the law so complex that judges and lawyers prospered from their exclusive right to understand and interpret it. The system was defended most eloquently by the philosopher and theologian William Paley, in whose *Principles of Moral and Political Philosophy* (1785) the image of a 'net' — called 'Paley's net' — was set forth to justify the situation where the judge exercised discretion as to whether anyone convicted of the one hundred and sixty odd offences punishable by the death penalty should actually be sentenced to death, pardoned or transported.[30] Such discretion in the form of punishment placed enormous power in a judicial establishment intent on upholding the status quo.

Many writers were unhappy with this arrangement. Juries were reluctant to convict people of trivial offences when they might suffer the death penalty. Criminals had little to lose and no incentive to choose less harmful offences during a crime. This system of terror failed to reduce crime and with the end of transportation to America in 1776 as the solution of what to do with criminals, the crisis deepened.

Bentham's approach was intended to deal with these problems, and especially with the idea of a proportion between crimes and punishments. He developed his ideas in a series of nine rules which attempted to refine or give meaning to the terms of the proportion. His approach will seem somewhat technical, but might better be described as severely analytical. Within each rule he advanced several concepts which were then rigorously defined and distinguished. His first

[28] *Ibid.*, p. 407 n.

[29] *Ibid.*

[30] W. Paley, *The Principles of Moral and Political Philosophy*, in *The Works of William Paley, D.D.* . . (5 vols., London, 1819), Vol. II, p. 8. See T.P. Schofield, 'A Comparison of the Moral Theories of William Paley and Jeremy Bentham', and J.E. Crimmins, 'Strictures on Paley's Net: Capital Punishment and the Power to Pardon', both in *The Bentham Newsletter*, XI (1987), pp. 4–22 and 23–34.

rule was that 'the value of the punishment must not be less in any case than what is sufficient to outweigh that of the profit of the offence'.[31] This rule assumed several key aspects of Bentham's penology. The first idea was that of an economic model that allowed him to write of the 'value' of the punishment and the 'profit' of the offence.[32] Bentham was well aware that the language of political economy had not yet been applied to punishment, and he saw in this language the possibility of the greater use of reason and calculation and the avoidance of passion and prejudice. Besides very crude and largely intuitive notions, such as that a thief should not receive the same punishment as a murderer, no one had devised a way to relate punishments to crimes or, for that matter, crimes to crimes and punishments to other punishments. Bentham believed that his economic model would facilitate his doing so. The pain of punishment was regarded as capital which was invested with the expectation of profit. The profit was the prevention of crime in the future; loss, the continuation or increase in crime. The idea of an economic punishment was one that produced its desired effect with the least possible cost of suffering. The economic model depended on the calculation of various interests which might be physical, financial or psychological, but were expressible in terms of pleasure and pain. Indeed, the economic model was a model about pleasures and pains and only indirectly about profit and loss in any financial sense.

The question then arises: does the model make the scale of punishment any more accessible than before? To answer this question it is necessary to see how Bentham used it to measure what ought to be the proportion between crimes and punishments.

As for the two terms in the first rule — the profit of the offence and the value of the punishment — Bentham meant by the former the force which urged the person to commit the offence, i.e. what one got from doing so, and by the latter, the force employed to prevent the crime. Even where the offence was easily quantifiable, Bentham was aware that the calculation was not a simple one. If an offender stole a pound, this first rule would indicate that he should at least be forced to repay the pound plus the costs of obtaining it. But such a simple equation of crime and punishment might not be adequate. If the offender had little reason to believe that he would be caught, he might be willing to steal again. A low detection rate might allow him to steal several pounds before having to repay only one. Furthermore, the offender might have stolen a pound but he might have so alarmed others by the audacity of his theft that he forced them to purchase expensive locks. This expense, plus the psychological pain suffered by the increased expectation of theft, might make the repayment of

---

[31] *An Introduction to the Principles of Morals and Legislation*, ed. J.H. Burns and H.L.A. Hart (London, 1970), p. 166.

[32] See H.L.A. Hart, *Essays on Bentham, Studies in Jurisprudence and Political Theory* (Oxford, 1982), p. 46.

only one pound too slight a punishment for the offence committed. On the other hand, the person who stole the pound might be very poor and at the point of starvation. The money might be needed to feed his family, and the punishment to repay the one pound might be not only far beyond his grasp but also no deterrent, because he was impelled to steal more by the pain of hunger and extreme suffering than by the fear of punishment.

How is one to decide when the 'value of punishment' exceeds the 'profit from an offence'? Some assistance comes from other rules which Bentham devised. The second was that 'the greater the mischief of the offence, the greater is the expence, which it may be worth while to be at, in the way of punishment'.[33] Bentham believed that this rule needed little argument in its support, though he admitted that so-called crimes against religion, like sacrilege, witchcraft and sorcery, were often severely punished though they caused little mischief. His rule would oppose that trend.

Unfortunately, we do not have the time here to do more than sample Bentham's powerful arguments which enabled the lawmakers who had read them to construct criminal codes based on these principles. The principles (and the codes) would be successful when, all circumstances considered, the minimum punishments were used to prevent the offences. It was easier to prescribe a greater punishment, and this was and has been the temptation of lawmakers. But such punishments are 'expensive' in the sense that they cause unnecessary pain and suffering, and may lead to an increase in criminality.

IV

The three writers, Montesquieu, Beccaria and Bentham, made the account of punishment the central aspect of the exercise of state power. As such, it was carefully limited to offences which injured individuals and was to be used as the main instrument of state power in protecting liberty. Criminality began to be seen as a social problem with social causes and solutions. While the reformation of the criminal was one end of punishment, it was not the sole end and was important mainly as it led to a reduction in crime. But the liberty and dignity of the criminal, even though that liberty would have to be restricted, remained an aspect of punishment to be enhanced by whatever institution was used to administer it.

These writers did not look forward to a period when, by revolution or other means, social institutions would be overturned, the people liberated, and punishment would be unnecessary. The human condition, as they saw it, required the continuing use of punishment to secure liberty. Human beings would continue, they thought, to invade the persons and property of others. Nevertheless, their vision was not a restricted one. They conceived of a society where

---

[33] *Introduction to the Principles of Morals and Legislation*, ed. Burns and Hart, p. 168.

each member should be free to make a plan of life and live it without fear of injury or invasion either by other individuals or by the state itself. Such a vision may seem modest to some; but in the world we inhabit nowadays, its very modesty gives it an unmistakeable appeal.

If this vision is not optimistic in believing that criminality can be wholly overcome, it is in showing that it can be made part of the rational organization of society, with the liberty of the population as a whole preserved, and criminals accommodated with as much dignity as possible. But perhaps even this modest aim is wildly utopian. We do not seem to be able to reduce crime through punishment. If we could, the current anxiety felt by many regarding growing lawlessness might be rejected as being exaggerated.

The real danger in the present circumstances lies in the possible abandonment of the principle of deterrence as the main object of punishment. This forward-looking principle underpins the emphasis placed on a proportion between crimes and punishments and prevents this doctrine from becoming a vindictive one. Punishment is designed to protect individual liberty by deterring the invasion of that liberty. It may serve related ends of reformation or example, but it is not concerned to save souls, put justice into them, or give satisfaction to the victims of crime or to society at large.

The threat to this system which has liberty at its heart comes mainly from the idea of retaliation, that is to say, that the object of punishment is to reflect somehow the crime itself and thereby give satisfaction to those who have suffered from it. It is important to distinguish between two aspects of retaliation. Montesquieu, as we have seen, wrote that punishments 'are a kind of retaliation'. 'A citizen deserves death', he wrote, 'when he has violated security so far as to take or to attempt to take a life.'[34] For Montesquieu, and later for Bentham, there was considerable profit in devising punishments which were analogous in some way to the crime committed. Even where exact analogy or retaliation was not possible, there could be a potent connection between a proposed punishment and the offence. Castration, observed Bentham, 'seems the most appropriate punishment in the case of rape; that is to say, the best adapted to produce a strong impression on the mind at the moment of temptation'.[35] Montesquieu's proposal of the death penalty for murder and Bentham's of castration for rape, are developed within the framework of devising punishments which will deter the criminal and reduce crime. For example, when Montesquieu advocates the death penalty for murder, he is in the process of proposing that it should not be used, for example, in cases of theft, where milder penalties will be equally effective and murder will receive the full force of an analogous punishment.[36]

[34] *SL*, XII.4.
[35] Bentham, *Works*, ed. Bowring, Vol. I, p. 411.
[36] *SL*, XII.4.

Bentham was well aware of the importance of both analogy and retaliation in punishment. At one point he wrote:

> The great merit of the law of retaliation is its simplicity. If it were capable of universal adoption, the whole penal code would be contained in one law: — 'Let every offender suffer an evil similar to that which he has inflicted.'
>
> No other imaginable plan can, for its extent, find so easy an entrance into the apprehension, or sit so easy on the memory. The rule is at once so short and so expressive, that he who has once heard it, is not likely to forget it, or ever to think of a crime, but he must think also of its punishment. The stronger the temptation to commit an offence, the more likely is its punishment to be an object of dread.[37]

In addition to these clear advantages, retaliation is also popular among the people in general. Though the idea of justice incorporated in it is somewhat rigid, it is simple and requires little sophistication to grasp its essence.

Bentham thus fully appreciated the significance of retaliation in punishment, but he was also aware of its limitations and especially its dangers. It is not applicable to numerous categories of offences, for example those of a public nature. How, he asked, is retaliation to be applied to the crime of high treason or having correspondence with an enemy? What he called semi-public offences (against the community at large) would also not allow for simple retaliation. Nor would offences against property, where (as was common) a thief has little or no property to compensate the person from whom he has stolen goods. In fact, retaliation is so limited that it is mainly used where 'blood will have blood'. 'Unless a murderer be punished with death', Bentham continued, 'the multitude of speculators can seldom bring themselves to think that the rules of justice are pursued.'[38]

The dangers lay precisely in the rigid conception of justice and the tendency towards severe punishments which make the idea of retaliation so popular. Those who used and exploited it tended to separate the idea from human happiness and utility. It was more popular, Bentham believed, among 'those of a vindictive character':

> Mahomet found it established among the Arabians; and has adopted it in the Koran, with a degree of approbation, that marks the extent of his talent for legislation . . . Either from weakness or ignorance he encouraged the prevailing vice, which he ought to have checked.[39]

Bentham clearly rejected retaliation as the sole end of punishment, and in the *Introduction to the Principles of Morals and Legislation*, he observed that 'no punishment ought to be allotted merely to this purpose, because . . . no such

---

[37] Bentham, *Works*, ed. Bowring, Vol. I, p. 410.
[38] *Ibid.*
[39] *Ibid.*, p. 411.

pleasure is ever produced by punishment as can be equivalent to the pain'.[40] In part, Bentham was pointing to an asymmetry between pain and pleasure; pain and the relief of it count for far more in human happiness than the simple pursuit of pleasure. He was also making a profound point about punishment. No matter how much pleasure or satisfaction is given to the community by the severe punishment of wrongdoers, the pain inflicted is always greater than the satisfaction afforded to the person wronged or to the public at large. When the popular maxim, 'hanging is too good for him', is invoked at a trial of a particularly vicious killer, one wonders what would be 'good enough', and one is reminded of the terrible catalogue of brutal punishments which have been associated with the idea of retaliation. Montesquieu, Beccaria and Bentham opposed the use of retaliation in this simple though appealing form and placed their emphasis on using punishment to secure individual liberty.

F. Rosen   UNIVERSITY COLLEGE LONDON

---

[40] *Introduction to the Principles of Morals and Legislation*, ed. Burns and Hart, p. 159 n.

JEREMY BENTHAM:
BIOGRAPHY AND INTELLECTUAL BIOGRAPHY*

*David Lieberman***

Abstract: The article examines Bentham's writings and activities during the period 1788 to 1803, when much of his energy was devoted to the unsuccessful Panopticon prison project. Focusing on the varied strategies pursued by Bentham to secure public notice for his legislative programme, the discussion emphasizes how far in his writings he had moved from the central core of his legislative theory by the first years of the nineteenth century. This perspective, in turn, clarifies the critical importance to Bentham's later career of the successful reception of Etienne Dumont's redaction of the Benthamite legislative science in the 1802 *Traités de législation.*

The unique contribution of Jimmy Burns to modern Bentham studies will ever be associated with his eighteen-year tenure as the first General Editor of the on-going edition of the *Collected Works of Jeremy Bentham*. In this capacity, he guided the Bentham Project through its initial labours and personally co-edited three of the first four volumes of works published in the series. Just as it is impossible to understand contemporary Bentham scholarship without appreciating the pervasive impact of the new Bentham edition, so it is no less impossible to imagine the edition itself without celebrating the pioneering achievements of J.H. Burns.

For the historian of political thought, equal appreciation attaches to the series of article-length studies that accompanied the work of Bentham's editor, in which Burns illuminated the major strands of Bentham's intellectual development and placed his writings in their biographical and broader historical contexts. In this article, I seek to pay my dear and distinguished teacher the compliment of imitation. My aim is to consider Bentham's activities and writings at the mid-point of his career; roughly in the years 1788 to 1803. One reason for taking up this particular period is that it concerns a stage of Bentham's intellectual biography that has curiously divided previous commentators. But further incentive is supplied by the opportunity to turn to an area of

* As in the case of my previous attempts to explore Bentham's intellectual development, my greatest debt is to Jimmy Burns' wonderful scholarship, teaching and example. In approaching this article, I also benefited greatly from the recent writings and helpful guidance of Philip Schofield. Final thanks are directed to Janet Coleman, for her generous and much-needed counsel during the preparation of this article.

** University of California, Jurisprudence and Social Policy Program, School of Law, Berkeley, CA 94720, USA.

Bentham scholarship where Burns' own contribution — in the form of his 1965 Royal Historical Society lecture on 'Bentham and the French Revolution' — has proved so deservedly influential.[1]

The period 1788 to 1803 can be treated as a distinct phase in Bentham's career, though some inevitable arbitrariness occurs in setting any firm chronological boundaries. In February 1788, a few days before his fortieth birthday, Bentham returned to London, following an absence of two and a half years. He had spent the intervening period chiefly in White Russia, where his younger brother, Samuel, was then employed as a naval architect and engineer in the Russian service. The year 1803 saw the close of another chapter of Bentham's career: the effective end to over ten years' worth of frustrated effort to secure the required government backing to construct, manage and reap the profits of a Panopticon penitentiary in the metropolis.[2]

In terms of published writings the period is roughly bounded by the appearance of two major, synthetic statements of the theory of law and the codification programme Bentham had developed during the 1770s and early 1780s. In this, the enormously productive first phase of his jurisprudential speculations, Bentham believed he had achieved 'a complete and pretty detailed plan of a complete body of the laws'; a legislative system in which 'there are no *terrae incognitae*, no blank spaces; nothing is at least omitted; nothing unprovided for'.[3] Having successfully identified this programme for 'a body of the law complete in all its branches', the great remaining task (as he then conceived it) was to supply a fuller exposition and fleshing out of this legislative system, and thereby present a 'complete body of law, a *pannomion*, if so it might be termed'.[4]

In 1789 Bentham published a long-overdue *Introduction to the Principles of Morals and Legislation*. The work, originally composed 'as an introduction to a plan of a penal code',[5] had been printed nine years earlier. By 1789 only half

---

[1] J.H. Burns, 'Bentham and the French Revolution', *Transactions of the Royal Historical Society*, Fifth Series, XVI (1966), pp. 95–114.

[2] Selecting 1803 as the termination point for the Panopticon project is somewhat arbitrary, given the brief revival of the scheme in 1811–12 and given Bentham's continuing preoccupation with the project's failure up until the time of his death in 1832. These later involvements are reviewed by Janet Semple in *Bentham's Prison: A Study of the Panopticon Penitentiary* (Oxford, 1993). Semple's book offers the fullest account of the Panopticon prison, and I am much indebted to this fine study.

[3] Jeremy Bentham, *Of Laws in General*, ed. H.L.A. Hart (London, 1970), pp. 233, 246.

[4] Jeremy Bentham, *An Introduction to the Principles of Morals and Legislation*, ed. J.H. Burns and H.L.A. Hart (London, 1970), pp. 6, 305. For fuller accounts of this first phase of Bentham's legislative theory, see Gerald J. Postema, *Bentham and the Common Law Tradition* (Oxford, 1986), Part 2, and David Lieberman, *Province of Legislation Determined: Legal Theory in Eighteenth-Century Britain* (Cambridge, 1989), Part 4.

[5] Bentham, *Morals and Legislation*, p. 1.

of the original printing of two hundred and fifty copies survived; and notwith-standing some efforts to publicize the publication and secure notice from the popular reviews, the book made no impact. In contrast, 1802 saw the appear-ance of Etienne Dumont's three-volume version of *Traités de législation civile et pénale . . . Par M. Jérémie Bentham, jurisconsulte anglois*; the publication which, in Burns' words, 'virtually established Bentham as a significant thinker with a substantial reputation'.[6] Two further French editions of the compilation appeared before Bentham's death in 1832; along with translations into Russian (1805), Italian (1819), Spanish (1821–2), German (1830), as well as English (1830).[7]

Any examination of Bentham's career during the period 1788 to 1803 must begin with a survey of his writing projects. As Burns reported in a similar setting, 'that [Bentham] was writing goes without saying, for he had written almost without intermission since coming of age in 1769. That he was writing on a wide range of different subjects is, again, only what we should expect.'[8] Several months after the 1788 return to London, Bentham's writing took an unanticipated direction in response to the unfolding political events in France, where he identified a promising opportunity for the sympathetic consideration of his reform doctrines. Exploiting contacts at home and a variety of French correspondents, Bentham composed a series of political tracts for revolutionary France. These included a substantial treatment of parliamentary procedures, the *Essay on Political Tactics*, composed in 1788/9; a proposed *Draught of a New Plan for the Organisation of the Judicial Establishment in France*, printed in 1790; and a roughly concurrent series of proposals on political representation and constitutional matters, which in turn led Bentham to a brief exploration of these same topics in the British context.[9] France's unbidden advisor was rewarded with honorary citizenship in the summer of 1792. But by the time notification of the honour reached Bentham later that year, he had begun to react against the increasing violence and radicalism of revolutionary politics. The reaction led to further writings, now in condemnation of French radicalism and in defence of Britain's unreformed electoral system. The most substantial of these critical polemics was Bentham's relentless mid-decade attack on the

---

[6] J.H. Burns, 'The Bentham Project', in *Editing Texts of the Romantic Period*, ed. John D. Baird (Toronto, 1972), pp. 73–87, p. 78.

[7] The publishing details and contrasting fortunes of the two publications are valuably explored in J.R. Dinwiddy, 'Bentham and the Early 19th Century', in J.R. Dinwiddy, *Radicalism and Reform in Britain, 1780–1850* (London and Rio Grande, Ohio, 1992), pp. 293–4.

[8] J.H. Burns, 'Dreams and Destinations: Jeremy Bentham in 1828', *The Bentham Newsletter*, I (1978), pp. 21–30, p. 22.

[9] For surveys of these writings, see Burns, 'Bentham and the French Revolution', and the reconsideration by James E. Crimmins, 'Bentham's Political Radicalism Re-examined', *Journal of the History of Ideas*, LIV (1994), pp. 260–74.

French Declaration of the Rights of Man, first conceived under the title *Pesti-lential Nonsense Unmasked*.[10]

By the time Bentham had begun writing *against* rather than *for* the politicians of France, his own attention had shifted dramatically as a result of the effort to construct under his direction and management an inspection-house penitentiary in the metropolis. The now-famous Panopticon project was initially described in a series of twenty-one brief *Panopticon Letters*, composed in Russia in 1786, and later qualified as merely 'the original rude sketch' of the scheme.[11] These effusively celebrated the potential of his brother, Samuel's, innovative archi-tectural device for managing labourers, and enthusiastically advocated the adoption of this 'inspection-house' design for any institution in which 'a number of persons are meant to be kept under supervision'.[12] In the first years of the next decade, Bentham saw opportunities for the realization of the project in such places as Dublin, Edinburgh and Paris. In 1792, however, opportunity was increasingly focused upon London. Bentham won the support of the Home Secretary, Henry Dundas, and less effectively courted the Prime Minister, William Pitt. In the summer of the following year, both ministers visited Jeremy and Samuel's London residence to view 'the Raree-show'[13] of assembled Panopticon models and prototypes. The result of the long-awaited meeting (to Bentham's understanding) was the even more-desired announcement by Pitt that the project enjoyed the ministerial support needed to ensure its speedy realization.[14] As the brothers confidently reported earlier to a friend from their days in Russia, 'the "Panopticon" plan . . . is approved by everybody'.[15]

From these propitious beginnings followed over a decade's worth of failure and disappointment, fury and grievance. The extent to which the Panopticon project eclipsed all other of Bentham's activities and interests during these ten-plus years is painfully evinced in his contemporary correspondence. His letters and papers of the period 1793 to 1803 document at crushing length the relentless efforts to rally parliamentary backers, the speed with which he alienated aristocratic landlords and lease-holders whose property he sought for the Panopticon site, the ease with which he was neglected and outmanoeuvred

---

[10] The work is now better known under the title, *Anarchical Fallacies*; see *Works of Jeremy Bentham*, ed. John Bowring (11 vols., Edinburgh, 1838–43), II, pp. 489–534.

[11] *Correspondence of Jeremy Bentham*, ed. Timothy L.S. Sprigge, Vols. I–II (Lon-don, 1968); ed. Ian R. Christie, Vol. III (London, 1971); ed. Alexander Taylor Milne, Vols. IV-V (London, 1981); ed. J.R. Dinwiddy, Vols. VI–VII (Oxford, 1984–8); ed. Stephen Conway, Vols. VIII–X (Oxford, 1988–94); Vol. IV, p. 290.

[12] *Panopticon; or, The Inspection-House*, in *Works*, ed. Bowring, IV, p. 40.

[13] So described by Bentham in a letter to his brother of 21 May 1793; *Correspon-dence*, ed. Milne, IV, p. 432.

[14] See *Correspondence*, ed. Milne, V, pp. 22–5, for Bentham's understanding of the meeting.

[15] *Ibid.*, IV, p. 320.

by unsympathetic politicians and Treasury officials, and the countless humiliations and insults he suffered at Whitehall.

Bentham's elderly obsession with the Panopticon disaster ensured the episode thereafter received due notice in sketches of his career. What, however, remains less familiar is the amount of writing and intellectual energy Panopticon absorbed and stimulated at this time. In 1790–91, Bentham composed two protracted *Postscripts* to the original *Panopticon Letters* which dwarfed the material they supplemented. Much of the standard scholarly characterization of the Panopticon, even before Foucault's well-known treatment in *Discipline and Punish*, focused on Bentham's chilling effusions in praise of inspection-house surveillance: 'a new mode of obtaining power of mind over mind, in a quantity hitherto without example'.[16] But, as Janet Semple rightly emphasizes, it is the *Postscripts* which contain the real plan for the prison.[17] There Bentham not only revised basic features of the penal design presented in the *Panopticon Letters* (such as the restricting of solitary confinement), but also went on to introduce major new features to the project (such as the creation of a network of panoptic-asylums for the support and monitoring of released prisoners).

In addition to the *Postscripts*, the prison campaign led to the drafting of a variety of substantial compositions: a printed *Proposal* and draft contract serving as the basis for Bentham's negotiations with the Treasury; two separate draft parliamentary bills of 1794 (the longer of which ran to two hundred and fifty-seven clauses and fifty thousand words), revising the terms of authorization specified in the earlier 1779 Penitentiary Act; two pairs of summary 'Memorials' to the Lords of the Treasury of 1794 and of 1800 (the longest of which ran to fourteen sections and roughly four thousand words), setting out the details of his obstructed efforts and mounting expenditures;[18] a body of scathing polemics of 1802–3, detailing the injustices of his treatment, denouncing the integrity and conduct of his opponents, and challenging the constitutionality of the rival regime of penal transportation.[19] Beyond all these was the most voluminous and ambitious of the companions to the original *Panopticon Letters*, Bentham's 1797 plan for the relief of poverty in England, *Pauper Management Improved!*. The proposal called for the construction of a national network of two hundred and fifty profit-making pauper-panopticons under joint-stock company management, which would function primarily as workhouses for the indigent but additionally supply collateral benefits as 'Register Offices, Loan Offices, Frugality Banks, Superannuation-Annuity Banks, Post-

[16] *Works*, ed. Bowring, IV, p. 39. For Foucault's characterization, see Michel Foucault, *Discipline and Punish*, trans. Alan Sheridan (New York, 1979), pp. 200–9.

[17] See Semple, *Bentham's Prison*, pp. 111–12.

[18] See *Correspondence*, ed. Milne, V, pp. 54–69, and *Correspondence*, ed. Dinwiddy, VI, pp. 316–19, 471–85.

[19] For a more detailed account of these polemics and their partial publication in 1812, see Semple, *Bentham's Prison*, pp. 218–53.

obit-benefit Banks, Charitable Remittance Offices, Frugality Inns, Dispensaries, Lying-in Hospitals, Midwifery Lecture Schools, Veterinary Lecture Schools, Military Exercise Schools and Marine Schools'.[20]

Bentham, in developing the pauper-panopticon project, sought to take advantage of the mid-1790s public debate over the poor laws and indigence which was aired in response to the food scarcities and steep rise in grain prices of these years. As such, the work can be grouped with a more heterogeneous set of compositions through which Bentham similarly responded to the varied social problems and parliamentary discussions that emerged during the first phase of the wars against revolutionary France. Some of these initiatives, such as the 1796 collaboration with Patrick Colquhoun which led to the drafting of two parliamentary bills for improved rural and metropolitan policing, enjoyed clear thematic connection with the kinds of social ills addressed by the two Panopticon schemes. But elsewhere Bentham tackled quite different issues, as in the case of a series of works concerning government fiscal policy in dealing with the steeply escalating wartime public debt. All but two of the sixteen tracts which Werner Stark assembled in his three-volume edition of *Jeremy Bentham's Economic Writings* were composed in the period 1788 to 1804.[21] These ranged widely in content and scope: essays identifying untapped sources of government revenue; proposals for the better regulation of banks and insurance companies, and for the introduction of an interest-bearing paper currency; and bafflingly complex explorations of the dangers and dynamics of price inflation.

Even this schematic and incomplete survey makes plain the remarkable pace and range of Bentham's literary output in the years under examination here. Nonetheless, previous commentators have disagreed strongly on the assessment of the compositions themselves. Elie Halévy maintained that the period following 'the year 1789' constituted 'as it were a pause in the history of Bentham's thought'. Leslie Stephen believed that the entire Panopticon episode rested upon a massive misdirection of talents. Werner Stark, responding to the frequency with which Bentham abruptly abandoned and left unfinished most of the works assembled in the edition of *Economic Writings*, likened the behaviour to that of 'a child that plays with a favourite toy for a time but then throws it aside and forgets about it'.[22]

In striking contrast, more recent commentators have ascribed critical importance to the writings of 1788 to 1803. One version of the counter-thesis has

---

[20] J.R. Poynter, *Society and Pauperism: English Ideas on Poor Relief, 1795–1834* (London, 1963), pp. 139–40. See also Charles F. Bahmueller, *The National Charity Company: Jeremy Bentham's Silent Revolution* (Berkeley, CA, 1981).

[21] Stark's introductions to each volume remain the fullest survey of this material; see *Jeremy Bentham's Economic Writings*, ed. W. Stark (3 vols., London, 1952–4).

[22] Elie Halévy, *The Growth of Philosophic Radicalism*, trans. Mary Morris (London, 1972), p. 153; Leslie Stephen, *The English Utilitarians* (3 vols., London, 1900), I, pp. 205–6; *Bentham's Economic Writings*, ed. Stark, III, p. 47.

been developed by treating the Panopticon programmes as encapsulating the fundamental core of Bentham's approach to public institutions and human welfare, thereby furnishing in themselves the (often revelatory) materials for an account of his more general moral and legal theory. Foucault's renderings of 'Panopticism' offers a complex example of the approach, which is also found in the treatments of more conventional interpreters, such as Gertrude Himmelfarb and Charles Bahmueller. Himmelfarb, emphasizing how much of the penitentiary plan was shaped by Bentham's immediate financial interests in the institution's anticipated profits from inmate labour, condemned an effort that was 'more and more a travesty of the model prison and the model reformer'. Bahmueller, noting the minute planning of the pauper-panopticons, proposed the institutions as 'a version of Benthamite society writ small' which afforded 'insight into [Bentham's] hopes and strategies for the government of society at large'.[23] Unfortunately, as critics have been quick to point out, the Panopticon schemes scarcely support the interpretative weight these scholars assigned to them. Their characterizations tend to mistake particular and selective institutional applications of Bentham's principles for his entire legislative programme.[24]

An alternative and more compelling case for the importance of the writings of this period has been made by scholars who find in them key moments in the development of Bentham's mature reform programme. The political tracts directed at revolutionary France thus have commanded attention as the setting in which Bentham first elaborated the utilitarian case for democratic representation which he did not publicly present until the 1817 *Plan of Parliamentary Reform*.[25] Likewise, the discrete and varied institutional designs of this period — the plan for *Judicial Establishment in France*, the two Panopticons, the police bills — have been heralded as the breakthrough investigations of those principles of public management and administrative accountability which furnished a central pillar of the democratic state elaborated in Bentham's *Constitutional Code*. L.J. Hume, in *Bentham and Bureaucracy*, meticulously charted and assessed this important line of intellectual development. By the time of the collapse of the Panopticon campaign, Hume explains, Bentham had acquired 'most of the elements that he was later to put into his programme' for the modern state's administrative apparatus. On this basis, the 1790s are re-

---

[23] Gertrude Himmelfarb, *Victorian Minds* (New York, 1968), p. 58; Bahmueller, *National Charity Company*, pp. 110, 155.

[24] On Foucault, see Janet Semple, 'Foucault and Bentham: A Defence of Panopticonism', *Utilitas*, IV (1992), pp. 105–20; on Himmelfarb, see L.J. Hume, 'Revisionism in Bentham Studies', *Bentham Newsletter*, I (1978), pp. 3–20; on Bahmueller, see David Lieberman, 'From Bentham to Benthamism', *Historical Journal*, XXVIII (1985), pp. 199–224, pp. 210–14.

[25] See Crimmins, 'Bentham's Political Radicalism', for the most recent treatment of this theme.

vealed to be an enormously fertile and valuable phase of Bentham's life, the period when he 'advanced most rapidly towards the detailed contents of the *Constitutional Code*'.[26]

While this recent emphasis on Bentham's achievements in the period 1788 to 1803 helpfully serves to qualify the picture of an intellectual hiatus fashioned by Halévy and others, important interpretative questions remain. In these accounts, the labours of the period are redeemed retrospectively by the subsequent use Bentham made of these materials in his radical political programme. It is hardly surprising that Bentham's intellectual biography should be plotted in these terms. Still, some suspicion emerges that the case for these compositions turns so extensively on Bentham's pursuits at the very final stage of his long career. Bentham, after all, was already in his mid-70s when he came in the 1820s to make the *Constitutional Code* his chief legislative project. Suppose Bentham had not been so blessed with such a long and intellectually active life: how, then, might the writings and pursuits of the Panopticon years be assessed? Again, in these accounts, it is the *intellectual* biography which supplies the critical measure of this phase of Bentham's career. Suppose attention shifts from the content of these varied writings to the more purely biographical circumstances of their composition: how then might these productions and this phase of Bentham's life best be appraised?

In what next follows, I seek to develop such a non-retrospective assessment of Bentham's career during the period 1788 to 1802. A useful way into this treatment is to explore the crude yet obvious question of Bentham's need to secure an audience and reputation on the basis of which he could promote his ambitious and intricate codification programme. Bentham, at the very beginning of his career, had come to recognize in himself 'a genius for legislation' and a lifelong vocation in the science of legislation.[27] The point of such theoretical pursuits was, of course, the promotion of human happiness; and the realization of this goal, in turn, required the mobilization of public authority. 'To frame weapons for the advocates of the reform of the institutions of his own country' and 'of all countries', Southwood Smith eulogized in 1832, 'was his daily occupation and his highest pleasure'. Bentham himself 'took no part in the actual business of legislation and government', instead 'he guided the minds of many of the most distinguished legislators and patriots'.[28]

Early on Bentham determined that the practice of law, for which he had been trained, would only distract or even corrupt the pursuit of this life's mission. The decision not only frustrated the designs of his father, it also denied Bentham a well-worn professional route to the public stage. This trajectory from legal practice to parliamentary law reformer is found in the careers of several of the important figures with whom Bentham intersected at various points in his own

[26] L.J. Hume, *Bentham and Bureaucracy* (Cambridge, 1981), pp. 13, 110.
[27] *Works*, ed. Bowring, X, p. 27.
[28] *Ibid.*, XI, p. 92.

life: William Eden, to whom in 1778 he directed his first essay on prison design, *A View of the Hard Labour Bill*; his friend and confidant of many years, Samuel Romilly; and his own half-brother, Charles Abbot.

Having rejected this particular professional course of self-promotion, Bentham's biography can be charted in terms of the various alternative routes to public prominence he tested and pursued. Perhaps the most obvious of these was the direct overtures Bentham often made to sovereigns and governments, advertising his services as a legislative draftsman and codifier. In the last two decades of his life — by which time his public reputation had been achieved — Bentham enumerated the conditions under which a modern code might ideally be drafted and debated, and further specified the terms under which his own services could be secured. Bentham published codification proposals addressed 'to all nations professing liberal opinions', and successively directed his attention to the governments in the US, Iberia, Greece and Spanish America.[29] In the earlier phases of his career, this strategy remained less explicitly elaborated and publicly aired. But even then Bentham looked just as opportunistically for the chance to find a sovereign or statesman who could directly translate his legislative theory into actual law. By the late 1770s, both Bentham brothers had come to identify Tsarist Russia as an especially promising target for their respective lines of expertise.[30] 'I work upon *Code* with more pleasure', Jeremy wrote to Samuel in 1778, 'now that I do it under a moral certainty of its finding it's way to my dear Kitty' [that is, Catherine II].[31] The subsequent visits to Russia, which began with Samuel's departure in 1779, were conceived from the start as a joint enterprise. But while Samuel successfully advanced his career as a naval engineer in Russia, Bentham's career as a codifier stalled. The projected *Code* remained unfinished, and the actual opportunity to meet the Empress of all the Russians was evaded.[32]

The tracts for France which Bentham composed soon after his 1788 return from Russia easily conform to this pattern of self-promotion. Moreover, the success he enjoyed in getting some of this material into circulation through such vehicles as Mirabeau's *Courier de Provence*, like the later award of honorary French citizenship, might be reckoned a respectable return on this initiative, especially in comparison with the previous Russian venture. Unfortunately, the radicalization of the French revolution and its repercussions for Britain rendered all the more fragile this general strategy for attaining public influence. Bentham's career can scarcely be reckoned another casualty of the French

---

[29] These codification proposals and personal initiatives of the 1810s and 1820s are treated by Philip Schofield in 'Jeremy Bentham: Legislator of the World', *Current Legal Problems*, LI (1998), pp. 115–47. I am much indebted to this valuable discussion.

[30] The brothers' Russian ventures are examined in Ian R. Christie, *The Benthams in Russia 1780–1791* (Oxford and Providence, Rhode Island, 1993).

[31] *Correspondence*, ed. Sprigge, II, p. 188.

[32] See Christie, *Benthams in Russia*, pp. 175–6.

Revolution: he simply lacked the kind of public reputation for which his initial French enthusiasms could cause embarrassment or damage.[33] At the same time, though, the general reaction against French militancy, which he came to share, created a most unpromising political climate for the reception of that kind of comprehensive codification programme which his own legislative science urged. If Bentham during the Panopticon years seemed to occupy himself with reform projects and proposals far more limited in scale than the great *pan-nomion*, some of this adjustment followed the dynamics of anti-French politics at home.

An alternative, more conventional path to political influence was afforded by the settled patterns of aristocratic patronage in the parliamentary system of Hanoverian Britain. The elderly Bentham took such pains to present himself as the gentle 'hermit of Queen Square Place', who carefully avoided partisan intrigue and whose reform programme took equal aim at the entrenched abuses of the Tory and Whig establishments, that it becomes nearly impossible to imagine him playing the part of Burke to another's Lord Rockingham. None-theless, in the 1780s and 1790s Bentham's career pursuits frequently came to depend on his developing connection and friendship with the Whig politician and reforming minister, the Earl of Shelburne. Initially it was the promotion of Samuel's career that led Jeremy into correspondence with Shelburne, and the diffident Jeremy avoided a personal meeting until Shelburne took the initiative in the summer of 1781. In the autumn of the year, Bentham enjoyed the first of several visits to the Earl's estate at Bowood, where the Earl pressed the writings of the still-unknown jurist on his prestigious legal advisors, Lord Camden and John Dunning. 'He raised me', Bentham later explained to his first biographer, 'from the bottomless pit of humiliation — he made me feel I was something.'[34]

In the years immediately following the 1788 return from Russia, Bentham in effect placed much of his fortunes under Shelburne's (now the Marquis of Lansdowne) wing. Bentham's turn to the affairs of revolutionary France de-pended fully on Lansdowne's encouragement and patronage. Major parts of his French writings were composed while a guest at Bowood and Lansdowne House. Lansdowne supplied Bentham with his French translator in the person of Etienne Dumont; and Lansdowne acted critically in helping to create an audience for these tracts by promoting them among his own French contacts. It was again Lansdowne who in some measure initiated the Panopticon cam-paign, when in 1790 he sent a copy of the still-unpublished *Panopticon Letters* to Sir John Parnell, the Chancellor of the Exchequer for Ireland. Bentham

---

[33] Even so, Bentham on occasion found it prudent to clarify any 'Republican' impression given by some of the French tracts; see *Correspondence*, ed. Milne, IV, p. 430.

[34] *Works*, ed. Bowring, X, p. 115. For Bentham's more contemporary account of these experiences, see *Correspondence*, ed. Sprigge, II, pp. 470–1; *Correspondence*, ed. Chris-tie, III, pp. 49–74.

quickly jumped on Parnell's announced enthusiasm for the scheme, looking
first to Ireland before shifting attention to London.

This, moreover, was a period of considerable personal intimacy between the
two men. He 'has opened to me a good deal of late', Jeremy reported to Samuel
in July 1989, 'and I am become one of the Cabinet Council [at Lansdowne
House], dining there regularly once a week'.[35] When Lansdowne's wife died
that August, the Marquis singled out Bentham to join him at Bowood and
remain with him during the first months of bereavement. Unfortunately,
Lansdowne's own parliamentary career was already in its period of long
decline, so that he could never provide the kind of political influence needed
by Bentham to realize the Panopticon scheme or any other of his diverse
institutional projects of the 1790s. But even had the Whig aristocrat been
differently situated, it is hard to imagine Bentham managing any long-term
posting in the 'Cabinet Council'. The temperamental difficulties were painfully
disclosed in an appalling letter of about ten thousand words Bentham sent to
Lansdowne in late August 1790, protesting the Marquis' failure to provide him
with a parliamentary seat. The prolix composition, challenging Lansdowne's
judgment and his sense of justice, shows the brittle insecurity with which
Bentham observed the Marquis' patronage of others in his circle, and was
menaced by the thought that he himself, in contrast, had been judged 'incapable
of every thing but proposing impracticable projects, and throwing out odd ideas
that would not have occurred to any body else'.[36]

Lansdowne countered with a predictably briefer, more measured and concili-
atory note. He readily repudiated Bentham's claims ('I am impatient to set you
right about your Foundation Fact, upon which we are very far from agreed'),
confirmed his affection and (no doubt correctly) suggested that the unexpected
epistolary explosion was chiefly due to Bentham's acknowledged distress at his
step-brother's recent election to the House of Commons under the patronage of
the Duke of Leeds.[37] Although the friendship survived this particular 'Ebulli-
tion', as Lansdowne termed it, contact between the two figures had largely
ceased by 1797. The termination of the relationship marked the closing of
another route to public notice that Bentham tested in these early stages of his
career.

Eventually of course, it was on the basis of his stature as a jurist that Bentham
secured the international reputation his 'genius for legislation' required. The
achievement rested above all on the reception of the published versions of his
legislative science, and from early on Bentham appreciated the need to make
his way by his pen. Here again the legacy of his later years easily clouds the
earlier biographical record. Bentham's mature prose notoriously became ever

---

[35] *Correspondence*, ed. Milne, IV, p. 83.
[36] *Ibid.*, p. 167.
[37] *Ibid.*, pp. 180–3.

more 'puzzling and tedious beyond mortal endurance'[38] such that it requires a near leap of faith to imagine him an author in search of a general polite readership. Nonetheless, his initial literary, no less than his philosophic, aspirations can be accurately measured in terms of the celebrity enjoyed by those philosophes Bentham routinely invoked as youthful mentors: Beccaria and Helvétius, Hume and Voltaire. In 1774 he began his career in print with an anonymous translation of Voltaire's *Le Taureau Blanc*, which he furnished with a lengthy, satiric preface that 'may just as well be read afterwards'.[39] That same year Bentham appropriated from his friend, John Lind, the project of publishing a critique of Blackstone's famous *Commentaries on the Laws of England*, noting the regrettable absence in Lind's first draft of the requisite 'Voltairian . . . legereté'.[40] The resulting *A Fragment on Government* of 1776, like the 1787 *Defence of Usury*, aimed at a large readership by riding on the coat-tails of the celebrated authors (Blackstone and Adam Smith) whose errant doctrines each tract scrutinized. Although each publication earned gratifying initial attention and second editions, neither work qualified as the kind of systematic and constructive undertaking upon which to establish a leading reputation in jurisprudence. As several close friends and supporters of the 1770s and 1780s observed, the disastrous combination of Bentham's perfectionism and his frequent distractions with lesser projects repeatedly frustrated the completion of his major legislative theory, which in turn denied him the recognition he both deserved and required.   No one was so diligent or brutally accurate in reminding Bentham of the damage thus caused to his career than George Wilson, an intimate friend of these years. Writing to him in Russia in 1786, Wilson reported the recent appearance of 'a book called Principles of Moral and Political Philosophy' by 'a Mr. Paley, a parson': 'it has gone through two editions with prodigious applause'. The work, Wilson noted, contained little that had not been better covered by Bentham himself in the yet-unpublished *An Introduction to the Principles of Morals and Legislation*. The broader lesson was plain. 'I am still persuaded', Wilson urged, 'that the way in which you are most likely to benefit the world and yourself is by establishing, in the first place, a great literary reputation in your own language and in this country.'[41] Two years later, Wilson resumed the well-rehearsed sermon. The public presentation of his 'system of Morals and general Jurisprudence' would 'raise your reputation more than anything you have yet published, and that reputation . . . will add

---

[38] So judged by William Cobbett in 1818; quoted in William Thomas, *The Philosophic Radicals* (Oxford, 1979), p. 29.

[39] *The White Bull, an Oriental History from an Ancient Syrian Manuscript, Communicated by Mr. Voltaire* (London, 1774).

[40] *Correspondence*, ed. Sprigge, I, pp. 204–5.

[41] *Ibid.*, ed. Christie, III, pp. 490–1.

greatly to the weight of whatever you may write hereafter on temporary subjects'.[42]

This background renders all the more significant the full literary failure of *An Introduction to the Principles of Morals and Legislation* which Bentham finally succumbed to making public in 1789. Although Bentham then supplied the treatise with a preface detailing the several ways in which his discussion proved inadequate as an introduction either to morals or to legislation, and although he acknowledged privately that 'no man conceives it possible for any other man to get through it',[43] the book nevertheless was still the fullest statement of the massive programme for law and legislation which constituted his most important intellectual pursuit since coming of age in 1769. At the time of its first printing, moreover, the work had been identified as the likely breakthrough-publication for his career. As Bentham's father enthused to a distant relation in 1780, Jeremy 'is now actually engaged in correcting the Press' of a book 'of much greater Consequence' than his previous publications, 'upon which principally will depend his reputation as a Writer'.[44] In 1789, however, that reputation remained unmistakably unrealized. The efforts and abortive projects of the 1790s thus stood in the shadow of this failed attempt to capitalize on the intricate jurisprudential labours of earlier years. 'I have written so much and to so little purpose', was Bentham's own verdict on his compositions in 1798.[45]

The political culture of Hanoverian Britain offered another route to the public stage (one perhaps better associated with Victorian-era administrative and social reform). This path to public prominence carried a variety of individuals who acquired their reputations and influence on the basis of their developed expertise or local accomplishments in particular and increasingly specialized areas of parliamentary concern. As Bentham in the period 1788 to 1803 came more and more to involve himself with designs for discrete institutional projects, he often was involved with figures whose careers conform to this broad pattern: Patrick Colquhoun, the London magistrate and established expert on urban policing; Frederick Morton Eden, the learned authority on poverty in England; Arthur Young, the widely-celebrated pundit and publicist for scientific agriculture. To the extent that this kind of career was exemplified for Bentham in the life of any single contemporary reformer, the model was provided by John Howard. Bentham's own doctrines concerning punishment and imprisonment differed in important respects from those advanced by Howard in the 1777 *State of the Prisons* and its later instalments. Nonetheless, the personal example of the unknown Bedfordshire squire who attained international acclaim as a reformer of prisons powerfully affected Bentham early in

[42] *Ibid.*, ed. Milne, IV, p. 16.
[43] See *ibid.*, p. 50n.
[44] *Ibid.*, ed. Sprigge, II, p. 425.
[45] *Ibid.*, ed. Dinwiddy, VI, p. 65.

his career. The two briefly met in 1778, and Bentham considered dedicating to Howard his *An Introduction to the Principles of Morals and Legislation*.[46] 'He is', Bentham rhapsodized in a 1778 letter, 'one of the most extraordinary men this age can shew'. But his importance extended well beyond the 'model for method' contained in his deservedly celebrated book. Howard's practice of philanthropy and advocacy helped shape Bentham's understanding of his own identity as a reformer. 'Law mending *sine privilegio* is a sad trade for a man to thrive by . . . Such as I am, I have given myself to the Public . . . Mr Howard and the public honour he has met with, are of more use to me than you would imagine'.[47]

In the period 1788 to 1803, Bentham thus can be understood to have engaged — without necessarily any settled or premeditated plan — in a number of stratagems for obtaining public notice. By 1793 such efforts increasingly narrowed on the Panopticon prison, which then dominated his activities for the next ten years. In following this particular path, he can be thought to have pursued the career model afforded by the example of Howard. Bentham was never disposed to underestimate the institutional potential of the 'inspection-house' design, nor the financial rewards he would gain as the prison manager. Still, he was throughout explicit that the ultimate value of the successful realization of his project was to secure a public reputation on the basis of which he could effectively promote his more substantial legislative programme. Writing in 1808 (by which time he reported having 'next to no expectation of seeing Panopticon set on foot'), he explained that the prison 'has never been more than a secondary object, [the] primary object being a reform in the state of the law . . . and in the state of the penal law in particular'.[48] Or as he put it at a time when he still cherished every expectation of 'seeing Panopticon set on foot': 'The Termination of my negotiations . . . relative to the Penitentiary business is an epoch of such importance to the remainder of my life, and will make so great a change in my position with relation to all sorts of objects, that I am got in to the habit of deferring to that period all sorts of undertakings, permanent and transient, considerable and inconsiderable.'[49]

As we have seen, an earlier generation of scholars found this obsessive pursuit of the Panopticon bafflingly misguided. 'He was well out of the plan', Leslie Stephen curtly noted of the scheme's final collapse.[50] But this reading neglects too much of the important biographical dynamics. By 1793, Bentham had already invested heavily in alternative strategies of self-promotion, none of which had proved successful and none of which offered any immediate prospects for success. While Bentham (as several government opponents

---

[46] See Semple, *Bentham's Prison*, p. 92.
[47] *Correspondence*, ed. Sprigge, II, pp. 106–8.
[48] *Ibid.*, ed. Dinwiddy, VII, p. 507.
[49] *Ibid.*, ed. Milne, V, p. 159.
[50] Stephen, *English Utilitarians*, I, p. 205.

charged) may have maintained quite unrealistic goals for his prison design, he appears far more realistic in viewing prison reform as a suitable vehicle for self-advancement. After all, model prison construction, inspired by the doctrines of Howard, secured the public repute of such less ambitious contemporary reformers as Gloucestershire's George Onesiphorus Paul and Manchester's Thomas Butterworth Bayley. Moreover, in the initial stages of the prison campaign external developments conspired to facilitate Bentham's commitment to this path. The Panopticon was always regarded as the joint endeavour of the two brothers and as the most important of the several ventures the brothers had formulated while in Russia. Samuel's own return from Russia in the spring of 1791 furnished the technical expertise and managerial experience required for realizing the financial objectives of the plan. The death of their father in March 1792, and Jeremy's subsequent inheritance, gave them the resources for developing the costly prototypes of the envisaged prison works-machinery; and by summer 1793, as we have seen, Jeremy could report that their penitentiary plan had 'been honoured by the acceptance of Mr Pitt and Mr Dundas'.[51]

Accordingly, there is little difficulty in explaining Bentham's decision to embark so zealously on the prison campaign or his belief that the venture would provide a stepping-stone for the promotion of his legislative programme. The real and terrible damage inflicted by the effort needs to be reckoned more precisely. There was, first, Bentham's utter incapacity to moderate his pursuit of the scheme or to extricate himself from the quest, notwithstanding the numerous warnings from his supporters of the obstacles in his path and the abundant evidence that these obstacles were not being surmounted. Bentham, in fact, never abandoned the campaign; his opponents ended it against his will. It was this obstinate perseverance which enabled Panopticon to drain so much of Bentham's fortune and energies for the better part of ten years.

Even more potentially ruinous was the manner in which Bentham, in the midst of his Panopticon frustrations, turned fitfully and graspingly to a variety of schemes and proposals as the means to restore his finances and salvage a career still lacking its public platform. Hence the rapid succession of projects and tracts suddenly initiated and abruptly discarded during this period: plans for new government revenue through a reform of the law of escheat; schemes for 'circulating annuities' and new forms of paper currency; experiments with 'conversation tubes' and commercial refrigeration; suggested visual aids for the improvement of parliamentary debate; techniques for the prevention of forgery; and so on.[52] These endeavours not only took him into topics well beyond his jurisprudential expertise, they also threatened to undermine the very credibility

[51] *Correspondence*, ed. Milne, IV, p. 441.
[52] For the revenue and financial schemes, see *Bentham's Economic Writings*, ed. Stark, I, pp. 279–367, and II, pp. 155–200, 203–300. For the other projects, see *Correspondence*, ed. Milne, IV, pp. 485–90; *Correspondence*, ed. Dinwiddy, VI, pp. 335–6, 346–9, 386.

he sought to secure through the Panopticon project itself. In the summer of 1800, his step-brother, Charles Abbot, issued the warning that he now risked alienating his supporters by acquiring the reputation of a mere '*Faiseur de projets*'.[53] Even more damagingly, the cumulative effect of these efforts was to lead Bentham steadily away from the central core of the codification programme he still avowed as his primary objective. By 1800, the would-be Newton of legislation seemed to lose sight of his own legislative science.

Bentham himself supplied the benchmark for measuring just how far he had travelled from his systematic legislative theory over the course of this period. In the 1789 preface to *An Introduction to the Principles of Morals and Legislation*, he reported that his 'present designs' comprised the completion of a voluminous ten-part exposition of the 'principles of legislation', to be followed by 'the body of law itself exhibited *in terminis*'.[54] Only a fraction of the writings and intellectual labours of the next ten-plus years could be treated as contributions to this declared goal.[55] Of course, at every other period of his career Bentham also routinely departed from the 'repulsive and thorny'[56] path of systematic legislative theory to compose more limited essays and polemics: the 1776 *Fragment on Government*, separated out from the more systematic critique of common law jurisprudence; the 1808 *Scotch Reform*, which accompanied the massive elaboration of judicial procedure; the critical papers assembled in the 1830 collection, *Official Aptitude Maximized; Expense Minimized*, which complimented the publication of the first volume of the *Constitutional Code*. What was exceptional about the projects and proposals of the period 1788 to 1803 was the general absence of systematic work on the 'principles of legislation' from which these writings could be viewed as digressions. While much of this material, as L.J. Hume has shown, came to serve Bentham well some twenty years later in the composition of his code of constitutional law, there is no evidence that Bentham was moving in this specific direction at the time. Indeed, the more pressing biographical question is how the frequent '*Faiseur de projets*' of the 1790s managed to reclaim his career in legislative theory in the years after 1803.

There is no reason to suppose any single or certain answer to this biographical question. Still, a discernable change in Bentham's writing and intellectual programme appears at this time. The Panopticon polemics of 1802 to 1803, and

---

[53] *Correspondence*, ed. Dinwiddy, VI, p. 342.

[54] Bentham, *Morals and Legislation*, pp. 5–6.

[55] Aside from the first essays for France, the works most directly relevant to the 1789 legislative programme are two unfinished accounts of the relationship between political economy and legislation (*Manual of Political Economy* (1793–5) and *Institute of Political Economy* (1801–4)), as well as the mid-decade critique of the Declaration of the Rights of Man. For these, see *Bentham's Economic Writings*, ed. Stark, I, pp. 219–73, and III, pp. 303–80; and *Works*, ed. Bowring, II, pp. 489–534.

[56] So termed in Jeremy Bentham, *The Rationale of Reward* (London, 1825), p. 190.

the 'magnificent invective' (in Semple's apt phrase)[57] with which Bentham
excoriated the government and Treasury officials who had undermined his
prison scheme, may well have served a cathartic purpose in securing release
from the project. Although Bentham's original hopes were to use these abrasive
narratives of injury and frustration to rally new support for Panopticon, there
is a sense that in these writings he for the first time grappled with the evident
defeat of the campaign. In 1803, for reasons which still remain unclear, Bentham took up the topics of judicial evidence and procedure which he had last
addressed in the 1790 proposal for the *Judicial Establishment in France*. By
1804 he was fully absorbed in this material. Writing to Dumont in March of
that year, he reported his decision to abandon writing on his study of 'the
influence of money on the increase of wealth', which contained 'few ideas' not
available elsewhere, so that he might 'go quietly back to Evidence'.[58] It is
tempting to think of this work on evidence — which eventually issued in the
single most substantial work in jurisprudence published in his lifetime[59] — as
leading Bentham back to the centre of his *pannomion*, and thus helping to
restore an earlier set of theoretical ambitions and priorities.

But in addition to these changes in orientation was another absolutely crucial
development, which figures as a kind of off-stage counterpoint to the biographical disaster of the Panopticon years. In 1792 the putative prison manager sent
to Etienne Dumont a great shipment of manuscripts, backed by the much-
needed disclosure 'not [to] wonder at the disorder in which you find my
papers'.[60] Dumont, who earlier translated Bentham's plan for judicial organization in France, then began the herculean editorial labour that finally secured
Bentham his public repute and salvaged from manuscript the Benthamite
legislative system elaborated decades before. Between 1796 and 1798, Dumont
published in the Genevan journal, *Bibliothèque britannique*, a series of eight
articles containing extracts of Bentham's works.[61] In 1802, the *Traités de
législation civile et pénale . . . Par M. Jérémie Bentham* made its noteworthy
appearance. As proofs of the edition became available in the spring of that year,
Bentham developed a lively concern for the edition, and no little elation at the
prospect of its publication. 'You have set me a strutting, my dear Dumont, like
a fop in a Coat spick-and-span from the Taylor's', he enthused. 'Between us, I
think we know something about legislation.'[62] But the reaction stands in sharp
contrast to the lack of attention Bentham gave the editorial project during most

[57] Semple, *Bentham's Prison*, p. 243.
[58] *Correspondence*, ed. Dinwiddy, VII, pp. 262–3.
[59] This was the five-volume *Rationale of Judicial Evidence* edited by John Stuart
Mill and published in 1827.
[60] *Correspondence*, ed. Dinwiddy, VI, p. 385.
[61] For bibliographic details, see *ibid.*, ed. Milne, V, p. 200n.
[62] *Ibid.*, ed. Dinwiddy, VII, p. 28.